The Control of Natural Monopolies

The Control of Natural Monopolies

Richard Schmalensee
Alfred P. Sloan School of
Management
Massachusetts Institute of
Technology

Lexington Books
D.C. Heath and Company
Lexington, Massachusetts
Toronto

Library of Congress Cataloging in Publication Data

Schmalensee, Richard.
    The control of natural monopolies.

    Bibliography: p.
    Includes index.
    1. Monopolies. 2. Industry and state. 3. Public utilities. I. Title.
HD2731.S34   338.8'2   78-6061
ISBN 0-669-02322-1

Published simultaneously in Canada

Printed in the United States of America

International Standard Book Number: 0-669-02322-1

Library of Congress Catalog Card Number: 78-6061

For Diane

Contents

Preface

This work attempts a systematic analysis of the basic problems associated with natural monopoly situations and of the policies that have been proposed or employed to deal with them. Although the analysis is primarily economic, I have generally avoided the use of formal economic theory. The stress is on drawing implications for policy design from the large body of relevant theoretical and empirical literature and on indicating important gaps in current knowledge.

This book should be of interest to academic specialists concerned with regulation and public utility industries. I have also tried to make it accessible to students and practitioners in these and related areas. Much of the book is a critical survey, so I cannot claim that well-read specialists will find much that is truly new. I do think that most will encounter some material that is at least unfamiliar, and I hope that there is some useful novelty in my organization and analysis.

A work of this sort cannot be opinion free, and this one is certainly not. Further my prejudices have inevitably affected my understanding and interpretation of the literature I discuss. I thus expect that I have unintentionally neglected, misinterpreted, or otherwise slighted some authors. I can do little about this beyond offering a blanket apology, however.

The research reflected here was initially supported by National Science Foundation Grant APR75-16563 to the Department of Economics of the University of California, San Diego. I am grateful to both the foundation and the department. This initial work benefited from the useful comments of Robert Gilpin and the research assistance of Bernard Poirine. I am also indebted to Victor Goldberg and Paul MacAvoy for helpful suggestions at this stage. A final report, skillfully typed by Judy Lyman, was submitted to the National Science Foundation in June 1977, shortly before I left UCSD to come to MIT.

I received useful comments on that report from William Baumol, Robert Gilpin, Paul Joskow, and Oliver Williamson. But for their help, this book would not have been written. I alone, of course, must take responsibility for any defects in the final product. Additional research and writing were done at MIT during the summer of 1978. Cynthia Works typed most of the final manuscript with diligence and good cheer.

Last by tradition, but far from least, my wife, Diane, provided essential support during this entire effort. I could not have completed it without her. The least I can do is to dedicate this book to her in grateful appreciation.

1

Introduction and Overview

Analysis and Reform

This book is concerned with alternative ways of controlling the conduct and thus affecting the performance of natural monopoly industries. In the United States, the standard device for imposing such control—administrative regulation—is the point of departure for much of the analysis.

Public utility regulation in the United States has rarely lacked vocal critics. In the 1930s, many of those who felt the performance of regulators and of regulated firms was inadequate proposed a shift to public ownership and operation of those firms. In the 1960s and 1970s, however, the most commonly discussed remedy for inadequate performance under regulation seems to be deregulation, after which market forces alone would be relied upon to determine industry performance. As Trebing (1976a) notes, this shift may have been clearest within the so-called Chicago school.

It is not unlikely that the most urgent items on the current regulatory reform agenda in the United States do involve total or partial deregulation of certain activities or industries. Numerous studies have predicted substantial net benefits from the deregulation of interurban transportation and natural gas production. But the case for total deregulation of the traditional public utilities (electricity, gas distribution, water and sewer, and telephone service) and intraurban public transportation is less clear and is less often made. Thus some situations exist in which there is at least a prima facie case that the market mechanism will not yield acceptable performance unless special control mechanisms are employed.

After any such case for control is made, the natural next step is to examine the properties of alternative control strategies. Breyer (1977) and Joskow and Noll (1978) note the logical importance of determining the best way to respond to particular political demands for intervention in the market process. Breyer, in particular, stresses the importance of matching regulatory tools to the characteristics of the problem addressed, though he does not consider alternative control strategies for natural monopoly situations.

If the decision to impose controls has not yet been made, it can be informed by an examination of alternative forms of control. Only if all forms of control are likely to worsen performance, for instance, is a no-intervention strategy indicated. To show that one form of control is likely to worsen performance does not make the case for nonintervention unless there are no alternatives. On

1

the other hand, if controls are to be imposed, analyzing alternative approaches is even more clearly important. Such analysis then has direct implications for unavoidable policy decisions, so that it is potentially of great value to policy makers. A study that shows, for instance, that some actual or proposed control strategy is imperfect is clearly less valuable in this context than a comparison of two or more feasible alternatives.

It is true that decisions about control strategies and tactics are made in a political setting. But the fact that politics is involved does not mean that analyzing the alternatives is pointless. Certainly research that shows the superiority of some new policy B to the current policy A cannot by itself ensure the adoption of policy B by the political process. But if affected parties are ignorant about the implications of these alternatives, research can build a constituency for policy B. If such a constituency exists, its size and influence may be enhanced by research that documents desirable attributes of policy B. Further policy makers who are under pressure from those who oppose policy A may embrace a study that provides policy B as a publicly defensible alternative.

Joskow (1977) indicates that academic research on peak-load pricing, for example, has affected regulatory practice through these and other related channels. Similarly research on the effects of regulation on natural gas and transportation markets has had an impact on political decisions in these areas. Analysis of alternative approaches to the control of natural monopoly sectors can also affect decision making.

In light of these considerations, it is at least somewhat surprising that, as Joskow and Noll (1978) note, little systematic research has been done on alternative institutional structures for controlling natural monopoly. Conventional rate-of-return regulation is one such structure, and it has been analyzed intensively. But most such studies have compared actual regulated outcomes with some ideal rather than with what might reasonably be expected from radically different approaches or from changes in the structure or process of regulation itself. Since there are situations in which total reliance on the market mechanism is unlikely politically and rarely advocated seriously even by academics, comparisons of real regulation with various ideal states are somewhat beside the point. The real choices are often among alternative imperfect forms of control; research that seeks to affect policy should focus on those alternatives.

This argument is hardly novel. At the end of his famous critique of public utility regulation, Horace M. Gray (1940, p. 20) argued against the assumption that the alternative to regulation in many sectors was public ownership. He contended, "If the spirit of 'institutional inventiveness' is given a free rein, many new types of control, not heretofore contemplated, may be developed." He went on to note that these may differ from currently employed regulatory or public ownership structures. But the public utility sector in the United States has not been much affected by institutional inventiveness since Gray wrote. In 1974, Trebing pointed out that, except for a few procedural changes, public utilities were still generally regulated much as they had been in the 1920s.

A wide variety of alternative control strategies for natural monopolies have been applied at various times and places, and others have been proposed and discussed. Subsequent chapters consider some of these. First, though, it is useful to indicate more precisely what *natural monopoly* means and why industries so labeled may require controls beyond those imposed by market forces.

The Natural Monopoly Problem

Lowry (1973) credits John Stuart Mill (1848) with introducing the concept of natural monopoly, though the phrase itself was apparently coined by economist Richard T. Ely in a series of newspaper articles in the 1880s. As Lowry notes, the concept was refined and modified by subsequent authors. In this section, the modern cost-based definition of natural monopoly is outlined and related to the desirability of imposing controls.

An industry or activity is said to be a natural monopoly if production is most efficiently done by a single firm or other entity. This concept is most easily analyzed when there is only one relevant commodity. Suppose that the total cost of producing any level of output, X, is given by the function $C(X)$. It is most natural to assume in what follows that prices of inputs are fixed, so that $C(X)$ reflects only the characteristics of the relevant technology. Let $\bar{X}$ be some particular level of output. Then costs are said to be subadditive at $\bar{X}$ if the following condition is satisfied:

$$C(X) = C(X_1 + X_2 + \ldots + X_n) < C(X_1) + C(X_2) + \ldots + C(X_n), \text{ for any } n > 2$$
$$\text{and any set of positive outputs } (X_1, X_2, \ldots, X_n) \text{ adding up to } \bar{X}. \quad (1.1)$$

Condition 1.1 says that any division of total output $\bar{X}$ among two or more firms using the same technology, with firm 1 producing X_1, firm 2 producing X_2, and so on, must raise total costs. Then if costs are subadditive at $\bar{X}$, the industry must be a natural monopoly for this output level, since costs are lowest with only one producer. If condition 1.1 holds for all positive total output levels (all positive values of $\bar{X}$), costs are said to be globally subadditive, and it follows that the industry is a natural monopoly for all levels of output. (See Baumol, 1977, on this.)

In fact, global subadditivity is ensured if condition 1.1 holds for all positive $\bar{X}$ when $n = 2$. Then any division of any total output between two firms raises costs. Since any division among more than two firms can be thought of as a sequence of divisions between two firms, costs are always minimized when there is only a single producer.

Natural monopoly is often discussed together with declining average costs (see, for instance, Kahn, 1971, p. 123). It can be shown that if average cost, $C(\bar{X})/\bar{X}$ declines with all increases in $\bar{X}$ (and if $C(0)$ is zero), then costs will be globally subadditive. But the reverse implication does not hold (Baumol, 1977);

condition 1.1 can be satisfied for all $\overline{X}$ even though there are some ranges of output for which $C(\overline{X})/\overline{X}$ is increasing in $\overline{X}$. Everywhere decreasing average costs imply but are not implied by natural monopoly. If natural monopoly is present, though, average cost must be falling for some range of outputs.

In a single-commodity context, with everywhere decreasing costs, monopoly is natural in two respects. First, since monopoly represents the cheapest way of producing any level of output, single entity production is a natural aim of intelligent public policy. Second, in the absence of public intervention, dominance of the market by a single firm is generally held to be the natural outcome. Larger firms always have lower costs than their smaller competitors. The largest firm at any instant is thus in the best position to compete for sales. If the largest firm is sufficiently aggressive, it will drive all rivals from the field and still earn substantial excess profits. This second story has never been made rigorous to my knowledge, however. It cannot be told in situations with global subadditivity but without everywhere decreasing costs.[1]

When multiple products are involved, the fundamental cost test for natural monopoly still involves subadditivity. (In basic condition 1.1, $\overline{X}$ and $X_1, \ldots,$ X_n become vectors, with one component for each product.) However, the relation between global subadditivity and decreasing average costs is no longer straightforward. One must consider the implications of the level of production of, say, commodity 1 for the costs of commodity 2. Natural monopoly can rest in large measure on such factors as the ability to use plant and equipment for the production of two products or services, such as daytime and nighttime electricity. These issues have been explored by Baumol (1977), Baumol, Bailey, and Willig (1977), and Panzar and Willig (1977a, 1977b) in recent papers, and more theoretical and empirical work in this area is likely to be forthcoming.

Several of the classic public utility industries, such as water and sewer services and the local distribution of gas and electricity, involve networks along which something is transmitted from (or to) a relatively small number of locations to (or from) a relatively large number of geographically dispersed demanders (or suppliers). Cable television also fits this model, though because of the necessity to provide connections between all pairs of customers, telephone service does not. Schmalensee (1978) shows that if there are everywhere decreasing average costs of transmission within the network, such distribution systems are natural monopolies. Water supply provides a simple illustration. It is often argued that a pipe's capacity is roughly proportional to its cross-section area, while cost is roughly proportional to circumference. If the cross-section of a pipe is doubled, the circumference less than doubles. If these assumptions about cost and capacity are correct and if pumping costs are nondecreasing in volume, water supply is a natural monopoly, because doubling the volume of water to be transmitted between any two points less than doubles cost, and average transmission cost is therefore everywhere declining. As in other contexts, it is possible to have a natural monopoly in distribution without everywhere declining transmission costs, though costs must decline for some ranges of output.

If costs are globally subadditive, the situation involves a *permanent* natural monopoly, since no matter what the level of output(s) at any time, production is most efficiently done by a single entity. Some of the distribution networks referred to above may be permanent natural monopolies. But if costs are subadditive only for some output levels, a *temporary* natural monopoly exists, since some but not all patterns of output require single-entity production for efficiency. A simple example would be the retailing of groceries. In very small towns, it is surely "natural" that there be but one grocery. But it is generally argued that average costs in this industry are constant after a relatively modest level of output has been attained. Thus in large cities, the grocery industry is not a natural monopoly. Various bits of evidence (see, for instance, Scherer, 1970, ch. 4) suggest that this is a not uncommon pattern. That is, temporary natural monopolies may tend to exhibit subadditivity only for low levels of total output, so that demand growth eliminates natural monopoly.

Weiss (1975) has argued that the generation (but not the distribution) of electricity may only be a temporary natural monopoly, since the tendency for average costs to decline with plant size may not continue indefinitely. (See also Trebing, 1976b. Waverman, 1975, provides a similar analysis of telecommunications.) Shepherd (1975, ch. 9) has argued, in effect, that there exist no permanent natural monopolies, though his seems an extreme position. The question is in any case empirical. The distinction between temporary and permanent natural monopolies has implications for control strategies.

Now we must consider why industries with the attributes that define natural monopoly might require special control policies. The reasons must have to do with the economic implications of those attributes, since global subadditivity is an economic concept with no direct legal, political, or social implications. The natural monopoly problem, which motivates consideration of special control strategies, must be that the economic performance of natural monopolies tends to be unsatisfactory without special controls.

A single firm or other entity on the supply side is required for cost minimization; this follows from the definition, and it may be brought about under natural monopoly by uncontrolled market forces. But any firm that is the sole producer of some commodity or set of commodities enjoys some monopoly power, some degree of control over price. If other goods or services are good substitutes for the outputs of such a firm, its monopoly power will not be great. But if a monopoly produces goods or services for which there are no close substitutes, its demand is likely to be relatively insensitive to the prices it charges. In such cases, the firm's monopoly power is substantial, and it will likely charge prices that are well in excess of costs. Such prices can have sizable adverse effects on the efficiency with which scarce resources are employed. By reducing allocative or economic efficiency, prices well in excess of costs impose losses on the community or nation as a whole. There is a potential gain from controls that would force prices down to the level of costs. The size of the gain depends on both cost and demand conditions; it is generally greater the less responsive is demand to price.[2] Thus one would worry more, on efficiency grounds, about an uncontrolled water supply monopoly than about a similarly situated cable television firm in a large city.

There is another way to look at the natural monopoly problem. Although this alternative approach is commonly encountered outside the academic world, it is less useful than the efficiency focus. High prices charged by a monopoly seller generally translate into high profit rates, where the standard is profit rates earned by firms in competitive markets. Such excess profits represent income transfers from buyers to the seller, and excess profits are potentially larger, all else equal, the smaller the effect of price changes on demand. It is sometimes held that the purpose of regulation or government ownership of natural monopoly is the protection of buyers against overcharges that become monopoly profits. This may be descriptive of the political rationale for some government intervention in natural monopoly sectors, but it is inadequate as a basis for specific policy formation. Although controls that enhance economic efficiency also generally reduce profits below uncontrolled levels, the reverse is not the case. That is, a control strategy that focuses only on the level of profits earned by a natural monopoly does not necessarily enhance economic efficiency. Profits can be reduced by allowing costs to rise or by forcing some commodities to be sold below cost; both actions waste scarce resources. Some may benefit, but the community as a whole loses in this situation. In order to deal with the special economic problems posed by natural monopolies, control mechanisms must focus on the efficiency of resource use directly and not limit attention to the level of profits.

Many texts note that demand for the outputs of the traditional public utility sectors tends to be relatively insensitive to prices (see, for instance, Farris and Sampson, 1973, pp. 18-19). Since these sectors are also generally viewed as natural monopolies, there is at least a prima facie case for special controls; such cases can be made elsewhere as well. But arguments of this sort cannot be dispositive; the operational properties of alternative feasible control strategies must be considered because no such strategy is perfect or costless. Even though there are potential benefits from detailed control in some particular case, the cost of feasible control may well outweigh the realizable benefits. To my knowledge, nobody seriously proposes detailed regulation of local grocery monopolies in small towns, for instance, though perfect and costless regulation would yield net benefits.

The inevitable imperfections of the control process make the distinction between temporary and permanent natural monopoly of some importance. Detailed controls should be imposed only when they will yield net gains, and they should be removed when they cease to do so. If a temporary natural monopoly is controlled, policy makers should be alert to the fact that changes in the level of demand may make removing those controls desirable. If competition becomes viable and does not entail cost penalties, the industry no longer has the special attributes that justified controls in the first place. Since controls generally require administrators, and since administrators are as attached to their jobs as the rest of us, the control mechanism probably cannot be relied upon to call attention to the desirability of its own demise. If, on the other hand, a natural monopoly is permanent, this problem may be less acute since changes in the level of demand cannot alter the industry's natural monopoly status.

Still, permanent natural monopoly does not necessarily imply permanent control. A change in the sector's technology may make cost-efficient competition feasible. Similarly a change in technology elsewhere in the economy may result in the availability of good substitutes for the natural monopoly's output, thus tending to reduce the potential benefits, and presumably the actual benefits, of detailed controls.

The interurban transportation sector in the United States has provided a number of examples of these sorts of changes in demand and technology. Its history also illustrates the tendency for unnecessary control systems to remain in place or even to expand their domain.

Some General Themes

At least three general themes run through much of the discussion in subsequent chapters. The first is that a great diversity of strategies for the control of natural monopoly is available. Even if one limits consideration to strategies that involve commission supervision of privately owned firms, considerable choice remains. Many critics implicitly deny the existence of real alternatives by implying that any form of regulatory supervision will exhibit exactly the same shortcomings as the present structure. I will argue that some problems are indeed intrinsic to the task of social control of natural monopoly but that different control strategies can be expected to exhibit nontrivial performance differences.

A second, related theme is that no social control strategy can be expected to perform perfectly in all situations. Humans are not perfect; neither are human institutions. All approaches to the social control of natural monopoly may not in practice commit the same sins as rate-of-return regulation, but all will sin. At least in principle, however, there is some hope of matching approaches with industries in which their particular sins will do the least harm. Such matching will not be attempted in great detail here, but the analysis will try to take note of the strengths and weaknesses of various proposals.

A third theme is the importance of institutional design. Much of the criticism of current administrative regulation focuses on the conduct of regulators and regulated firms. This literature is helpful only indirectly in institutional design. It indicates the responses that relevant actors have made to current institutional and legal structures, and it may suggest some general hypotheses about behavior. But criticism of conduct does not by itself help Gray's "institutional inventor" devise legal and institutional structures that will induce more desirable behavior. It certainly seems impossible to design an administrative structure capable of dealing with reasonably complex situations that does not allow administrators some discretion. On the other hand, it does seem possible to influence the costs and benefits of various sorts of managerial and regulatory discretionary activity by the choice of institutional structure.

Institutional structure is not fully defined by, for instance, the number of regulatory commissioners and the details of their appointment or election process. The whole matrix of laws and of political and administrative relations affecting behavior must be considered. Some potentially relevant elements of structure are considered in subsequent chapters.

In discussions of antitrust policy, it is often argued that the way to produce competitive performance is to move toward competitive market structure. It is not enough to instruct firms to ignore rivals in their pursuit of profit. Similarly, individuals involved in the management and control of natural monopolies will not ignore their own interests. It may not be enough to write articles telling them how to behave. In order to affect performance in natural monopoly situations with a high degree of reliability, it may be necessary to design and install the appropriate social control structure. Unfortunately the techniques of institutional engineering are not very well developed; the details of the structure-conduct linkage in administrative contexts are not well understood. (This problem is considered in some detail in chapter 4.) But some clues as to the conduct and performance implications of alternative structures do exist and are discussed in this book.

Plan of the Book

My concern is with natural monopoly situations in which at least a prima facie case for the imposition of special controls has been made. Such situations exist, if only in the traditional public utility sectors. The focus of the analysis is on alternative control mechanisms and their properties.

In order to evaluate such alternatives and even to limit the set of mechanisms to be considered, one needs to specify the objectives that control of natural monopoly should seek. Chapter 2 considers this question and argues that economic efficiency should be the dominant objective. The contention is not that society is not legitimately concerned with other values but rather that natural monopoly control mechanisms are inherently ill suited for the task of balancing efficiency against other goals.

Chapter 3 spells out the main features of efficient natural monopoly operation. These are used to evaluate current utility regulation in the United States, and in subsequent chapters they serve as normative standards against which proposed alternatives can be judged.

Chapter 4 is concerned with aspects of natural monopoly industries and of human behavior that serve to limit the possibilities for effective control of performance. I argue that some entity must serve as the buyers' agent if control is to be effective, and I survey some of the literature on administrative and regulatory behavior for insights into likely agent behavior under alternative structural conditions.

Using the discussions in chapters 2-4 as background, I examine a variety of alternative control structures in chapters 5-8. The focus is on likely performance along dimensions of economic efficiency, and only proposals with some promise in this respect are considered. (There is thus no detailed discussion of moving commissions into executive branches or establishing specialized administrative courts.)

The devices considered in chapter 5 flow from economists' inclination to employ the market as an incentive creation and control mechanism. Natural monopoly renders direct product market competition inadequate for these purposes in general, so that these proposals focus on the input markets for capital funds and for managerial services. At the ideologically opposite extreme, public ownership and operation has been advocated in order to reduce the potential for harm inevitably associated with the pursuit of profit in monopoly situations. Structures involving various forms of public ownership and operation are considered in chapter 6.

The proposals discussed in chapters 7 and 8 are generally less radical from a U.S. perspective in that they involve reforming rather than replacing commission regulation of privately owned firms. Chapter 7 considers proposals that seem designed primarily to increase the responsiveness of the regulatory process to change, and chapter 8 analyzes suggestions mainly concerned with increasing regulated firms' incentives for efficient operation. Because several proposals discussed are viewed by their advocates as potentially helpful in both these and other dimensions, the division between these two chapters is necessarily somewhat arbitrary.

Chapter 9 summarizes the conclusions of the analysis and makes a few general and specific suggestions for improving natural monopoly control mechanisms.

In order to keep the length of this study within bounds, I generally do not consider detailed problems that might be associated with changes from one social control structure to another.[3] Similarly, while an attempt is made to refer to and to reflect the findings of much of the relevant literature, it would have required a much longer book to discuss it all in detail. Readers are advised to seek out items in the bibliography for additional information and analysis.

A number of the specific proposals discussed in chapters 5-8 are similar or identical to control schemes that have been employed at various times and in various places. In principle, this means that much historical evidence could be used in their analysis. In fact, however, it appears that many potentially informative experiments in the control of natural monopoly have never been rigorously evaluated. In many instances, the best available evidence seems to be the judgment of contemporary observers, and that judgment is reported. Such informed opinions are not all that might be desired, but they are often a useful antidote to a priori theorizing.

Notes

1. I return to this point in subsequent chapters; it relates to the notion of sustainability analyzed by Panzar and Willig, "Free Entry," and by Baumol, Bailey, and Willig, "Weak Invisible Hand Theorems." See also Faulhaber, "Cross-subsidization."

2. This is true when demand is linear in price; see Schmalensee, "Estimating the Costs and Benefits." If demand is absolutely unresponsive to price, of course, resource use is unaffected by price, and there can be no efficiency loss. But this is a textbook case in which an unregulated monopoly's optimal price is infinite; in all real situations there must exist large but finite price increases that will lower demand.

3. For discussions of such problems, see Clark, *Social Control of Business,* p. 335; and, more generally, Tullock, "Transitional Gains Trap." As a matter of principle, if control strategy B is more efficient than the status quo strategy A, there must exist a transition from A to B (perhaps involving special transition-period taxes and subsidies) that will make all affected parties better off. Devising and promoting such a scheme in any particular case may be both difficult and essential if change is to occur.

2 Appropriate Control Objectives

Criticisms of Current Regulation

Almarin Phillips (1974, p. 320) has argued that "it may be time for revolutionary reform of regulation." Although many critics of regulation, with a wide variety of backgrounds, would probably agree, they would not agree on the direction the revolution should take. Among those who have argued that regulation has failed to live up to the expectations of its Progressive enthusiasts, there is no consensus as to the basic nature of its failure.[1] Three distinct conceptions of the central problem of contemporary U.S. regulation can be identified in the literature. (See McCraw, 1975, for a summary of the evolution of various views of regulation and its problems.) Each reflects a different opinion about the appropriate basic goals of the regulatory process.

The first conception of regulatory failure is economic. Its proponents argue that the central shortcoming of current public utility regulation is its failure to pursue and promote economic efficiency (Trebing, 1960a; Posner, 1969; and MacAvoy, 1970a).[2] (Much of the relevant critical literature is surveyed by Joskow, forthcoming.) A central theme is that regulators tend to be primarily concerned with the welfare of those they regulate (see Gray, 1940 and Stigler, 1971, for examples and Noll, 1971b, ch. 3, and Jordan, 1972, for surveys). Noll (1971b, ch. 4) and others have stressed the link between this concern and regulators' pursuit of their own interests. The efficiency consequences of apparent regulatory blunders and of inflexibility during inflation have also received attention (see, for instance, MacAvoy, 1971a, and Joskow and MacAvoy, 1975). Some proponents of the economic view of regulatory failure contend that regulation in principle can cure itself, while others argue that such failure is inevitable (compare Trebing, 1976a, and Stigler, 1971). By focusing on the implications of current regulation for economic efficiency, however, these critics all implicitly assert that pursuit of economic efficiency is an appropriate objective of public utility regulation. Some contend that efficiency is the only appropriate objective.

The second widely held conception of regulatory failure is political. Proponents of this view generally treat public utility regulation as only an important example of government regulation of private activity in general. The economic considerations that set natural monopolies apart from other industries rarely receive more than passing mention. The ideal in these discussions is not the perfect market competition or fully efficient resource allocation of the economist but rather some generally ill-defined notion of perfect political competition among interest groups. This seems to reflect a relatively recent shift in norms; among political scientists in particular, responsiveness to interest group competition seems generally to have replaced pursuit of the public interest as an ideal. A comparison of the implicit norms in Bernstein (1955) and Cutler and Johnson (1975) reveals this shift clearly as it relates to regulation. (See also McCraw, 1975, pp. 175-79.) A critique and defense of the pluralist ideal of interest group competition in the context of administrative regulation are given by Lowi (1969, esp. ch. 5) and Auerbach (1972), respectively.

Critics taking the political view of regulatory failure describe the central shortcoming of current regulation as its lack of appropriate responsiveness to the whole spectrum of legitimate interest group pressures. Cutler and Johnson (1975, p. 1399), for instance, explicitly define regulatory failure as occurring "when an agency has not done what elected officials would have done had they exercised the power conferred on them by virtue of their ultimate political responsibility." Such failure is endemic when, as a former Interstate Commerce Commission (ICC) administrative law judge (Pellerzi, 1974, p. 84) notes, "The basic nature of the regulatory process has been *ad hoc* adjudication or balancing of the interests of the litigants to the particular proceeding." Interests not represented by litigants are clearly not heard. The Progressives' attempt to "remove regulation from politics" is held to have been fundamentally misguided and to have facilitated the capture of regulatory agencies by special interests (see Bernstein, 1955, and Wilson, 1974, for general discussions). Within this tradition, Huntington's (1952) portrait of a feeble ICC dominated by the railroads is classic. That portrait has been sharply criticized by Jaffe (1954), however, who argues that a number of special interests, including the regulators themselves, generally exert important pressure on the regulatory process. (Posner, 1974, and Peltzman, 1976, have recently argued that the economists' "capture by the regulated" model must be similarly generalized.) This diagnosis of regulatory ills implies that increased politicization is an appropriate general remedy, and tighter control by the elected chief executive is a common specific prescription.[3]

A third conception of regulatory failure is administrative. Some critics of regulatory agencies place primary stress on the inefficiency with which these bodies perform their tasks, often calling particular attention to the delays and costs inherent in case-by-case decision making. Proposals that stem from this conception often involve changes in the administrative structure of regulatory bodies (see, for instance, Bernstein, 1972, and Thomas, 1971). Friendly (1962) and McConnell (1966, ch. 8), among many others, have urged regulatory bodies to increase their efficiency by relying more on rule making and standard setting instead of treating individual cases one at a time. (Robinson, 1970, provides a comprehensive critique of various proposals in this tradition.)

The administrative conception of regulatory inadequacy and the reform proposals that flow from it have been strongly attacked for focusing on procedure rather than policy. This conception implicitly assumes that politics and administration can be separated, a possibility that most students of politics now seem to reject. (See, for instance, Bernstein, 1955, 1961, Massel, 1961, and Seidman, 1970.) Most of the specific reform proposals in this tradition have been criticized as inadequate. Thus Robinson (1970) argues convincingly that it is possible to be consistent in adjudication but inconsistent in rule making so that greater reliance on rule making need have no beneficial effects. Further, as Bernstein (1955, ch. 7), Landis (1961), and Wilson (1974), among others, have noted, procedural changes can have substantial unintended effects on policy. Increased regulatory efficiency certainly need not benefit all interests; some parties may be well served by delays. Finally, it is frequently and persuasively argued that the structural changes proposed by administrative critics lack sound empirical support; their ultimate impacts on both policy and administrative efficiency are uncertain. Noll (1971b) makes this key point quite forcefully, as do Bernstein (1961, 1972), Massel (1961), and Thomas (1971).

These criticisms of the administrative conception of regulatory inadequacy seem persuasive; especially telling is the failure to relate reform proposals arising from this critical tradition to changes in the substantive consequences of regulatory activity. If these criticisms are accepted, we are left with two alternative diagnoses of the basic problem with current regulatory practice: the economic view that it fails to enhance efficient resource use, and the political view that it fails to respond to legitimate interest group pressures. There correspond two opposed implicit assertions of the appropriate objectives of regulation, particularly when it is used to control natural monopolies. The economic conception of regulatory failure implies that regulation should be primarily concerned with attaining allocative efficiency, while the political conception implies that regulation should strike an appropriate balance among all relevant interests and thus, indirectly, among all competing social goals.

It is not my intention to choose between these two diagnoses of regulatory failure. There seems to be more point to asking which of these two opposed views of appropriate regulatory objectives is the more productive basis for consideration of alternative control devices in the natural monopoly context.

Efficiency versus Responsiveness

In the abstract, economic efficiency is logically an instrumental or derived objective, not a basic social goal. All else equal, any citizen ought rationally to desire that the allocation of scarce resources among competing ends be done efficiently. But the relative importance to be attached to alternative ends or conflicting social goals is at least to some extent a matter for collective decision by the political process. Market competition can promote economic efficiency, but it can hardly determine the goals of government policy. Attainment of economic efficiency provides nobody (except, possibly, professional economists) pleasure or gain directly. If it were to prove necessary to sacrifice efficiency in the pursuit of important basic social goals, even economists would often be willing to make the sacrifice (Okun 1975). Thus the political pressure for economic efficiency in the abstract is unsurprisingly slight.

It follows that there is no general philosophical reason why control of natural monopoly should be concerned exclusively or especially with economic efficiency. In principle, government ought to coordinate all the instruments at its disposal in pursuit of all its policy objectives. As Tinbergen (1956, chs. 1, 8) has emphasized, rarely can one associate sets of instruments uniquely with ultimate goals. That is, most government actions have implications for numerous social concerns. Utility regulation, for instance, can be employed to tax undesirable activities or persons and to subsidize desirable ones. As Posner (1971) argues, such taxation by regulation is not *a priori* any less efficient or effective than other available taxes. Munk (1977), in effect, makes this same point formally in a general equilibrium model.

The preceding two paragraphs outline the case that control of natural monopoly, like any other government activity, should consider all ultimate policy objectives and be directly or indirectly responsive to all legitimate interest group pressures. Missing from that outline, and from the case it summarizes, are any considerations of administrative feasibility, which are important in the present context.

Tinbergen's (1956) perfectly administered government efficiently pursues ultimate goals selected and valued in the political process. Since any government action may have implications for all such goals, perfect administration requires close coordination of all actions. Trade-offs among competing goals must be made consistently whenever and wherever they arise. Any branch or agency of government contemplating an action that might affect the distribution of real income, for instance, must consult with all others that could also affect the income distribution. This means, at a minimum, that all price regulation and taxation decisions must be closely coordinated. Some central authority must ensure that all strike the same balance between, for instance, equalization of real incomes and protection of the environment.

This clearly requires an authority with considerable power and resources, especially because many of the concerns of modern governments can be dealt with in quantitative terms only with great difficulty, either because of inadequate data, inadequate theoretical knowledge, or deeper problems. It is possible to quantify the impact of property tax reform on the income distribution in the short run, though severe data problems are likely. It is harder to relate changes in the property tax to the incidence of crime in the long run, though quantification seems possible here in principle. But absent a universally accepted breakthrough in political philosophy, it seems impossible to quantify the impact of any tax reform on the fairness or justice of the overall tax system. There is no way a chief administrator or executive (let alone a legislature) can deal with such issues on the basis of a few numbers supplied by subordinates; a different order of knowledge and understanding is required. It is hard to imagine any single individual or working group that can bring such knowledge and understanding to bear on all the decisions of a modern government. Tinbergen (1956, ch. 8) does note that the extreme centralization and universal coordination required for ideal administration is not descriptive of actual governments, but he does not explore the causes or implications of this discrepancy.

Similar discrepancies exist elsewhere. No modern corporation of any size is run so that all decisions are made by those legally responsible to the shareholders, even though all business decisions have implications for shareholder returns. The managers are not lazy or irresponsible; rather their rationality is bounded (Simon, 1957). No single individual can possibly analyze and evaluate carefully all the decisions that must be made daily in any large firm. As long as managers are human, complete and perfect centralization of decision making must result in action taken without adequate analysis. Well-run modern firms deal with this fundamental problem by seeking forms of organization that permit top management to delegate substantial decision-making authority to subordinates yet provide incentives for the resultant decisions to be consistent with top management's objectives. The use of internal profit centers is a clear response to the problem of bounded rationality.[4]

If corporations, concerned in principle with the single objective of shareholder wealth, find it necessary to decentralize decision making, then it must be true *a fortiori* that the bounded rationality of politicians and civil servants, concerned with a variety of conflicting and ill-defined goals, implies that perfect centralization and coordination of government decision making is incompatible with intelligent action. Indeed some argue that one of the great virtues of the federal system in the United States is its avoidance of excessive centralization of decision making. In any case, as Davis (1969) and Auerbach (1972), among others, have pointed out, those ultimately responsible to the electorate must delegate some decision-making authority to others if government is to cope with the complexity of the modern world. No single body, no single chief executive can possibly do an adequate job of making or reviewing all the detailed decisions required of most modern governments.

Let us now see what bounded rationality implies about the operational value of the political view of the proper objectives of control of natural monopoly. If regulation or any other control device is to respond to shifts in the balance of political forces, some agency must be involved. No computer or set of contracts can possibly possess the requisite sensitivity to interest group pressures. In addition, this agency must have some freedom to make decisions that are not subject to detailed review.

Indeed under virtually any workable arrangement, control of natural monopoly requires an agency of some sort with specialized skills. If nothing else, history demonstrates that this task cannot be performed adequately on a part-time basis by either the executive or the legislature. (See, for instance, White, 1921, on the failures of control without specialized agencies in Massachusetts in the nineteenth century.)

An agency with some freedom from detailed administrative scrutiny of its every action might be made responsive to the whole range of legitimate interest group pressures in two ways. First, it could be directly responsible to the electorate in some way, perhaps by the direct election of regulators or by legal requirements to hear and weigh all affected interests. Second, it could somehow be made to internalize the values and objectives of the elected chief executive, thus doing (without review of its actions) what he or she would have done. Neither approach seems to have great promise.

Voters' rationality and time available for political action are bounded. If all agencies of a modern government were, in effect, transformed into miniature legislatures, no single voter could intelligently participate in all aspects of the (quasi-) legislative process. Instead interest groups would concentrate their attention on a subset of agencies, with the result that different agencies would face and thus respond to different balances of forces.

Regulatory agencies are now, in at least some important respects, responsive to a spectrum of interest groups, and some concentration of attention does occur.[5] For example, environmentalists have concentrated much of their energy on electric utility regulation (Joskow, 1974). Their effect on that process, however, exceeds their impact on government policy across the board; that is, more weight seems to be given to the objective of environmental protection vis à vis other objectives in electric utility regulation than in other government decisions. But this form of control differs from complete capture by special interests, which the political critics decry, only in degree. It is certainly incompatible with elementary notions of efficient administration, which require that conflicting objectives receive the same relative weights in all decisions.

One might seek to mitigate this problem by making some but not all agencies directly responsive to the electorate, though there seems no reason why regulators of natural monopolies would logically be selected for inclusion in this set. Local police departments probably make decisions with more impact on most citizens; the Department of Defense may control a larger fraction of pretax income; and public assistance programs seem to arouse stronger emotions. The list of more plausible candidates for direct voter control could be extended almost indefinitely.

For these and other reasons, critics who adopt the political conception of regulatory inadequacy take something like the second approach mentioned above when they propose reform; the most common proposals involve tighter control over regulatory agencies by the elected chief executive. Since detailed review of all decisions is impossible, such control must involve making sure that agencies internalize and pursue the executive's objectives. But this approach has apparently insoluble problems as well.

First, it is difficult to imagine that any elected chief executive could articulate fully the precise objectives he wishes pursued. And it is impossible to imagine such articulations accompanied by clear indications of the relative importance of those objectives. Governments do not deal with easily quantified basic goals, to which numerical weights can be attached; the executive cannot easily express the relative values of competing goals.

If agencies cannot be given clear objectives, the details of their decision making are not susceptible to effective review and their overall performance cannot be evaluated in any precise way by executive, legislative, or judicial review. This situation contrasts sharply with the business world, where managers of profit centers can be judged, at least in large part, on quantitative indicators provided by an accounting system.

Still, if one could be confident that administrators would earnestly and capably strive to understand and pursue the appropriately weighted objectives of the relevant elected officials, delegation of decision-making authority without the possibility of objective performance review might not pose severe problems. But administrators are human. As Downs (1967) and others have noted, they can be expected to pursue their own interests. Sometimes those interests will be well served by trying to do what elected officials would have done themselves, but this will certainly not always be the case when those officials have no good way of monitoring performance. (As Cleveland, 1956, shows vividly, many forces affect modern bureaucrats.) Thus some degree of regulatory failure as defined by Cutler and Johnson (1975) is inevitable.

Administrators' necessary freedom of action opens the door to the possibilities of special interest domination on the one hand and the arbitrary exercise of power on the other hand. As Bernstein (1972) has emphasized, the possibility of capture by special interests applies to executive branch agencies as well as to independent regulatory commissions. The classic study of the U.S. Army Corps of Engineers by Maass (1951) illustrates both this general point and the importance of legislative committees as loci of pressure. Wilson (1971, 1974) discusses the incentives for arbitrary and erratic administrative actions, and Davis (1969) grapples with the problem of preventing such behavior.

In short, the political view of appropriate regulatory performance is an inherently unattainable ideal; effective interest group competition on all decisions and effective decision making are incompatible. In order to permit regulators to consider the whole spectrum of collective goals and to respond directly or indirectly to all interest group pressures, they must be given considerable freedom of action. But the relative lack of control that must accompany the delegation of broad authority increases the difficulty of ensuring that desirable trade-offs are made and makes special interest dominance and arbitrary action or inaction more likely. It is simply not possible, desirable though it seems in principle, to use the control of natural monopoly effectively to pursue a number of potentially conflicting social goals.

A way around these problems with the political view of regulatory objectives is suggested by the use of profit centers in large corporations. If one can provide subordinates with clear objectives that are consistent with the overall goals of the organization, one can evaluate performance without monitoring the details of decision making. The ability to review performance makes control possible. If individual agencies are charged with the pursuit of well-defined objectives, their performance can be reviewed. It is the notion that regulators should pursue and strike an appropriate balance among a variety of ill-defined goals that makes effective control difficult. Moreover if regulatory objectives were clearly defined by statute, judicial review could concentrate on society's substantive goals rather than focus on highly derivative issues of procedure.

Just as not all functions in most businesses can be set up as profit centers, not all government agencies can be given sensible and well-defined objectives. But where this can be done, the potential for increased effectiveness and simplified administration (and adjudication) is considerable. Both Posner (1976) and Bork (1978), for instance, have argued that economic efficiency should be the sole objective of antitrust policy. Although some of their case is built on analyses of legislative intent and statutory language that often do not have direct analogs in the context of regulation, some of their other arguments are directly relevant.

Posner (1976, ch. 2) notes that protection of small business has also been proposed as an appropriate goal of antitrust. Although he does not deny the legitimacy of that goal in the abstract, he argues that antitrust is not an especially good instrument to employ in its pursuit. Further, he contends, to require courts to assess the impact of their decisions on small business would greatly complicate the antitrust process. Similarly Bork (1978, pp. 110-2) argues that to require antitrust to consider the distributional consequences of proposed actions would bog the process down in complexity. Posner (1976, ch. 2) holds that if courts are given the conflicting goals of enhancing efficiency by promoting competition and of protecting small business, they must strike a balance between them in particular cases without clear guidance, thus inevitably rendering decisions that are fundamentally arbitrary. Similarly Bork (1978, ch. 3) argues that to require courts to decide the proper trade-offs among economic efficiency and diverse other objectives is to transform the courts into legislatures not subject to review by the electorate. Since a positive case can be made for economic efficiency as the sole appropriate objective of antitrust, and since adopting it as such would avoid these and other problems, both authors argue strongly for its adoption.

I contend that control of natural monopoly is another policy area where a single clear objective can be productively adopted and, as Posner and Bork have argued in antitrust, that objective should be economic efficiency.[6] The administrative arguments for adoption of a single goal whenever it is sensible to do so do not indicate what the goal should be in any particular case. But there are strong reasons for choosing economic efficiency as the appropriate objective of control of natural monopoly. After all, the defining characteristics of natural monopoly are economic, and the only coherent justification of which I am aware for singling out natural monopolies for special treatment rests on economic analysis and argues that economic performance in the absence of control may be unacceptable. If one must pick a single objective for telephone pricing, for instance, economic efficiency is surely much more natural than, say, distributive justice. The tax system, after all, has a much more profound effect on the distribution of real income, while telephone regulation can much more directly and precisely affect resource use in that industry than any other available government instrument.

Pursuit of economic efficiency in natural monopoly industries may, of course, conflict from time to time with other legitimate social goals, just as pro-competitive antitrust policy may conflict with a legitimate social interest in fostering small business. But there is a fundamental and important sense in which economic efficiency is consistent with almost all imaginable basic social goals. If policy B promotes more efficient resource use than policy A, society's options are generally greater under B than under A. In particular, there will generally exist a policy C that only redistributes income such that if B and C are adopted together, all affected parties will be made better off than they were under A. Attainment of economic efficiency implies a potential improvement in the well-being of all. This is surely an attractive general property.

If C is not adopted, a shift from A to B will likely make some individuals worse off, though the gains to others will in aggregate be larger. And regulatory agencies generally do not have the power to make lump-sum income transfers. Thus regulatory actions in pursuit of economic efficiency will in general harm some and help others.

The argument that economic efficiency should be the dominant or sole objective of public utility regulation is hardly novel. Donahue (1971, p. 209), for instance, concludes from a literature survey that "the sole function of price and entry regulation is to compensate for market failure—to perform the allocative function of the competitive market in a situation in which that market could not operate." Kahn (1970, 1971, 1975) has persistently advocated the adoption of economic efficiency as the dominant goal of utility regulation, and he has deplored the tendency of regulators to impose their own values on the industries they regulate. Kahn and Zielinski (1976a, 1976b) explore in detail the implications of this viewpoint for telephone rate structures. At the close of their analysis, they argue that "it is time regulators stopped trying to play legislator with this industry" (1976b, p. 23). Unless regulators focus on only one objective, however, the arguments of this section imply that they have no choice but to "play legislator" and to resolve conflicts among alternative goals in light of their own preferences and values.

Beyond Economic Efficiency?

Although economic efficiency should be the only objective of government control of natural monopoly industries, other objectives may be much more important. Indeed, economic efficiency is not an ultimate objective at all, merely a means to a variety of ends. Many other goals are more fundamental and, in my view, more important. Yet I do not think that they should be consciously pursued in the control of natural monopoly. The average person may not worry about economic efficiency, but those in charge of natural monopolies should, and they should not have to decide conflicts between efficiency and other goals.

This prescription is apparently at odds with current utility regulation, which seems—on the surface at least—to be greatly concerned with questions of fairness and justice, to the partial or total exclusion of efficiency considerations. At least two general principles of fairness seem to surface in this context. The first states that regulatory (or other administrative) actions should not be arbitrary and capricious; they should follow from the careful application of principles developed in the political process. I see no conflict between this principle and regulation that carefully and diligently seeks economic efficiency; the actions of such a regime must be more easily predicted than those of an agency trying to maintain a balance among competing goals and interest groups over time. (This echoes Bork, 1978, ch. 3, who says that only by focusing antitrust policy on a single objective can the courts avoid rendering arbitrary decisions.)

The second principle of fairness is that regulation should avoid robbing the poor to help the rich, or, more generally, robbing the deserving to help the undeserving. A variety of regulatory decisions apparently have been motivated at least in part by some version of this principle (see Kahn, 1970, pp. 190-92, for instance). A regulator's view of who should be taxed or subsidized in any particular case may differ from that which would emerge from the political process, however. Even if it did not, it is hard to ensure in advance or to determine after the fact that departures from efficiency in any particular case were motivated only by a concern for distributive justice; regulators, like the rest of us, do not always listen only to their consciences. In any event, as Breyer (1971) and Kahn (1975) have pointed out, regulatory attempts to subsidize the deserving and tax the undeserving have generally been based on inadequate study of either efficiency or equity impacts of policies selected and on unclear ultimate objectives. Peltzman's (1976) theoretical analysis of regulators' cross-subsidization decisions suggests that these would not have any desirable properties even if informed by good analysis (also Hilton, 1972, and Russell and Shelton, 1974).

Feldstein (1972a, 1972b) and Munk (1977), among others, have analyzed the problem of setting natural monopoly prices so as to take account of the differential effects of price changes on different groups in the economy. In principle, this problem can be solved. It requires the ability to evaluate the ultimate incidence on various groups of consumers of prices charged business, however, and economists do not yet seem capable of this. (See Schmalensee, 1977, for a discussion.) More importantly, its operational solution also requires a set of explicit weights to be attached to the real incomes or welfare levels of different households or groups of households in society. Munk (1977), in particular, notes the sensitivity of optimal price policy to those weights. It is difficult to imagine any such system of distributive weights being given to regulators by elected executives or legislatures. But the only alternative is to allow regulators to devise their own weights, hardly an appealing prospect. The relative importance of the well-being of individual citizens or groups of households is surely a basic and fundamental political issue, which regulators have no special competence or legitimacy to settle. But without a set of explicit distributive weights, there is no systematic, nonarbitrary way to factor concern with distributive justice into regulatory decision making.[7]

The result is that although control of natural monopoly will affect the division of real income between rich and poor and between the deserving and the undeserving, no control mechanism can evaluate those effects in a systematic and satisfactory way. In the interests of administrative feasibility and rationality and to avoid arbitrary and capricious actions, control should focus on economic efficiency. The system should be aimed at efficient resource use and evaluated by its success in meeting that goal.[8]

This argument resembles Harberger's (1971) call for the neglect of incidence analysis in cost-benefit studies on grounds of administrative feasibility. But at the level of analysis rather than that of decision, I would disagree with him here. Regulatory actions in pursuit of efficiency may have important distributional impacts from time to time. Regulators have no special competence or legitimacy to pass judgment on such impacts, but they should be in a good position to describe them. It seems both appropriate and productive for them to develop such descriptions and to provide them to the relevant elected officials. (Willig and Bailey, 1977, provide tools that should be useful in such efforts.) The distribution of real income may be a legitimate social and political concern. If that distribution is noticeably affected by particular regulatory actions, those responsible to the electorate may wish to offset those effects through tax or other policies. This division of concerns will not produce perfect policy coordination, but that is impossible anyway.

Economists should be encouraged to perform systematic analysis of the incidence of regulatory policies on various groups in the economy, not to help regulators impose their own notions of fairness but to inform those constitutionally responsible for value judgments. Economists should obviously not abandon their traditional concern with allocative efficiency; if the normative conclusions of this chapter are accepted, efficiency analysis should be the main guide to the design and execution of policies to control natural monopoly sectors.

Similar reasoning applies to the role of other social goals in the natural monopoly control process. The regulated industries have important impacts on both the environment and the pattern of energy consumption, for instance. Regulators should be able and willing to analyze such impacts. But there is clearly little to be said for having national energy or environmental policies emerge willy-nilly from the isolated deliberations of a host of regulatory agencies. If the government has energy use and environmental policies, these must affect the regulated sectors. But regulators themselves have no special competence or authority to make such policies. Ideally they should inform but not dominate policy making in these and other areas. Regulatory decisions should follow Harberger's (1971) advice to analysts and assume the correctness of market prices and the decisions of other administrative agencies. For example, it makes no sense to delegate to the ICC, explicitly or by default, the authority to determine the appropriate value to be placed on rail service to rural areas, though rural development may be a legitimate goal of the federal government. (On this example, see Kahn, 1970, pp. 190-92.)

Further, the analysis of Federal Power Commission (FPC) planning by Breyer and MacAvoy (1974) suggests strongly that there is no special role for regulators in that activity. Planning that relates specifically to a single regulated industry can be done by managers, as it is in the unregulated sector. Policy planning that relates to several industries, as in energy or transportation, is logically unrelated to the basic tasks of natural monopoly control and ought to be done, if at all, by other parts of the government's administrative apparatus.

Implications for Regulatory Reform

The preceding discussion provides a potentially useful objective and a set of evaluative standards, not a reform proposal. There are a host of reasons why regulators cannot be expected to maintain an exclusive concern with the systematic pursuit of efficiency under current arrangements. The incentives facing them tend to encourage a balancing of opposed interests rather than pursuit of any single goal.[9] It remains to be seen whether alternative social control structures exist that can be confidently expected to induce economic efficiency in natural monopoly industries.

But restricting attention for the moment to conventional rate-of-return regulation, the analysis here does seem to have at least two immediate implications for desirable reform that deserve discussion. First, statutory mandates should be narrowed. Second, experts, and in particular economists, should play a larger role in the regulatory process.

An important characteristic of utility regulation is that statutory mandates have been too broad. As Spengler (1969, p. 3) puts it, "Economically, regulatory legislation usually embodies the principle of the just price." This principle leaves regulators with considerable apparent freedom since virtually any price can be plausibly defended as just by a skilled advocate. (There are, of course, a host of procedural restrictions affecting the form, but only indirectly if at all the substance, of commission decision making; see Jones, 1967, pp. 146-58.)

As Bernstein (1955, 1972), Jaffe (1954), Noll (1971a), and others have argued, the vagueness of regulatory statutes serves to enhance regulators' freedom to pursue their own interests, increasing the likelihood of arbitrary and inefficient decisions. Noll (1971b, chs. 4, 8), for instance, considers in some detail the undesirable consequences of the increasing vagueness of the ICC's mandate (see also Locklin, 1966, chs. 11-13). At the same time, the comparative absence of legislative or executive constraints on their actions has made regulators both more attractive and more vulnerable to special interest groups. Further, when a vague mandate in effect asks regulators to do everything, they often respond by trying to avoid decisions that might offend any strong interest groups; the response to statutory overload is often refusal to make decisions. MacAvoy (1971b) provides a good example by documenting the high ratio of paperwork to decision making in FPC activity (see also Wilson, 1971, 1974, and Noll 1971a).

If economic efficiency is accepted as the single appropriate goal of natural monopoly control, the mandates of regulators of such industries should attempt to require them to pursue only that goal. Their freedom of action to pursue other objectives, whether society's, their own, or those of special interests, should be reduced as much as possible. Limiting regulators' authority in this way should facilitate administrative and political control, contribute to overall administrative and economic efficiency, and reduce potentially adverse consequences of the inevitable exercise of administrative discretion.

Writers, such as Bernstein (1955, ch. 4) and Massel (1961), who adopt the political conception of regulatory failure tend strongly to oppose the domination of regulation by experts. If, after all, the task of regulation is to pursue the public interest, or in more modern terms, to respond appropriately to the legitimate concerns of all affected interest groups, broad statesman, not narrow economists, are needed as regulators. Breadth, vision, and sensitivity are needed to produce fair and just rulings, in this view.

On the other hand, Smith (1978) notes an increased tendency for economists to be appointed to state public utility commissions, which he attributes to the increasing technical complexity of the regulatory process. Even defining *economist* rather broadly, though, Smith finds only 13 economists among 226 state commissioners. Still, this tendency is quite appropriate if the goal of monopoly regulation is taken to be the attainment of economic efficiency. Indeed as Donahue (1971) has argued forcefully, it is hard to see why the process should not be dominated almost entirely by economists. Questions of sensitivity and breadth of vision do not arise with much force if there is a single, clear goal to be pursued rather than a host of competing claims to be arbitrated.

As Donahue (1971), a lawyer, argues, the lawyer's skills of advocacy and compromise are wasted in such situations; dominance of regulation by lawyers has a clear historical basis, but its continuation can be justified only by the assertion that multiple goals should be pursued and balanced.[10] Acceptance of economic efficiency as the only goal of natural monopoly control would seem to imply directly that the relevant experts, economists, should play the dominant role in the control process.

Of course, simply replacing lawyers with economists on existing commissions will not automatically produce efficient regulation. Certainly professional background affects behavior, as Seidman (1970) illustrates, so that one would expect some changes in regulatory conduct. Spengler (1969), for instance, plausibly argues that replacing lawyers by economists would be likely to produce more flexible regulation, with the economist's respect for the market replacing the lawyer's respect for precedent. But economists are human, and the same sort of forces that now cause some apparently civic-minded lawyers to regulate poorly along a variety of dimensions would also act on economist commissioners. The notion that economists should play the major roles in controlling natural monopolies is a consequence of acceptance of economic efficiency as the only appropriate goal of that process; it is not a proposal that can ensure that goal's adoption or achievement.

Notes

1. On those expectations and the reasoning that supported them, see Bernstein, *Regulating Business,* ch. 1.

2. The remainder of this paragraph is intended neither as a complete survey nor as an endorsement of this literature. The efficiency implications of current utility regulation in the United States are considered in some detail in chapter 3. Chapter 4 provides a more systematic discussion of the literature on regulatory behavior.

3. The reform proposals surveyed by Bernstein, "Independent Regulatory Agencies," and Thomas, "Politics, Structure, and Personnel," embody varying mixtures of the political and administrative views of regulatory inadequacy. See also Cutler and Johnson, "Regulation and Political Pressure," and the literature they cite.

4. For more on the need for and problems of decentralization of business decision making, see Chandler, *Strategy and Structure,* and Williamson, *Markets and Hierarchies.*

5. See Stewart, "Reformation of American Administrative Law," on this trend.

6. This is intended as a prescription, not a description. I am not arguing that utility regulation was ever instituted solely for the purpose of pursuing efficiency or that it has ever engaged exclusively in that task.

7. Willig and Bailey, "Income Distributional Concerns," propose an interesting approach to the evaluation of the incidence of price changes that does not require explicit distributive weights. Unfortunately their approach, even in principle, can label only some price changes as acceptable or unacceptable; it cannot evaluate all changes or serve to select an optimal price structure. For more discussion of this proposal, see Schmalensee, "Income Distributional Concerns." See also Williamson, "Administrative Decision Making," on the incorporation of some equity concerns directly in efficiency analysis.

8. Some monopoly control decisions must involve equity considerations. In a single-product natural monopoly with everywhere declining costs, pursuit of efficiency implies marginal cost pricing, which in turn implies a deficit. If such a deficit must be covered, some sort of tax must be imposed, either by the treasury or in the form of a price above cost. Tax policy cannot in general be derived entirely from efficiency considerations. For a number of reasons, it seems best to postpone discussion of this problem until chapter 3.

9. See Bernstein, *Regulating Business;* Jaffe, "Effective Limits"; Noll, "Behavior of Regulatory Agencies," and *Reforming Regulation;* Pallerzi, "Conceptual View of the Regulatory Process"; Peltzman, "Toward a More General Theory of Regulation"; Seidman, *Politics, Position, and Power;* and Wilson, "Dead Hand of Regulation," and "Politics of Regulation." On the difficulty of inducing systematic, consistent regulatory activity in any direction, see Auerbach, "Pluralism and the Administrative Process"; Cutler and Johnson, "Regulation and the Political Process"; Davis, "New Approach to Delegation"; Lowi, *End of Liberalism;* Friendly, *Federal Administrative Agencies;* McConnell, *Private Power,* ch. 8; and Wilson, "Politics of Regulation."

10. In the terminology of Selznick, *Leadership in Administration,* the contention here is that if natural monopoly control is targeted on efficiency, the ratio of routine to critical decisions will rise. The importance of efficiency (in Selznick's sense) rises relative to that of leadership if organizational mission is fixed. Kahn, *Economics of Regulation,* ch. 1, and "Between Theory and Practice," has sensible observations on the role of economists in regulation.

3 Utility Regulation and Economic Efficiency

Traditional Regulatory Practice

As bases for subsequent discussions, this chapter sketches and compares procedures and results under traditional utility regulation in the U.S., on the one hand, with the requisites for efficient resource use, on the other. This introductory section briefly describes typical regulatory procedure in U.S. public utility sectors as it had stabilized by the late 1960s.[1] The remainder of this chapter is devoted to comparing utility performance under regulation with the 4Ps necessary for efficient resource use: *prices* based on incremental cost, appropriate *products* offered for sale, *production* that minimizes cost, and *profits* just sufficient to provide necessary capital.

Most regulated public utility firms have legal monopolies over specified geographic areas. Firms providing telephone service or electric power, for instance, generally have assigned franchise areas from which they cannot expand but within which they are more or less immune to entry. (There are exceptions, of course; see Primeaux, 1975, on competition in the distribution of electricity.) Only in rare instances do regulators, especially at the state level, concern themselves with the identity of suppliers or with the possibility of new entry. The task before them is control of the historically determined legal monopolies under their jurisdiction.

Regulators' mandates focus on prices, which are to be "just and reasonable" or to satisfy some other similarly vague standard. Prices are set in rate cases and, except for the operation of automatic adjustment clauses, remain fixed between cases. Rate cases resemble in many procedural respects civil cases tried by state or federal courts, and the regulatory commission's role is much like that of a panel of judges. Witnesses are heard and cross-examined; rules of evidence and procedure must be followed; appeal to higher courts is possible. Rate cases are most frequently initiated by regulated firms seeking the authority to change prices. (For an interesting behavioral model of firms' decisions to seek price changes, see Joskow, 1973.)

The quantitative analysis that must be done in a rate case in order to justify particular new prices focuses on a *test period,* traditionally a year in the past. The key issue facing the commission is the level of profits necessary to provide the utility a *fair rate of return* on its invested capital, or *rate base.* New prices are set so that if they had been in effect during the test year, they would have yielded such a rate of return. Basic accounting defines the rate of return as follows:

$$\text{Rate of Return} = (\text{Revenues} - \text{Expenses})/\text{Invested Capital}. \qquad (3.1)$$

In typical rate cases, expenses are primarily determined by test period accounting results; they are not subjected to systematic examination during the case. Similarly, the total invested capital or rate base is usually determined by the depreciated original cost of the firm's assets. Even when this is not the case, the rate base is computed according to more or less stable and well-defined procedures.

Controversy in rate cases usually centers on the appropriate rate of return to be allowed. Generally the fair rate of return is taken to be that necessary to attract new capital funds, which in turn implies that equity holders are to be provided returns on their investment commensurate with those provided by other enterprises of comparable risk.[2] This standard is reasonably clear in principle, but it has not proven capable of routine and uncontroversial application. One must have some model of capital market operation and investor behavior that permits translation of such concepts as *comparable risk* into potentially operational terms. Then the model must be calibrated with some set of data in order to produce numerical estimates. In a typical rate case, a number of expert witnesses present and defend a variety of models and a range of estimates of the fair rate of return.

The commission, usually not composed of individuals with much expertise in finance or economics (Smith, 1978), chooses a fair rate of return on the basis of this testimony and whatever other factors it finds relevant. Given the expenses, rate base, and rate of return thus determined, equation 3.1 can be solved for the *revenue requirements* of the test period:

$$\text{Revenue Requirements} = \text{Expenses} + (\text{Fair Rate of Return}) (\text{Rate Base}). \quad (3.2)$$

The regulated firm is then typically instructed to submit a set of prices that would yield the required revenues when applied to actual test period sales. The structure of prices submitted in response to such requests generally does not receive systematic analysis; if it seems "just and reasonable" and if the firm's arithmetic is correct, it is approved.

This process, even in this simplified version, can take some time to operate. Hyman (1975, table 3) found an average lag of about one year in the early 1970s between the initial filing of proposed rates by regulated utilities and the issuance of a *rate order* by the relevant commission that finally authorized new prices. If the firm or some other party decides to appeal the commission's decision to the courts, much longer delays can result.

As Trebing (1974) has noted, the basic features of rate-of-return regulation remained unchanged from the 1920s until the 1970s.[3] The rapid inflation that began in the late 1960s, however, put severe strains on utility regulation, as Joskow (1974) and MacAvoy (1978) describe. The responses to these strains by regulators, regulated firms, and others have been diverse; some of them will be mentioned in the remainder of this chapter and discussed in chapters 7 and 8. But it is useful to keep in mind that the process of utility regulation as described (or caricatured) above represents the starting point from which recent changes in regulatory practice have originated. Change has generally been evolutionary, not revolutionary; the foregoing describes a reasonably close relative of most of the current population of regulatory practices.

Pricing and Product Selection

A key requirement for efficient resource allocation, in natural monopoly industries as elsewhere in the economy, is that prices be based on marginal or incremental costs; they should reflect the actual costs that would be incurred as the result of increases in demand, not some measure of the average historical cost of meeting historical demand levels. Only then do the prices that influence demanders' decisions reflect the costs that those decisions impose on suppliers and thus on society as a whole. Kahn (1970, p. 65) correctly describes equality between price and marginal cost as "the central policy prescription of micro-economics."

Most regulated monopolies offer a variety of products or services, though pricing policy often does not reflect this. Electricity consumed at 5:00 P.M. on a hot summer day is a commodity with different cost and demand characteristics than electricity at 2:00 A.M. on a winter morning. The same statement holds for water. Gas that can be interrupted at the supplier's discretion differs in cost and demand aspects from noninterruptable gas service. Long-distance telephone calls are not the same commodity as local calls, and even local calls may have different costs depending on whether they involve urban or rural subscribers. Industrial firms that use electricity supplied at high voltage clearly purchase a different commodity than do typical residential users of electricity.

If economic efficiency is an important goal of utility regulation, then the structure of utility prices or rates should be a central focus of regulatory attention. This has not been the general pattern, however. Regulators' neglect of rate structure issues has been noted and deplored by numerous authors, including Kahn (1970, pp. 45-54), A. Phillips (1974), and Shepherd (1975, ch. 9). To my knowledge, no estimates have been made of the overall efficiency costs of this clear regulatory failure in natural monopoly sectors, but the central importance of price and the general neglect of marginalist pricing principles suggest that those costs may have been substantial.

To the extent that utility regulators in the United States have been concerned with rate structures, they have tended to focus on prices paid by different classes of users. But this focus has typically been motivated and informed by considerations of equity or fairness rather than efficiency. Thus it is standard practice to require statewide uniformity in basic residential telephone rates, even though the costs of serving rural households may be well above the costs of providing service in urban areas.[4] (See Posner, 1971, for further examples and discussion of this sort of cross-subsidization.)

In a seminal article, Lipsey and Lancaster (1956) showed that efficiency considerations can in principle justify prices that diverge from marginal costs.[5] Suppose an economy has twenty-six markets, labeled A to Z, with only the price charged in A subject to direct government control. Suppose further that because of uncontrolled monopoly, excise taxation, or other distortions, buyers in markets B to Z do not face prices equal to marginal costs. The best government policy would be to eliminate all the distortions in the economy and to induce marginal cost pricing in all markets. But if this is not feasible, Lipsey and Lancaster show that the *second-best* price policy for industry A alone is not always marginal cost pricing. In an economy with distortions elsewhere, second-best analysis establishes that efficiency-seeking monopoly control should not necessarily require marginal cost pricing.

There is no problem in principle here, of course; nothing is sacred about marginal cost pricing. But the theory also shows that in order to compute the most efficient second-best price in any particular case, a staggering amount of information about the nature and effects of distortions in other markets is required. To my knowledge, nobody has ever even attempted a full computation of the second-best price policy for a natural monopoly firm or industry; the task seems well beyond economists' current and likely future abilities. Thus just as virtually any set of prices can be defended as fair, almost any prices can be asserted to be optimal on second-best grounds since the calculations necessary to prove this assertion incorrect are apparently impossible to perform. If one must show beyond doubt that they are inefficient, regulatory cross-subsidization policies are immune to attack.

But this seems an inappropriate placement of the burden of proof. In the first place, the theoretical literature does indicate that in many cases, the second-best optimum is still marginal cost pricing (see Dusansky and Walsh, 1976, for a recent contribution). Basically this occurs when the industry considered is not closely and directly related (as a major supplier of inputs or buyer of outputs, or as a producer of important substitutes or complements) to a market that is severely distorted. (See Kahn, 1970, p. 196, and the references he cites.) If one considers the U.S. economy to be generally competitive, it would seem to follow that marginal cost pricing must provide a good approximation to second-best optimality in many cases. Then since the real choice is between social control based on marginal cost pricing and social control with no operationally defined objective, it seems most sensible to take marginal cost pricing as a starting point for efficiency-oriented control. In some cases, good second-best arguments for departing from such pricing may exist (see Kahn, 1970, pp. 195-98, and 1971, pp. 241-43, for a general discussion and an example). In such cases, it seems reasonable that regulators or other control agents charged with the pursuit of efficiency be required to make those arguments explicitly in order to defend prices that diverge from marginal costs. That is, in order to make pursuit of efficiency an operational goal of natural monopoly control, the burden of proof should be on those advocating departures from *first-best* marginal cost pricing. This will not ensure second-best optimality in all situations, of course, but as long as the economy is generally competitive, it should provide sensible, efficiency-enhancing decisions in most cases. And there would seem to be no better feasible and consistent policy.

This policy implies that regulators in most cases should take prices set in other markets as efficient and correct. On this view, equity-based regulatory cross-subsidization cannot be defended by simply arguing that its second-best optimality cannot be disproven; such nonmarginalist pricing is likely inefficient and should thus be treated as in conflict with regulation's appropriate objective in the absence of persuasive supportive analysis.

Perhaps the most serious public utility rate structure problem, and certainly the one that has received the most attention in recent years, is the failure of U.S. utilities and their regulators to move to peak-load pricing schemes, in which price varies regularly over time as marginal cost does. (The term derives from the general prescription that price should be higher when demand is at its peak than at other, off-peak times.) The only cost of meeting additional demand for electricity at 2:00 A.M. in the winter is likely to be the cost of fuel, while in order to expand output at 5:00 P.M. in the summer, it may be necessary to add new capacity as well as to consume more fuel. Marginal cost is thus lower in the first instance than in the second, and price should accordingly also be lower. For small residential users, the gains from prices that vary by time of day may in some cases be outweighed by the additional metering costs that would be incurred. But this is unlikely to happen for large commercial or industrial customers. In any particular case, the size of net efficiency gains, net of metering costs, can be estimated reasonably easily. Even seasonal variation in prices, which would entail no special metering problems, can produce sizable gains in electricity (Wenders and Taylor, 1976), gas (Tzoannos, 1977), and other sectors.

The basic theoretical rationale for peak-load pricing based on marginal cost in utility sectors was developed in the early 1950s, and refinement has proceeded to the present day.[6] Peak-load pricing principles have been widely applied abroad, apparently beginning with electricity supply in Britain and France in the 1950s. These principles were persistently advocated (and, in part, developed) by American economists. Yet Shepherd's (1966a) survey of telephone and electricity rate structures in the United States in the mid-1960s shows very little penetration of marginal cost pricing. On the commission side, this may have reflected lawyers' general hostility toward technical economic arguments, perhaps supplemented by a feeling that such abstractions and minutiae were beneath the concern of those in pursuit of either the broad public interest or their own private welfare. Managers of regulated firms could also be expected to resist new and difficult-to-comprehend approaches to pricing. Finally Bailey's (1972) theoretical analysis implies that if the provision of additional peak capacity is capital intensive, regulated firms have an incentive to resist peak-load pricing because it would lower their rate base and thus their allowed profits.[7]

Whatever its sources, the resistance to marginal cost pricing seems to have melted away in the last few years, at least in the electric utility sector. State utility commissions are moving rapidly toward time-of-day pricing (Joskow, 1977), and federal legislation mandating consideration of peak-load pricing of electricity was signed in November, 1978. Economists in the United States seem to be newly fascinated by the practical problems of implementing marginal cost principles in electricity supply (see, for instance, Cicchetti, Gillen, and Smolensky, 1977, and Scherer, 1977).

It is much too soon to draw the conclusion that marginal cost pricing will soon be the rule rather than the exception in U.S. public utility sectors. As Joskow (1977) makes clear, the main reasons for the move toward peak-load pricing of electricity are noneconomic and peculiar to that industry; economists have not become noticeably more persuasive. Adoption of marginal cost principles in other industries seems to be proceeding much more slowly. Further, in spite of its theoretical elegance and good press coverage, peak-load pricing is not the only potentially important application of these principles. Traditional questions having to do with, say, residential versus commercial rates, should also be addressed in marginal terms. Similarly as Kahn (1970, ch. 5) and McKie (1970) discuss, a number of delicate and potentially important pricing issues arise when regulated firms face competition (see also Baumol, 1967). In spite of the recent flurry of activity in the electric utility industry, the general adoption of prices based on marginal costs in the U.S. public utility sectors is far from certain in the foreseeable future. Peak-load pricing of electricity is an important step in the right direction, if one accepts economic efficiency as the appropriate goal of natural monopoly control, but many other important steps toward the full use of marginal cost pricing will remain after it has been taken.

Related to the structure of prices to be charged by a natural monopoly is the question of the appropriate array of products to be produced. As Spence (1976) and others have recently shown, the competitive market mechanism cannot be relied upon to produce a solution to the product selection problem with any particular optimality properties. Under natural monopoly, the limitation to one producer and the tendency for costs to fall with the output of any single product may impose particularly tight restrictions on the array of products that can be produced economically. If it is not efficient for an electric utility to sell interruptable power to residential customers, for instance, they can purchase only service with a single level of reliability. Since residential customers have no choice along this important dimension of product quality, they cannot directly reveal their willingness to pay for increments to system reliability by their market behavior.

In such situations, the utility's choice of capacity (often a key determinant of reliability) and other quality-related decisions become public goods in certain respects. (The general public good dimensions of product quality choices are analyzed by Drèze and Hagen, 1978.) Government spending for national defense, the classic example of a public good, directly affects all citizens. In spite of their different preferences for national defense, all must somehow collectively choose a single level of spending. Similarly the quality attributes selected by a public utility directly affect the happiness or profits of its entire set of customers, whose preferences for different aspects of quality may vary considerably (see Donahue, 1971, pp. 213-14, for a suggestive discussion). Buchanan (1968) and Sherman (1970) examine the public good dimensions of utility investment decisions in general.

Fully optimal solutions to the collective choice problems that are intrinsic to situations involving public goods are never easy to obtain (see Tideman and Tullock, 1976, for an exposition of some interesting recent developments in this area). On the other hand, careful analysis that neglects the incidence of costs and benefits can yield reasonable operational solutions to quality choice problems (see Telson, 1975, for an unfortunately rare example).

As Hunter (1917) documents, most early attempts to regulate monopolies focused on maintenance of service quality. In many of these cases, prices were fixed by law or long-term contract, so that the firm's incentive to degrade quality was obvious. In contrast, modern utility regulation has not been much concerned with defining and enforcing quality standards (see Kahn, 1970, pp. 20-25). The consequences of this neglect have not received systematic empirical study.

Regulatory neglect of quality decisions may leave regulated firms with strong incentives to provide high-quality products, especially if quality is capital intensive. Kahn (1970, pp. 20-25) and Spence (1975) make this point in general terms. Focusing on situations involving stochastic changes in demand, Crew and Kleindorfer (1978) note that regulated firms may enhance their profits by choosing excessive reliability, and Telson's (1975) study of electrical utilities provides some support for this prediction. Excess reliability can also be useful politically by protecting both regulators and regulated firms from the storm of criticism that usually follows a major service outage.[8] (This point echoes Lindsay's, 1976, general observation that agents tend to concentrate on those aspects of performance most easily evaluated by their principals.) Still, excess quality is no better than deficient quality in efficiency terms. The product selection problem exists and may be important in many cases, in spite of regulators' tendency to ignore it.

Cost Minimization

A critical prerequisite for overall economic efficiency is efficient production, minimization of the total cost of providing goods or services. As Comanor

(1970) and Schmalensee (1974) note in the natural monopoly context, a little production inefficiency can do more harm than a lot of irrational pricing. In the short run, output must be produced at minimum cost from existing facilities. In the long run, investment must be made at appropriate times and in appropriate amounts, and new technology should be developed and adopted at the optimal rate. The costs associated with social control processes should be as low as possible.

As Kahn (1970, pp. 26-41) notes, regulators have traditionally not subjected the operating expenses and investment outlays of public utility firms to close scrutiny. In the unregulated sectors of the economy, of course, market forces give firms strong incentives to hold down costs; a dollar of cost savings translates into a dollar of profits. Under regulation, these forces are inevitably attenuated.

Indeed in a paper that has become the basis for analysis of the regulated firm in most of the economics literature, Averch and Johnson (1962) argued that rate-of-return regulation gives firms a positive incentive to produce at excessive costs by employing too much capital. This so-called AJ effect arises formally if the fair rate of return is set above the firm's cost of capital funds and if the firm can always earn the fair rate of return (but no more) on all its investment. Then the possibility of earning excess returns (above the cost of capital) on its investment in plant and equipment gives a profit-seeking regulated firm an incentive to overinvest and, more generally, to distort its pricing and other decisions so as to increase its rate base over levels dictated by economic efficiency.[9]

Stelzer (1969) and Joskow (1973, 1974), among others, have argued that the assumptions of the Averch-Johnson model are inadequate characterizations of the regulatory process. In particular they question the assumptions that the actual rate of return is forced to equal the allowed rate of return at each instant and that the regulated firm does not behave strategically toward the commission. (On the second point, see Spence, 1975, Wendel, 1976, and Baron and Taggert, 1977.) The empirical importance of the AJ effect is also a matter of some controversy. Econometric analyses of the electric utility industry by Courville (1974), Spann (1974), and Petersen (1975) find evidence of overuse of capital, but these studies have been tellingly criticized by McKay (1976). In a recent analysis of electric utilities, which permits disequilibrium behavior, Smithson (1978) fails to detect overcapitalization. Indeed Baron and Taggert (1977), using a model of regulation that departs from that of Averch and Johnson in a number of respects, find evidence suggesting undercapitalization in this industry. This last result can be rationalized within the Averch-Johnson tradition, though. If firms maximize sales revenue instead of profit, it follows from an AJ-like model that they will generally underuse capital (Bailey 1973, ch. 5). Edwards (1977) and other authors have suggested that regulated firms' managements are likely to be concerned with objectives other than profits, and Callen (1978) finds evidence of revenue-maximizing behavior in his study of regulated pipelines. In any case, while the principle that regulation can bias firms' input choices is clear, the existence of such biases, let alone their importance, in U.S. public utility sectors does not seem to have been firmly established.

After surveying the existing literature on the AJ effect, Baumol and Klevorick (1970, pp. 180-81) argued that a more important problem is what Leibenstein (1966) christened *X-inefficiency,* the tendency for management in protected situations to fail to pursue production efficiency with much vigor. Obvious measurement problems have inhibited empirical work here, however, so that the extent of this effect is unknown. It has also been argued that regulation leaves management without incentives to resist union demands; workers in regulated firms could earn "excess wages" even though shareholders do not receive excess profits, but recent work by Hendricks (1977) fails to provide much support for this hypothesis. Some comparative cost studies have been undertaken to explore the implications of public versus private ownership for electric utility costs. They do not, however, alter the conclusion that we have no good estimates of the extent of production inefficiency in U.S. public utilities. Regulation may or may not have failed in major ways here; we do not know.

An important aspect of production efficiency is the appropriate development and use of new technology. Kahn (1970, pp. 117-20) and others have argued that U.S. public utility regulation can give firms incentives to retard the introduction of new technology. (Kahn focuses on problems associated with depreciation policy in the face of unpredictable technical change.) Weintraub (1968), on the other hand, has argued that since new capital tends to be the carrier of new technology, the AJ effect may enhance progress. As the various essays in Capron (1971) indicate, the processes of regulation and of technological change are sufficiently ill understood that it is hard to go beyond the anecdotal level in analyzing the effects of the first on the second. It is not obvious to the casual observer that public utilities in the United States are greatly ahead of or behind their counterparts in other developed nations in terms of technology in use, but I know of no systematic comparative studies in this area.

A potentially important impact of regulation on costs is developed by Faulhaber (1975), Panzar and Willig (1977a), and Baumol, Bailey, and Willig (1977). (See Joskow and Noll, 1978, for a general discussion of this literature and its implications.) These authors point out the possibility that a set of commodities can involve natural monopoly (by globally subadditive costs), and yet a monopoly producer may not be immune to profit-seeking entry. That is, even if a single firm produces all the relevant commodities and even if prices are regulated so that costs are just covered, outside firms may be able to offer a subset of the commodities at prices below those charged by the regulated firm. The conclusion is that there can exist situations in which entry restrictions are necessary in order to sustain efficient production.

The implication that entry should generally be restricted in markets served or commodities provided by regulated firms does not follow. Empirical work has yet to demonstrate the existence or importance of situations where breakeven natural monopoly pricing cannot be sustained. Further, although entry restrictions may permit efficient production, firms thus protected may not have much incentive to hold costs down. In some cases, it may be better to sacrifice potential efficiency to obtain effective market pressures against X-inefficiency. Finally, as Joskow and Noll (1978) point out, the sustainability literature does not consider the original monopoly's response to entry and the impact of likely response patterns on the attractiveness of entry. These are not simple issues, of course, especially in the presence of regulation, but assuming that the existing supplier is passive likely overstates the attractiveness of entry.

The sustainability literature nonetheless establishes the possibility that regulation or any other control device can increase production costs by permitting entry in situations that truly involve natural monopoly. This may not have occurred to any important extent in U.S. public utility sectors, however. Most commentators have criticized utility regulators for being blindly hostile to new entry, not for carelessly allowing it to occur (see, for instance, Kahn, 1971, pp. 11-14, Shepherd, 1973, and Wilcox and Shepherd, 1975, ch. 13). On the other hand, policies toward new entry have changed recently in some arguably natural monopoly industries, particularly telecommunications, and proposals to relax entry restrictions elsewhere have been made. The sustainability literature does bear on these changes and proposals.

Two additional costs associated with conventional utility regulation deserve mention. First, the operating costs of the regulatory process itself may be substantial, particularly when the administrative costs imposed on regulated firms are taken into account. (See MacAvoy, 1970b, pp. 276-86, for some interesting evidence on this point.) Even if regulation or other forms of control with comparable costs induce no production inefficiency, these direct costs imply that public control should cease when it is no longer necessary. Shepherd (1973; 1975, ch. 9) has stressed this point, and Kahn (1971, ch. 1) discusses and illustrates the resistance of conventional regulation to this sort of change. While the operating costs of public utility regulation in the United States are undoubtedly substantial, however, it is not obvious that they greatly exceed the costs of alternative control systems of comparable effectiveness. That is, it is not apparent to what extent, if at all, the direct costs of current utility regulation are excessive in any operational sense.

Second, utility regulation or any alternative control device can affect the social cost of risk bearing. Individuals are made worse off when they are required to bear risk; real costs are thus imposed upon them. For economic efficiency, the risk inherent in any natural monopoly should be borne by those best able to do so, and, perhaps more importantly, the process of public control should not add to total risk. In general particularly erratic control will increase the total risk associated with a firm's operation, thus producing inefficiently high real costs. In the context of regulation, erratic or inflexible regulators can raise a utility's cost of capital, which they then expend considerable energy trying to estimate. The actual or potential importance of such effects in U.S. practice is unclear, however.[10] On the other hand, if earnings are stabilized through frequent price changes, the cost of capital may fall as risks are shifted from shareholders to a utility's customers (see Sherman, 1970, for a discussion). Commissions do not seem to have attempted seriously to consider the appropriate division of risk between the parties involved. The issue is not simple, and it does not vanish under alternative control systems. Under public ownership, for instance, risk is often borne to some extent by the relevant set of taxpayers.

Limitation of Profits

The final condition associated with economic efficiency requires that if capacity is not to be contracted, profits should be limited to the amount necessary to attract needed capital. In other words, the natural monopoly should earn zero economic profit on average or, alternatively, its actual rate of return should equal its cost of capital funds on average.

This condition has a rather different status from those discussed so far. Protection of consumers from the profitable exercise of monopoly power may have motivated or served as a public rationale for regulation or public ownership from time to time. But the fundamental natural monopoly problem is not potential excess profits but rather potential economic inefficiency, and the appropriate goal of natural monopoly control is the prevention of inefficient resource use. Assuming efficient production and appropriate product selection, economic efficiency is generally enhanced by marginal cost pricing. Under natural monopoly, marginal cost pricing need not imply zero economic profit for the enterprise as a whole. Indeed in the classic natural monopoly case of everywhere declining average cost and a single product, marginal cost pricing implies price below average cost and thus negative economic profit. Although this result is not inevitable in more general natural monopoly situations, it is still true that the zero-profit prescription does not follow from the basic analysis of economic efficiency.[11]

For some time the prevailing view among academic economists seems to have been that in the classic case, price should be set equal to marginal cost and the resulting deficit covered by general taxation. (See Henderson, 1947, and Coase, 1970, on these issues.) This prescription is now generally rejected, for a number of reasons. First, raising taxes to cover such a deficit generally imposes distortions and efficiency losses elsewhere in the economy; these cannot be assumed to be small. Second, there is a serious equity question: why should taxpayers in general subsidize those who most intensively consume the natural monopoly's output? Finally, there are problems of investment decision making.

If the enterprise's deficit under marginal cost pricing exceeds the value that consumers place on its existence, the enterprise should not exist. But that value, or consumers' surplus, is hard to estimate precisely. One can be sure that the enterprise is worth having if its customers show that they are willing to cover its total costs by actually doing so. Requiring the enterprise as a whole and any new investments it makes to cover total costs imposes a valuable market test that guards against excessive investment or maintenance of unjustifiable operations. For these and other reasons, most authors now seem to accept the desirability in principle of requiring natural monopolies to recover their total costs.

It is obvious, of course, that if a natural monopoly is to be privately owned and operated without subsidy, and if capital is to be attracted, total costs (including the cost of equity capital) must be covered. In most cases, rates of return of either private or public enterprise that are in excess of the cost of capital funds imply avoidable efficiency losses, so that there is rarely any justification for positive economic profits. Since privately owned natural monopolies will generally seek to earn such profits and, in situations where the imposition of controls makes any sense, will be able to do so if special controls are not imposed, profit limitation becomes a valid goal of efficiency-oriented natural monopoly control.

That goal generally translates into the specific target of zero average economic profit. But the important qualifier "if capacity is not to be contracted" is present. If it is impossible to cover the total costs of a natural monopoly enterprise that has plant and equipment already in place, production should still occur as long as variable or operating cost is covered. In most such cases, capacity should not be expanded, so that the inability to attract investment funds that must follow from failure to cover capital costs does no harm. Public control need not guarantee total cost coverage (including capital costs) in an obviously declining industry; pure and perfect competition would not do so.

Similarly the requirement of zero economic profit *on average* can generally be taken to imply that the market value of a utility's common stock should not persistently deviate from its appropriately computed book value. (See Clark, 1939, pp. 328-32, on this point, which has been made in more modern terms by Leland, 1974, Baron and Taggart, 1977, Myers, 1976, and Smiley and Green, 1978, among others.) But avoidance of persistent deviations does not mean that market and book values must always be equal or that revenues and total costs must exactly match in every accounting period. Under pure and perfect competition, an industry can be in full long-run equilibrium in spite of short-run fluctuations in earnings; such fluctuations are thus not always undesirable. Further, to eliminate them is to shift all risk from suppliers of equity capital to some other parties, and this is not always desirable either.

Given the general soundness of profit limitation as a goal of natural monopoly control, two questions arise. First, if first-best marginal cost pricing is not generally consistent with profits that just cover capital costs, what sorts of second-best pricing should be adopted to provide cost coverage on average? Second, how well has utility regulation in the United States performed along the profit limitation dimension?

If marginal cost pricing would result in losses (in economic terms), and if a natural monopoly enterprise's customers are nonetheless required to cover its total costs, some sort of tax over and above marginal cost prices must be imposed on them. (Henderson, 1947, provides a clear statement of this point.) The theoretical literature has focused on two types of price discrimination that might be employed to collect the necessary extra revenues efficiently.[1][2]

First, following Ramsey's (1927) fundamental contribution to the theory of optimal taxation, a number of authors have suggested that natural monopoly prices should generally be in excess of marginal costs, with the percentage gap between price and marginal cost generally larger the less responsive demand is to changes in price. A standard example of this sort of discrimination under regulation (though in what few consider a natural monopoly sector) is discount air fares for those willing to make reservations relatively far in advance. Such individuals are likely to be vacationers, who are presumably price sensitive. Businessmen, who are typically less price sensitive and less able to plan trips far in advance, are more likely to pay the full fare. Railroad value-of-service pricing provides another example. Theoretical work on this sort of discrimination, often termed *Ramsey pricing,* has been done by Baumol and Bradford (1970), Feldstein (1972a), Baumol, Bailey, and Willig (1977), and others.

A second type of discrimination that figures prominently in the theoretical literature involves *nonlinear pricing,* in which a buyer's average cost generally declines with the quantity consumed; bulk discounts are granted. (In principle, average cost could rise with consumption in some cases; the nonlinearity occurs because outlay is not proportional to consumption.) A standard example here is declining-block rates for electricity, in which the charge per kilowatt-hour falls with the amount of power consumed. Such pricing is discriminatory only if costs do not similarly decline, of course. A *two-part* electricity tariff, in which a residential customer pays a fixed monthly amount regardless of consumption in addition to a constant price per unit of power demanded, could be precise marginal cost pricing, since some costs—metering and wires, for example—do not vary with the amount consumed, while some—fuel and labor—do. Recent work on nonlinear pricing schemes has been done by Feldstein (1972b), Leland and Meyer (1976), and Willig (1978); Willig (1978) provides a useful bibliography.

Willig's (1978) paper is of particular importance. It demonstrates the general superiority of nonlinear pricing to Ramsey pricing when both are feasible, in that one can always move from the latter to the former (without simultaneously redistributing income by other means) in such a way as to keep total enterprise profit constant and yet make all customers better off. (The analysis of Leland and Meyer, 1976, points in this same direction.) Willig further shows that under efficient nonlinear pricing, some sales must be made at marginal cost. *Marginal price* will be defined here as the price an individual customer must pay for one additional unit of the good or service in question. The marginal price will generally decline with a customer's demand under nonlinear pricing. Then Willig's result is that marginal price must equal marginal cost for at least the customer with the greatest demand. The average price paid by that customer or any other will generally exceed marginal cost under nonlinear pricing; that is how the enterprise's total costs are covered.

In both Ramsey and nonlinear policies, marginal cost is the indispensable starting point for price determination. Since we must employ taxation when simply setting price equal to marginal cost produces inadequate revenue, equity issues inevitably arise. In the Ramsey approach, these are resolved by treating all customers identically. The total efficiency cost of enabling the enterprise to break even is minimized, and no attention is paid to the incidence of the tax burden. The superiority of nonlinear pricing arises because a smaller efficiency cost is incurred.[13] Nonlinear pricing also provides somewhat more flexibility as to how the tax burden is to be shared among buyers. In application, and following the discussion in chapter 2, it seems appropriate to follow the Ramsey literature and to ignore incidence. Since there is no hope of providing those in charge of natural monopoly control with an explicit set of relative weights to be assigned to the real incomes of different groups in society, and since there is little to be said for having the control system generate its own explicit or implicit weights, the natural prescription is to ignore the incidence of benefits and costs and to focus on net benefits. Thus the net efficiency cost of covering a natural monopoly's total cost should be minimized, considering, of course, any costs associated with increasing the complexity of the price structure. Incidence might be analyzed in some cases, and such analysis might be of interest to others, but it should not be used by regulators to impose their own values on the firms they regulate and the customers of those firms.

Let us now turn to actual performance under regulation. The fundamental importance of marginal cost in pricing decisions has not been widely recognized in practice. It is thus hardly surprising that the even more refined notions of Ramsey pricing and nonlinear pricing have not to my knowledge been explicitly used to set rates by any commission or regulated firm. The interesting performance questions relating to profit limitation must therefore deal with more basic issues. First, have public utility regulators in the United States on average held profits down to the cost of equity capital (in other words, have economic profits generally averaged zero)? Second, have regulators been sensitive to relevant differences among firms in the process of profit control?

Most empirical examinations of the general effect of regulation on profits have focused on the electric utility industry. In an important paper, Stigler and Friedland (1962) examined data for states with and without state regulation over the period 1900-1937 and concluded that regulation had no effect on prices. Though Comanor (1970) and DeAlessi (1974b) argued that the Stigler-Friedland evidence actually showed that regulation had significantly reduced prices, the conclusion of no regulatory impact was widely accepted for some time. (This conclusion supports theories in which regulated firms inevitably capture their regulators; see, for instance, Jordan, 1972.) Jackson (1969) essentially confirmed the Stigler-Friedland conclusions for 1940 and 1950, but he did find regulation-induced reductions in prices to commercial and industrial customers (though not to residential customers) in 1960. Moore (1971), however, found that the ratio of actual prices to uncontrolled monopoly prices in the early 1960s did not differ significantly from unity. Recently Smiley and Green (1978) have found that regulation did have a significant effect on prices and profits in 1970, though they suggest that regulators did not generally manage to hold total revenues down to total costs.

The pattern that emerges from these studies is one of relatively ineffective profit limitation by electric utility regulators until the late 1960s. Joskow (1974) supports this by noting the passivity of commissions and the small number of rate cases actually decided in the early and mid-1960s, a period of generally declining real costs of producing electricity. In the rapid inflation that began in the late 1960s and that has continued, the situation has changed dramatically. The backward-looking and time-consuming regulatory process described at the start of this chapter proved ill suited for dealing with rapidly rising costs. Commissions instituted a variety of procedural changes designed to cope with this problem; nevertheless, during most of the 1970s, electric utility profits were probably held down below capital costs. Joskow (1974), Joskow and MacAvoy (1975), and MacAvoy (1978) make this case persuasively.

If this pattern applies to other public utility industries, and the results of Keran (1976) and MacAvoy (1978) indicate that it does, it seems clear that regulation has generally failed to achieve appropriate profit control. In periods of little or no inflation, utilities have been allowed to earn excess profits. While slack regulatory control of this sort provides strong incentives for production efficiency (in particular, the AJ effect does not operate unless control is tight), prices that yield excess profits also generally produce efficiency losses. During the recent period of rapid inflation, utility revenues seem to have been held below real costs, though this seems to have occurred as a more or less unintentional by-product of adherence to an insufficiently flexible set of regulatory practices. When profits are inadequate, utilities have difficulty attracting necessary capital funds, and capacity expansion is inefficiently retarded. The costs of such erratic behavior may well have been substantial in both inflationary and noninflationary periods, though I know of no precise estimates of their magnitude.

Whatever the average level of profit control they have exerted, commissions have not generally been sensitive to important differences among the firms they regulate. Regulators do devote considerable energy to determining the costs of capital of the firms they regulate; these then translate into allowed or fair rates of return. The basic problem in such endeavors is that the cost of risk bearing, as it is reflected in the cost of equity capital, cannot be immediately related to any observed market price. Using stock market data, however, the cost of capital funds can be reasonably well estimated using modern techniques of financial analysis (see Myers, 1972, and Pettway, 1978, and the references they cite). As Pettway notes, such estimates have been presented to regulatory commissions on numerous occasions. Donahue (1971) cites the power of these techniques and the inability of lawyers to understand them in building his case for regulation by economists. Smith (1978) suggests that the use of modern financial analysis has been an important force in increasing the actual participation of economists in the regulatory process as commissioners in recent years.

Still the evidence suggests that profit regulation has been inefficient in that the implications of these techniques have not been reflected in commission decisions. Joskow's (1972) successful behavioral model of the New York commission in the 1960s, widely regarded as one of the more able, supports this assertion. In a more recent study, Hagerman and Ratchford (1978) investigated the determinants of rates of return recently allowed to electric utilities in thirty-three states. They found that the key riskiness measure according to modern finance theory (the β coefficient) was not a significant determinant of allowed returns. It appears that discrepancies between the cost of capital and the allowed rate of return across firms have been, in average absolute magnitude, larger than they could have been.

Summary and Conclusions

The four main requisites of efficient natural monopoly performance—prices based on marginal cost, appropriate product selection, efficient production, and zero economic profits on average—serve as yardsticks in subsequent chapters dealing with proposals to reform or replace conventional rate-of-return regulation. All four of these conditions must be satisfied for performance to be fully efficient. Ensuring that no excess profits are earned does little good if costs are inflated, the price structure is capricious, and the wrong products are produced. Profit control by itself need not produce any improvement over unfettered monopoly. (See Shepherd, 1975, ch. 9, on these points.) A good social control structure must induce at least adequate performance along all four relevant dimensions.

My evaluation of U.S. utility regulation along these dimensions showed that pricing and profit control have likely been the loci of sizable efficiency losses, while the evidence on product selection and production efficiency under regulation does not support firm judgments. Conclusions of this sort, however, do not by themselves call for elimination, reform, or replacement of conventional regulation. It remains to be seen whether there exist alternatives likely to do better.

Notes

1. The description that follows is distilled from a variety of sources. See, for instance: Breyer, "Reform of Economic Regulation"; Farris and Sampson, *Public Utilities,* chs. 5-8; Jones, *Regulated Industries,* chs. 1-3; Joskow, "Determination of the Allowed Rate of Return," "Pricing Decisions," and "Inflation and Environmental Concerns"; Kahn, *Economics of Regulation,* 1: ch. 2; MacAvoy, "Present Condition of Regulated Enterprise"; and Wilcox and Shepherd, *Public Policies,* chs. 13-14.

2. This standard was promulgated by the Supreme Court's decision in the *Hope* case: FPC v. Hope Natural Gas Co., 320 U.S. 591 (1944), and has been nominally honored since.

3. One important change does deserve mention: the proper computation of the rate base was a lively issue until the *Hope* decision of 1944.

4. For more on regulation-induced distortions in telephone rate structures, see Kahn and Zielinski, "New Rate Structures" and "Telephone Rate Structuring," and Littlechild and Rousseau, "Pricing Policy of a U.S. Telephone Company."

5. Lipsey-Lancaster, "General Theory of Second Best," has stimulated a large amount of theoretical work. Kahn, *Economics of Regulation,* 1: pp. 69-70, discusses and refers to some of this literature. Two recent contributions with useful bibliographies are Hatta, "Piecemeal Policy Recommendations," and Kawamata, "Price Distortion."

6. The literature on the theory and application of peak-load pricing is huge. Joskow, "Theory of Marginal Cost Pricing" and "Electrical Utility Rate Structures," and Joskow and Noll, "Regulation in Theory and Practice," provide useful surveys and references.

7. Her analysis is an extension of the Averch-Johnson, "Firm under Regulatory Constraint," model discussed in the next section. See also Bailey and White, "Peak and Offpeak Prices"; Wenders, "Peak-Load Pricing"; and Nguyen and Macgregor-Ried, "Interdependent Demands."

8. The formal analyses of Spence, "Monopoly," and of Crew and Kleindorfer, "Reliability," apply the Averch-Johnson model discussed in the next section. Kahn, *Economics of Regulation,* 1: 20-25, refers to AJ effects, but he also discusses the political motivations referred to in the text.

9. Most of the theory related to the AJ effect is clearly presented by Bailey, *Economic Theory;* see Kahn *Economics of Regulation,* 2: esp. chs. 2-3, for interesting discussions. Pegrum, *Public Regulation,* pp. 697-98, argues that managers of public enterprises generally face a below-cost price of capital funds, leading to a similar incentive to overcapitalization.

10. One utility's estimates of the capital cost savings from a sharp increase in regulatory flexibility are given in "A Utility's Experiment in Rate-Setting." It is not obvious how accurate or how generally relevant those numbers are, however.

11. See, in particular, Baumol, "Proper Cost Tests," and Panzar and Willig, "Economies of Scale." In an interesting recent paper, Starrett, "Marginal Cost Pricing," demonstrates that in a dynamic setting in which declining costs occur only in the acquisition of capacity, marginal cost pricing is consistent with nonnegative economic profits.

12. *Discrimination* is used here as a technical, not a pejorative, term. Kahn, *Economics of Regulation,* 1: ch. 5, discusses some of the earlier literature. Other strands of the optimal cost coverage literature have employed the game-theoretic concepts of the core—Littlechild, "Common Costs"; Faulhaber, "Cross-subsidization"; and Sorenson, Tschirhart, and Whinston, "Game Theoretic Approach to Peak Load Pricing"—and the Shapley value—Littlechild, "Game-Theoretic Approach," and Loehman and Whinston, "New Theory of Pricing," and "Axiomatic Approach." Sherman, "Club Subscriptions," "Private Ownership Bias," and "Design of Public Utility Institutions," has attempted to apply the theory of clubs, as developed by Buchanan, "Economic Theory of Clubs," and Pauly, "Clubs, Commonality, and the Core," and "Cores and Clubs."

13. This is formally related to the reasonably well-known point that while price discrimination through bulk discounts generally increases efficiency relative to an uncontrolled monopoly equilibrium with a single price, discrimination by charging different prices to different groups on the basis of demand characteristics need not do so; see Sherer, *Industrial Market Structure,* pp. 253-59, and Yamey, "Monopolistic Price Discrimination."

4

On the Design of Control Mechanisms

In a perfect world, one not affected by any of the various frictions and transactions costs that impede resource allocation processes in real economies, there would be no general case for government intervention in natural monopoly situations. The essence of the natural monopoly problem in real economies is that in the absence of special controls, natural monopolies selling products without close substitutes find it profitable to charge prices well in excess of marginal costs, thus producing inefficiency in resource use. As a matter of definition, such inefficiency implies the existence of a scheme of reallocating resources and redistributing wealth that can make both parties, the monopolist and its customers, better off. A natural scheme of this sort would have the monopoly sell at marginal costs, with its customers making payments to it totaling somewhat in excess of the profits it would receive from monopoly pricing. (They might also make payments to each other.) Because monopoly pricing results in inefficiency, such a scheme making all better off must exist.

In the absence of frictions that make bargaining and resource reallocation difficult, it follows from pursuit of self-interest that such an efficiency-enhancing scheme would be agreed to and put into operation.[1] The inefficiency associated with natural monopoly would vanish, and with it the natural monopoly problem. There would remain some difficulties of reaching collective agreement on such things as reliability and quality of service, but these could certainly be resolved by negotiation in a frictionless world at least as satisfactorily as by government fiat. In this wonderful place, there would also be no special need for government action to prevent price fixing or to control pollution; bargaining among affected parties would serve to forestall economic efficiency losses that might arise from these or any other activities.

Discussions of frictionless worlds can be amusing, but outcomes in a world of perfect and costless bargaining do not always correspond well to observations on this planet. Few would argue that negotiation can replace utility regulation, antitrust, and environmental policy. But the frictionless model does provide an important starting point for analysis. It indicates that frictions or impediments to transactions must underlie the natural monopoly problem, along with the cost characteristics described in chapter 1. Identification of the important frictions involved may help one evaluate alternative control schemes for natural monopoly, since those schemes will have to deal with whatever frictions are inherent in the situations they face.

Drawing on work by Williamson (1973, 1975) and Goldberg (1976a, 1976b,

1977), this task is attempted in the next section. There I describe some important transaction problems that serve as frictions in monopoly situations. The third section discusses the implications of these frictions for effective control devices.

Much of modern welfare economics is written for the guidance of an omniscient, benevolent despot. But as Buchanan (1968) has emphasized, no such beings are available for employment in the control of natural monopoly. That process must be entrusted to imperfect, self-interested humans who, whether employed as buyers' agents or in other control capacities, will not always bring about performance that always perfectly satisfies the four conditions of efficient natural monopoly performance. In order to design control mechanisms likely to induce acceptable levels of economic efficiency, one would like to be able to predict with precision what sorts of institutional and legal arrangements would make various sorts of undesirable controller or regulator behavior more or less likely. The fourth section of this chapter considers the literature on administrative behavior in general and on regulatory behavior in particular, in order to see what implications it has for the design of control structures.

Problems with Market Transactions

In recent work, Williamson (1973; 1975, esp. ch. 2) has proposed an interesting framework that can help one to predict when market processes will do a poor job of allocating resources. Williamson identifies two human factors, two environmental factors, and one derivative condition that predispose markets to bad performance. The two human factors are bounded rationality, a phrase coined by Simon (1957), and opportunism. The two environmental factors are uncertainty/complexity, and small numbers, and the derivative condition is information impactedness. To this list I think it is useful to add a second derivative condition: public goods.

Bounded rationality refers to the finiteness of human intellect. As Simon (1957, p. 199) puts it, "Human beings are limited in knowledge, foresight, skill and time." Human decision making is not costless and rarely perfect. In situations of any complexity in which the future is uncertain, it may not be feasible to anticipate and plan for all possible events. Since human intellect is a scarce resource, it may not be efficient to do such planning even if it is possible. Thus in a situation involving *uncertainty/complexity*, bounded rationality implies the likelihood that contracts written in a market setting will not anticipate all possible events. They are thus apt to break down when the unforeseen occurs, and awareness of this possibility may inhibit transactions.

In complex situations, even when uncertainty is not an issue, the real costs of the sort of bargaining that eliminates inefficient resource use in frictionless worlds can be substantial. In reality, complexity can become part of an otherwise simple situation if a large number of persons must reach agreement. Bounded rationality paired with complexity and, possibly, uncertainty, tends to make market allocation of resources costly and thus possibly inferior to other approaches. In much of Williamson's work, he contrasts market allocation and allocation within a firm or other organization, where uncertainty/complexity can be dealt with by adaptive procedures that require the absence of explicit contractual provisions and the presence of certain implicit obligations. Much of the discussion in chapter 2 was concerned with the implications of the bounded rationality-uncertainty/complexity pairing for organizational design, an issue that Williamson (1975, chs. 8-9) considers at length.

Similarly *opportunism* creates problems in market situations with *small numbers* of (actual or potential) buyers or sellers. Williamson (1975, p. 26) describes opportunism as "self-interest seeking with guile." He notes that two common manifestations of opportunistic behavior are less than complete and candid revelation of information and the making of promises that one intends to break. In market settings with many buyers and sellers, market pressures serve to control such conduct. On the other hand, in a market with only one buyer, for example, sellers may be victimized by opportunistic buyer behavior, and fear of victimization may prevent mutually beneficial transactions. When these two conditions are paired, Williamson argues, vertical integration (in particular) may be superior to market contracting, since the enterprise's top management can to some extent enforce adherence to a common set of objectives, thus reducing the likelihood of opportunistic exploitation of small numbers advantages.

Williamson (1975, p. 31) defines the derivative condition of *information impactedness* as present when important information "is known to one or more [of the] parties [involved] but cannot be costlessly discerned by or displayed for others." He describes the condition as derivative, since it depends on uncertainty/complexity, opportunism, and, less centrally, bounded rationality. When information impactedness is present, market processes may be adversely affected, as uninformed parties either inefficiently try to inform themselves, try to avoid entering into agreements that may later turn out to have been mistakes, or fail to exercise caution and find themselves at the mercy of better informed opportunists.

A second derivative condition, added above, obtains in situations involving *public goods.* In such situations, a set of economic actors (individuals, households, firms, or other entities) must directly or indirectly reach a single decision with implications for all. (Chapter 3 discussed the quality or reliability of public utility service as an example of such a choice.) Different decisions imply different costs and benefits for the actors involved. As Samuelson (1954) pointed out in his pathbreaking theoretical analysis of public goods problems, actors in such situations have incentives not to reveal their unobservable true preferences, and this can cause complete breakdown of the market mechanism. If tax payments to finance national defense were voluntary, for instance, I would have an incentive to announce that I cared not at all for missiles, tanks, and warships, regardless of how I really felt, and to withhold my taxes. Such opportunistic behavior would raise my spendable income noticeably but would have little effect on the level of defense protection I received. If all citizens reasoned similarly, there would be no national defense. This is an extreme case, of course, and the market need not always fail so dramatically in public goods situations.[2] Still since decisions concerning public goods can depend critically on individual preferences that cannot be directly observed and since individuals may have strong incentives to misrepresent their preferences, situations involving public goods may raise problems broadly similar to those associated with information impactedness. Though both conditions derive in part from opportunism, an important difference is that public-good problems tend to worsen, not improve, as one moves from small-numbers to large-numbers situations, since the potential for opportunistic behavior is enhanced, not diminished.

Let us now see what this framework implies about the ability of the unaided market mechanism to cope with natural monopoly problems. More specifically, why don't natural monopoly sellers and their customers simply negotiate schemes under which sales are at marginal cost but the seller receives monopoly profits, thereby removing any need for regulation or other special control devices? (I am assuming here that the monopoly has acquired a property right to its position as sole supplier. This is not essential to the present argument, however.) In order to strike such a bargain, buyers and the seller must agree on (1) marginal cost, (2) the level of profits the firm would earn as an ordinary monopolist, and (3) the division of the burden of providing those profits among the firm's customers.

In any realistic situation, (1) marginal cost and (2) monopoly profit are not likely to be easy to compute. Even if the logic of striking the sort of bargain described above can be persuasively communicated to all the monopoly's customers, their bounded rationality and the complexity of the task suggest that they will not do a particularly accurate job of estimating these magnitudes. The negotiation costs that would be incurred in reconciling a large number of marginal cost and profit estimates are staggering to contemplate. Further, these would not be once-only costs; demand and production cost conditions change over time. The complex uncertainty surrounding such changes suggests that these key magnitudes cannot simply be updated by formula; significant changes will require new estimation and negotiation.

The obvious small-numbers situation on the supply side joins with opportunism to create additional problems. The monopoly's incentive to have both marginal cost and the level of profit overestimated are clear. Unless some special arrangements are made, this motivation for opportunistic behavior cannot be checked by market forces.[3] This can produce information inpactedness with a vengeance; the firm's estimates, even if truthfully and correctly derived, are unlikely to be believed by sophisticated customers. But individual customers can hardly afford to acquire the skills and to invest the time required to check all the accounting detail that must support such estimates. Indeed if the number of customers is substantial, there is a public good problem here. If any one customer does this work, others may be able to rely on it. If all think that someone else will check the monopoly's estimates, none will feel an incentive to do so. Finally, item 3 involves cost sharing for a public good (the reduction of price to marginal cost), and getting agreement here runs up against the classic problems, which are especially severe if there are a large number of customers.

All of these points could be elaborated upon further, and additional related problems could be discussed. (What happens, for instance, when households or firms move into or out of a natural monopoly's service area?) But the main point should be clear: all the factors and conditions discussed in general terms above are present here and combine to establish the general impossibility of eliminating the natural monopoly problem by negotiation among the parties involved.

Implications for Control System Design

We will now consider the implications for the design of control devices of some of the key transactional difficulties that make the unaided market mechanism generally incapable of solving the natural monopoly problem. The mere existence of a natural monopoly problem that the unaided market cannot solve does not imply the desirability of imposing an inevitably imperfect control system. The discussion that follows assumes that the decision to control has been made, but the case for or against control may not be clear-cut in many instances.

The need for some entity to act as the buyers' agent, making decisions for them as a group, seems clear. The agent then engages in mass production of contact terms with the monopoly supplier for classes of customers (Goldberg, 1977). Such an agent can serve both to reduce negotiation costs and as a locus for collective decision making on issues with public-good dimensions. The need for an agent is reinforced by the complexity of many natural monopoly industries and the consequent need to acquire and comprehend massive amounts of specialized information in order to evaluate intelligently a supplier's conduct and performance at any instant. The agent thus serves to mitigate the buyers' problem of bounded rationality in the face of complexity.[4] Under private ownership, it is unlikely always to be in a monopoly seller's interest to assist its supervisors in the task of monitoring it accurately. It is difficult to see how this sort of opportunism can be adequately countered except by an agent with specialized skills and some legal right to acquire valid data.

The need for a buyers' agent may also exist under public ownership because collective choice problems and the requirement for expertise remain. Further, under any but the purest cooperative ownership structures, possibilities for monopolistic abuse remain. Governments can use public enterprises as major revenue sources and have done so at various times. Widely separated examples of this practice are provided by Meyer (1905, chs. 1-4), Colberg (1955), and Strauss and Wertz (1976); Wilcox (1912) gives an early argument against it. The enterprise's management may sometimes serve adequately as the buyers' agent under public ownership, but this is by no means certain, as Pegrum (1940) argues. In this context, some states still feel it necessary to regulate municipally owned utilities (see Mann and Seifried, 1972, p. 78, Foster, 1934, p. 23, Clemens, 1950, ch. 23, and Wilson, Herring, and Eutsler, 1938, pp. 535-36). Nash (1925, pp. 107-08) indicates, however, that regulators were intended to serve in part as taxpayers' agents to guard against their unknowingly providing heavy subsidies to utility operation. (Beigie, 1974, p. 188, notes that most government-owned utilities in Canada are also subject to commission regulation.)

A second general implication of natural monopoly characteristics, stressed especially by Goldberg (1976b) and Williamson (1976), is that detailed explicit contracts cannot be relied upon as the sole control device. This follows basically from the pairing of bounded rationality and uncertainty/complexity. The traditional public utility sectors employ relatively large quantities of long-lived, specialized assets that are not easily moved (see, for instance, Wilcox and Shepherd, 1975, chs. 15, 16, 21). This implies that long-run considerations are important in the direction of such enterprises; investment decisions are central and must be based on forecasts of the future. The history of utility control in the United States (as outlined below) seems to imply that in order to have investment decisions sensibly made, management and ownership structures must remain relatively stable. This means that the relationship between buyers and seller must be relatively long-lived.

But the bounded rationality of human actors and the inevitable uncertainty about costs, demand, tastes, and technology in the relatively distant future imply that it is impossible to control such long-lived relationships by means of contracts that anticipate all contingencies. In many situations, it is impossible to write contracts that provide for all conceivable relevant events, and in more it is not worth the effort. As MacNeil (1974) and Goldberg (1976a) have noted, such situations are not unique to natural monopoly industries. (See also Radner, 1968.) In most cases, observed long-term contracts are incomplete, in that no attempt is made to describe responses to all contingencies; rather they serve mainly to provide a constitution-like framework within which the relationship between the parties evolves. Much that is not explicitly stated in the contract affects that evolution. (MacNeil's, 1974, fascinating essay provides a wealth of illustrations.) Macaulay (1963) notes that many transactions between firms occur without any explicit contracts at all. Informal understandings are heavily relied upon to settle differences that arise. (On this last point, see the analysis of employment relations in Williamson, Wachter, and Harris, 1975.)

Conventional regulation is well characterized by what Goldberg (1976b) has called an administered contract. Even though commissions, buyers, and sellers are not noticeably bound by explicit contracts, the implicit contractual structure of due process requirements and statutory and precedential restrictions serves to establish rules within which disputes are settled. Under workable alternative social control structures, this same sort of relationship would prevail, as it does in many nonregulatory contexts. No control structure can determine precisely the actions or rewards of all relevant actors under all possible circumstances; some degree of flexibility and thus of contractual incompleteness is a sensible response of boundedly rational humans to complexity and uncertainty.

Many of these points can be productively illustrated by some aspects of the history of public utility control schemes. In the United States, the primary mechanism for control of local public utilities until roughly World War I was the municipal franchise, a contract between the city and a utility firm.[5] (Franchise contracts still exist, but they generally no longer serve much of a control function.) Similar contractual arrangements were employed elsewhere.[6] These contracts seem to have encountered three basic operational difficulties, all of them consistent with the general discussion here.

First, if the franchise period was long, it was difficult to write contracts that would ensure reasonable performance over the entire period. As Bauer (1939), for instance, notes, many early franchises simply specified maximum prices that could be charged over the contract life. This provision was excellent for utility firms in the deflation of the late 1800s, but it brought many to their knees in the inflation of World War I.

An interesting example of this sort of contractual breakdown is provided by gas supply in Paris. Gas was provided after 1907 by a private firm operating municipally owned works under contract (see Holcombe, 1911, and Normand, 1910). The contract fixed an upper bound on the price of gas and a lower bound on the operating firm's profit. Wartime increases in the price of coal quickly raised the cost of manufactured gas above the maximum sales price. By 1918, unit cost was roughly double the price charged. Under the terms of the contract (which clearly did not anticipate inflation of the magnitude experienced), the city was forced to pay large sums to subsidize the sale of gas at prices well under costs. It did so from 1915 until 1918, when it was finally possible to increase the price of gas.[7]

Utilities in the United States operating under fixed-price franchise contracts typically did not have minimum profit guarantees. They were forced by wartime inflation to attempt renegotiation of contract terms. Many very long-term franchise contracts were abolished in such renegotiations, and commission regulation was extended to cover the firms involved. (See, for instance, Wilson, Herring, and Eutsler, 1938, ch.2.)

Even before the inflation of World War I, many observers argued that a good franchise must provide for rate changes (see, for instance, King, 1912b, and Wilcox, 1910, pp. 41-42). Such provision could have avoided some of the dramatic breakdowns actually experienced. In order to allow for future rate changes, either a formula for such changes must be built into the franchise contract or some provision for continuing supervision or periodic renegotiation of contract terms must be made. In the latter case, some skilled entity would be required to act as buyers' agent in supervision or negotiation.

Suppose, on the other hand, that franchise contracts attempted to provide fixed formulas for rate changes. Late in the franchise control period, in fact, variants of the service-at-cost contract were employed, particularly for street railways. As Morgan (1923, p. 191) observed, the basic intent of these plans was to guarantee the utility's rate of return on its investment over the life of the franchise.[8] Guarantees of this sort pose obvious efficiency problems. If there are no rewards to efficient management, managers are unlikely to be efficient. Most people find it more enjoyable to play golf or to take long lunches than to cut costs; such behavior produces Leibenstein's (1966) X-inefficiency and is not generally unpleasant for those able to engage in it.

The French railroads appear to provide an excellent example of this sort of problem. As Dunham (1955, ch. 4) notes, the French government in the nineteenth century generally sought tight control over railroad construction and operation. By 1883, control over privately owned railroads was extensive, and their return on investment was guaranteed (Clough 1939, pp. 236-37). (Meyer, 1905, ch. 5, and Buckler, 1906, describe the situation just after the turn of the century.) In modern terms, control was responsive to virtually all affected interests except the traveling and consuming public. The government was forced to spend large and growing sums to meet the return guarantees until major institutional changes were made in 1921 (see Clough, 1939, pp. 236-37, 336-37). The necessity for heavy subsidies of private railroads in the period before major auto and truck competition makes at least a prima facie case for substantial inefficiency.

Under rate revision by formula, negotiation cost considerations imply that some expert agency will be required to judge the validity of the monopoly's announced costs and, unless the contract is unusually detailed or unworkably rigid, to consider rate structure and product selection (service quality) issues. Given that a buyers' agent must perform this sort of supervision, it seems natural to increase the flexibility and potential efficiency incentives of the arrangement by allowing the utility's rate of return to vary, thus moving to something very like conventional regulation. This move, of course, was generally made. As Glaeser (1957, p. 113) succinctly puts it, "Widespread dissatisfaction with franchise regulation after 1907 brought state commissions authority over street and interurban railways, and gas, water, electric, and telephone utilities." While other approaches to price changes by contract under franchise control might have avoided the particular problems encountered in practice, it is implausible to suppose that humans can write contracts that will avoid all problems that might have arisen or that might arise in the future. Absent such ability, the historical experience argues strongly that control of natural monopoly requires a buyers' agent and that it cannot rely entirely on written contracts.

A second major operational difficulty with franchise regulation concerns planning and investment incentives. Many observers noted that financing arrangements generally could not exceed the length of the franchise, and the necessity of raising money under such conditions tended to increase capital costs. This situation suggested the desirability of long-term contracts. But firms with only short periods remaining on franchise grants of any initial duration had a tendency to avoid both new investment and maintenance on existing plant and equipment.[9] Since many local franchises called for tangible assets to revert to the municipality after contract expiration, this behavior is hardly surprising. But even where arrangements were made to permit franchise renewal or purchase at "reasonable" prices, the uncertainty regarding asset valuation tended to discourage expansion of capacity. Higgins (1900), for instance, attributed the sharp decline in street railway construction in the United Kingdom relative to that in the United States to this problem. (See also "The Effects of the English Tramways Act.")

The general tendency in the United States was to follow the lead of Wisconsin in 1907 by moving to indeterminate or terminable franchises. Under these arrangements, the contract period is not limited in duration, but the municipality reserves the right to purchase the utility's assets at any time (usually after giving some notice) if service has been unsatisfactory. Most contemporary observers viewed this as a desirable reform; it solved the problem of investment incentives near the end of the franchise period by effectively making the period infinite except under exceptional circumstances.[10] Wilson, Herring, and Eutsler (1938, ch. 2) noted that municipal finances and voter attitudes often make takeovers impossible (see also Bauer, 1946).[11] At any rate, the investment incentives problem experienced during the franchise control period would seem to reinforce the case for relatively long-lived arrangements under natural monopoly conditions.

The third difficulty associated with franchise control concerns enforcement of the franchise contract. If a utility breaches a contract designed to control its performance, someone must detect the breach and take the appropriate action. Since such action likely benefits all the firm's customers, a public-good issue arises, and a buyers' agent is the natural way to handle it. Hunter (1917) documents the presence of specialized enforcement bodies in the earliest monopoly control structures in the United States, many of which were built around contracts between private firms and state governments. White (1921) describes a set of unsuccessful attempts to control performance without expert enforcement agencies. Many observers give the lack of expert agencies in most cities as an important cause for the weakness of control by municipal franchise. (Municipal corruption was also a severe problem in many cases, of course; see, for instance, Myers, 1900, esp. ch. 8.) Near the close of the period of franchise control, King (1912b, p. 206) stated the basic point here quite clearly: "A franchise is not self-enforcing. In this simple fact lies the justification for the creation of public utility commissions."

By the start of World War I, utility commissions existed in most states, and the case for such expert bodies seems generally to have been accepted. The only remaining doubts seem to have related to the appropriate roles of state and local commissions.[1][2] These doubts have generally been settled in favor of the states; as Troxel (1947, p. 66) notes, "Cities have only a vestige of their former regulatory powers." Local utility regulation has not completely vanished, of course; Smiley and Green (1978), for instance, observe that three states still had local regulation of electric utilities in 1970. Municipalities generally seem to have considerable responsibility for oversight of cable television systems.

The historical experience seems to support the primary conclusions of the general arguments presented earlier. Under any workable scheme for the control of a natural monopoly, some entity with appropriate skills and resources must act as buyers' agent, ownership and management arrangements for the monopoly enterprise must be relatively long-lived, and contracts involved in the scheme must of necessity be incomplete and thus must be supplemented by some sort of adaptive decision making over time. A number of caveats and qualifications are in order, however.

First, the historical case for these three aspects of workable control cannot be extended to a "survival of the fittest" defense of current regulatory structures, as Trebing (1976a) attempts to do. It is true that rate-of-return regulation embodies these features, and it is also true that this structure survived a fairly long period of experimentation ending roughly in the 1920s. But contemporary regulation has many other features, and much of the criticism of it after the 1920s argues that regulation evolved to fit a particularly confining niche in the political ecology, a niche that should not have been created.

Second, the proper function of a buyers' agent is not to press for ever lower prices. As Goldberg (1977) has discussed in detail, one must be clear as to what sorts of conflicts are and are not inherent in natural monopoly situations. In the long run, buyers' desire to be served at the lowest possible price generally coincides with the efficiency goal of social control. But in order to ensure service at all in the long run, the lowest possible price under private ownership must provide an adequate return to equity suppliers. That is, a buyers' agent concerned only with buyers' interests and totally in control of all details of a natural monopoly operation must generate sufficient returns on investment so that additional capital funds will be supplied on appropriately favorable terms when they are needed. The difficulty under private ownership of the monopoly firm is in deciding how much generosity to current equity holders and what guarantees (explicit or implicit) of future stability are necessary to bring this about.

Finally, even though natural monopoly control apparently cannot be accomplished through total reliance on explicit, written contracts, it does not follow that control should involve only implicit, unwritten contracts. Contracts between regulated firms and their customers or their regulators are now almost entirely of this form. (Exceptions are contracts between cities and utility firms that give the latter the right to lay cables, pipes, and so on in exchange for provision of service on "reasonable terms." Also, contracts between cities and cable television firms are sometimes much more detailed; see, for instance, Williamson, 1976.) If the explicit goal of natural monopoly control were economic efficiency rather than some ill-defined notion of just and reasonable conduct, it would seem that the key contractual provisions involving regulated firms' rights and obligations could be more precisely framed than at present. Shepherd (1973) has argued persuasively that the typical implicit regulatory contract assumes the permanence of regulations and of legal monopoly and is thus inconsistent with the long-term pursuit of efficiency in a dynamic economy.

There is nothing deeply wrong with the use of contracts that do not attempt to anticipate all contingencies. Their prevalence in the business world suggests that they represent a rational response to common problems. But in the present context, the necessity for such contracts between a natural monopoly and its customers to be administered and in fact generally negotiated by an agent of those customers can create basic obstacles to the pursuit of efficiency. The flexibility necessarily given the agent and the specialized and difficult-to-transmit information that the agent inevitably acquires mean that his performance can neither be precisely monitored nor easily evaluated. The case for limiting the agent's legitimate goals is thus strengthened. (Problems of a similar sort can arise in large businesses, where the suppliers of equity capital are forced to delegate authority to an agent, usually the enterprise's management.)

Politics and Administrative Behavior

A key issue in the design of systems for the control of natural monopolies is the likely behavior of the buyers' agent. It is not necessarily sufficient to declare or legislate that efficiency is the agent's or regulator's objective; the inevitable imperfection of the administrative process must leave those to whom authority has been delegated some freedom to deviate from rigorous and efficient pursuit of their nominal goals. We thus seek tools of institutional engineering that will tell us what sorts of institutional and legal arrangements make various types of undesirable administrative conduct more or less likely.

There have been many studies of administrative behavior in general and of regulators in particular. This literature, however, does not seem to provide a basis for the scientific design of most aspects of natural monopoly control structures.[13] It has been mainly concerned with identifying typical patterns of behavior; theoretical and empirical studies of comparative performance implications of alternative institutional and legal structures are disappointingly rare. Further, the relevant works in law and political science seem to deal almost exclusively with federal regulation, in spite of the importance of state control of most public utilities and the variation in the structure of state control systems.

One of the most influential hypotheses about regulation in recent years has been the *producer protection* theory of its origins. Bernstein (1955) and most other authors before the 1960s seem to have held the view that regulation in the United States was historically initiated for the purpose of protecting the public from actual or potential abuses. Termed the *public interest* theory of regulation by many subsequent authors, it was challenged by MacAvoy (1965) and Kolko (1965), who argued that ICC regulation of the railroads in 1887 was initiated in order to stabilize railroad cartels, not to protect the public. (On the evolution of academic views of regulation in general, see McCraw, 1975.) In earlier studies, which had apparently been forgotten, Gray (1900) and White (1921) showed that the origins of the Massachusetts Gas Commission, established in 1885, were even more clearly in conflict with the public interest theory. The MacAvoy-Kolko findings, and other observations pointing in the same direction (involving, among other things, state occupational licensing laws) were formalized into the producer protection theory by Stigler (1971) and others.

This theory rests on the notion that the political process responds only to groups able to devote resources to advancing their points of view on particular issues. Since the nature of regulatory policy has a greater effect on producers than on consumers, the potential benefits from organization in this area are generally greater for producers. Moreover since there are usually fewer affected producers than consumers, the costs of organizing a political effort are generally smaller. Thus producers are held to be more likely to be organized to deal with regulatory issues than consumers, so this theory predicts that regulatory legislation is generally responsive to producer interests. (See also Jordan, 1972, and, for a critical discussion of this sort of analysis, Posner, 1974.)

Those adopting the producer-protection view often draw from it the implication that regulation must continue to serve those it regulates, the firms that brought it into being in the first place. Were this view correct, it would provide a simple model of regulatory behavior with clear (and depressing) implications for other control structures.

Fortunately, or unfortunately, there are severe problems with the producer-protection view as a general theory. The MacAvoy-Kolko conclusions have recently been criticized by Ulen (1977), who finds no impact of early ICC regulation on railroad cartel stability. While Spann and Erickson (1970) find that consumers as a group did not benefit from this regulation, they do note that benefits were received by a subset of the population (primarily farmers), and Weingast (1978) points out that this group did lobby for railroad regulation. It is thus at least plausible that railroad regulation was instituted to benefit this group and did so initially. (If it did not benefit them, their lobbying becomes the sort of irrational activity that producer-protection theorists find implausible.) Weingast (1978) notes other cases where the initial effects of regulation do not support the inference that it was put in place to serve the regulated. (Consider, for instance, Schwert, 1977, who found that Securities and Exchange Commission regulation of securities exchanges imposed sizable capital losses on New York Stock Exchange members.)

Even if regulation did have dubious parentage in some cases, it is hard to see how parental sins alone can serve to condemn the current behavior and future prospects of the mature offspring. The nature and aims of regulatory behavior can change over time. However, Bernstein, (1955, ch. 3), who felt that regulation often had legitimate consumer protection origins, argued that eventual capture by the regulated was inevitable. His famous *life-cycle* theory of regulation described an inexorable decline from youthful vigor in pursuit of the public interest to senile protection of regulated firms and resistance to change.[14] This theory is certainly consistent with a public-interest view of the origins of the ICC and also with what Huntington (1952) described as its progressive emaciation into a feeble creature of the railroads. (But see Jaffe, 1954, for a rather different view of the ICC.) Weingast (1978) notes other cases that seem to fit the life-cycle model of eventual capture by the regulated better than the producer-protection model of capture from the outset. If the life-cycle theory is correct, it implies that the behavior of mature agencies, at least, tends to be concerned primarily with benefiting the regulated, regardless of the agencies' origins.

But there are problems with this theory as well. As Sabatier (1975) and Weingast (1978) point out, it is hard to derive Bernstein's (1955, ch. 3) theory from any model of the political process. The mechanisms that make inevitable the political decline of all relevant forces except those exerted by regulated firms are not obvious, and forces that can offset such declines in particular cases do exist. Indeed as Weingast (1978) notes, one can point to examples of mature regulatory agencies that have regained vigor and shifted to policies opposed by those they regulate. The pro-competitive decisions of the Federal Communications Commission (FCC) beginning in the late 1960s and the recent moves of the Civil Aeronautics Board (CAB) toward deregulation of the airlines are obvious cases in point.

In short, it does not appear that either the producer-protection or the life-cycle theory is adequate to explain regulatory behavior. (The pure public-interest theory, in which regulators always seek to advance the interest of consumers or of the general public, is clearly not adequate.) Mature regulatory agencies do not always seek the welfare of those they regulate. One must go beyond or beneath broad statements of historical inevitability to a closer examination of the forces acting upon regulators and other administrators and of the behavior that these forces produce. Only such an investigation is likely to produce a model capable of explaining the diversity of conduct observed.

A natural way to structure such an examination, at least to an economist, is to look at the objectives of the relevant actors and the constraints that confront them. If regulators or other officials behave more or less rationally, a framework of this sort can serve to generate predictions about the likely results of shifts in constraints. This approach, however, requires reasonably sharp descriptions of both objectives and constraints. In the present context, little is implied by the widely accepted assumption that regulators and other government officials pursue their own self-interest in the face of political and administrative constraints. Unfortunately, going beyond this sort of imprecise general statement has proven difficult. Both objectives and constraints appear to be complex and multidimensional in administrative and political contexts, and no generally accepted workable simplifications have been proposed.

The literature contains at least three distinct conceptions of regulators' basic objectives. A *bureaucratic activist* view, following Downs (1967) and Niskanen (1971), among others, emphasizes maximization of such objectives as authority, activity, budget, and salary. Thus Jaffe (1954, p. 1113) states as a principle that "the administrator develops a presumption in favor of regulation." Similarly McKie (1970) and Kahn (1971, pp. 28-32) note a general tendency for regulation to spread to previously unregulated areas as regulators seek to make their control more effective. Peltzman (1971, 1976) and others have advanced a *political activist* conception according to which regulators and other officials seek to maximize their political support. This is at least consistent with the general tendency of regulators to worry about the differential effects of their decisions upon various groups. On the other hand, Hilton (1972), Joskow (1974), Noll (1971a), and others seem to have a generally *passivist* view, in which regulators seek to avoid conflicts and responsibilities. The discussions by Kahn (1971, pp. 11-28) and many others of regulators' conservatism and tendency to protect regulated firms lend support to this view. An example is the FPC's reluctance (in the 1950s at least) to regulate the wellhead price of natural gas (see Wilcox and Shepherd, 1975, pp. 420-26).

The problem is that most investigators frame their hypotheses about objectives from evidence on behavior, and behavior is shaped by both objectives and constraints. Depending on the circumstances, apparently similar behavior patterns can serve quite different ends. Consider, for instance, the general tendency of regulators to eschew rule making in favor of case-by-case decisions, which Friendly (1962) and others have deplored. (Robinson, 1970, who also notes this general tendency, discusses the aggressive rule-making by the Federal Trade Commission in the 1960s as an important exception.) On the one hand, as Noll (1971a) and Hilton (1972) have noted, such behavior makes it easier for a passive commission to maintain equilibrium among competing interests. On the other hand, as Wilson (1971, 1974) suggests, erratic behavior may serve to increase an activist commission's power. (See also Williamson, 1967, for an interesting related discussion of the value of ambiguity and uncertainty to both parties to defense procurement contracts.) Similarly, while the regulated firm behavior modeled by Joskow (1972, 1973) is not inconsistent with the usual assumption of profit maximization, his behavioral model of the corresponding regulatory commission sheds little light on that body's ultimate objectives. Finally, a commission can seek a balance among competing interests in order to increase its political support (Peltzman, 1976) or to gain freedom to pursue private goals (Hilton, 1972).

It is probably most sensible to view bureaucratic activism, political activism, and passivism as modes of behavior that arise in response to various environmental circumstances. Thus depending on the circumstances, either political activism or passivism may serve an appointed official with ambitions to elective office. Similarly some structures may attract career bureaucrats interested in salary maximization, and others may tend to be populated by idealists with other aims. On this view, the ultimate goals of regulators and other officials may be determined by the processes and circumstances that select them. Or those goals might be sufficiently complex and plastic as to render simple, static descriptions impossible. Still one might hope that the empirical literature would indicate the sorts of regulatory structures likely to give rise to different mixtures of these and other behavior modes; unfortunately it does not.

Eckert (1973), for instance, argues with some force that activism is more likely in bureaus within an executive branch, while independent commissions are more likely to be passive, but he provides rather weak evidence. Hilton (1972) seems to believe that shortness of tenure inclines regulators toward passivism, but the relevant empirical work surveyed by Thomas (1971) does not seem to support this hypothesis. Indeed recent work by Hagerman and Ratchford (1978) and Smiley and Green (1978) on electrical utility regulation suggests that short terms may improve performance. In general, the literature has a disturbingly high ratio of hypotheses to conclusive tests.

Let us now consider the constraints that regulators face. From a narrowly economic point of view, the most obvious limitation on regulators is their necessarily incomplete control over regulated firms. (Problems of bounded rationality, opportunism, and information impactedness are intrinsic to regulatory situations.) Following Averch and Johnson (1962), most formal economic models of regulation treat firms as simply reacting naively to commission or other directives. But as a number of scholars have recently argued from a variety of different perspectives, this assumption is not plausible.[15] Regulated firms are not obviously more naive than those who regulate them. Regulators necessarily have incomplete information, and regulated firms can gain by strategic or opportunistic behavior. Unless regulators are dedicated to the interests of those they regulate, such behavior can have important implications for optimal or actual regulatory policy. The implications of sophisticated behavior by the regulated are just beginning to receive the serious scholarly attention they deserve.

The most commonly discussed constraints on regulators and other government officials are political, but there is considerable diversity in the treatment of the political process in the relevant literature. Joskow and Noll (1978), in an informative survey of that literature, make a useful distinction between legislative and bureaucratic models of agency behavior. In the former, the agency essentially deals directly with the electorate; in the latter, the forces on the agency are filtered through the legislative and administrative structures to which it is attached.

Even a superficial inspection of the political environments of most regulatory agencies reveals a complex set of forces and constraints, shifting in strength and direction over time. Even if the simple capture or producer protection models of regulation are not always correct, regulated firms generally exert an important political force on the regulatory process. But the direction of that force may shift over time. Thus Joskow (1974) notes a change in utilities' attitudes toward regulatory delay caused by their experience in the last decade's inflation. As Joskow (1974) and Wilson (1974) discuss, environmentalist and consumerist groups have emerged as important political forces in the 1970s.

Casual observation and the discussions of Cleveland (1956), Seidman (1970), and others indicate that regulatory and other agencies are subject to a variety of political forces exerted within the relevant governmental structure itself. In an influential study of the Army Corps of Engineers, for instance, Maass (1951) identified what has come to be called the "iron triangle" of a special interest, a government agency, and a legislative appropriations or oversight committee. As Maass showed, such triangles can persistently take actions of which the general electorate would disapprove. Legislative appropriations committees have historically wielded considerable influence even over nominally independent regulatory commissions, and no agency is likely ever to be totally immune to executive influence, even if it has nominal independence. Such influence is often exerted through the appointments process. (See Bernstein, 1955, ch. 10, and Thomas, 1971, on these points.) Agencies and agency personnel are also subject to a variety of pressures originating elsewhere in the bureaucracy.

The legislative models of agency behavior essentially ignore forces acting within the governmental structure and treat regulators as redistributing wealth so as to maximize their effective political support in the electorate. Important works in this tradition include Stigler (1971), Posner (1971, 1974), and Peltzman (1971, 1976). As Posner (1971) notes, cross-subsidization, wherein prices are set so that one group of customers subsidizes another, can be an important way of redistributing wealth by regulation. The level of profit allowed a legal monopoly is another obvious tool. Legislative models do not simply predict that regulators will adopt the most popular decisions, since effective political support depends on organization and the expenditure of resources. Benefits translate into votes only if the beneficiaries organize effectively. Thus regulated firms, for which the costs and benefits of organizing tend to be more favorable than for other groups, are predicted to exert an influence on the process of regulation out of proportion to the votes they represent. But as Peltzman (1976) stresses, this sort of analysis does not generally predict complete capture by regulated firms; other groups are likely also to receive benefits from a support-maximizing regulator.

The legislative approach has been subjected to considerable criticism. DeAlessi (1974b, pp. 23-25) and Hirshleifer (1976) have argued that treating effective political support as an ultimate goal is inappropriate. While such support may be a direct source of pleasure to some individuals, these critics argue that it is more sensibly thought of as providing a means to some more basic end or ends. Hirshleifer suggests that regulators' ultimate objective is wealth, the same objective postulated for other groups in these models. But this may also be a troublesome oversimplification in some instances. The studies that describe passivity as a common mode of regulatory behavior, for instance, suggest that leisure or freedom from stress also enters the objective function of at least some actors in common bureaucratic/administrative situations.

The analytical power of the legislative approach derives from the relatively simple and thus tractable models it employs. Tractability is enhanced both by the assumption of a single objective and the neglect of forces impinging on regulators from legislatures, executives, and other administrators. While many such forces may derive ultimately from the electorate, the transmission mechanism may not be straightforward. Other forces may originate in the nature of the bureaucratic/administrative process. A number of authors, including DeAlessi (1974b), Hirshleifer (1976), Tullock (1976), and Weingast (1978), have argued that the neglect of these forces or constraints is not a harmless simplification; rather it results in a distorted model of agency behavior.

The bureaucratic approach eschews the extreme simplification of legislative models. It attempts to do justice to the important forces arising within the structure of government that affect agency behavior and to the implications of the structural and procedural conditions within which the agency functions. Authors such as Jaffe (1954), Bernstein (1955, 1972), Noll (1971a, 1971b), Hilton (1972), and Weingast (1978) are associated with this approach. Its central weakness is that realism is often purchased by the sacrifice of analytical power; this literature provides a wealth of narrative detail, general observation, and provocative suggestion, but it offers little in the way of rigorous derivation or formal testing of hypotheses.

Weingast (1978) provides an interesting recent example of this conflict between realism and power. In his model, regulators are entirely passive; all important decisions are assumed to be made by the relevant legislative oversight committee. Weingast then carefully considers how procedural rules and legislators' self-interest affect the response of that committee's make-up to changes over time in the political power of various groups in the electorate. The assumption of perfect legislative control seems overly strong, and it is hard to be completely comfortable with the neglect of other forces and constraints. But to add more realism to Weingast's formal structure would likely rob it of any predictive power.

As Joskow and Noll (1978) point out, these attempts to model regulatory behavior are not sharply different from general ones to construct models of the behavior of democratic governments. As in that more general area, no single view or approach has emerged with much power or with universal scholarly support. This lack is disturbing; we do not seem to have a framework that would enable us to predict the behavioral implications of alternative institutional arrangements for the control of natural monopoly.

Even in the absence of a satisfactory general theory, empirical work might provide at least some relevant suggestions. But, as Joskow and Noll (1978, p. 63) note, "Very little research is available on the comparative outcomes of different regulatory structures." Two recent comparative studies do deserve mention, however. Hagerman and Ratchford (1978) investigated the effect of a variety of political or structural variables on the rates of return allowed electric utilities in recent rate cases. Their only positive result was that commissioners with shorter terms tended to allow lower returns. Using more sophisticated measures of regulatory effectiveness and a larger sample of electric utilities for 1970, Smiley and Green (1978) found some support for this result and also noted that regulatory performance seemed to be better when commissioners were appointed rather than elected.

These are interesting findings, but they raise at least as many questions as they answer. More work is obviously needed in this area. Bernstein's (1972, p. 26) assessment of our knowledge here seems to remain correct: "We are unable to identify, on the basis of rigorous analysis rather than impressionistic judgments, the requisites of acceptable administrative performance."[16]

After a review of the relevant literature, Thomas (1971) passes a similar judgment on the state of institutional engineering knowledge. But he does note that Jaffe (1954), Friendly (1962), and Lowi (1969) had made a persuasive case that the vagueness of statutory mandates is often an important cause of observed regulatory inadequacies. Bernstein (1972) and Noll (1971b) have strengthened this case. This literature thus supports the argument in chapter 2 that regulators' mandates should be narrowed. If one cannot predict well how administrators will exercise authority delegated to them, it is sensible to try to delegate as little as possible. This is a rather disappointing and negative conclusion to draw from a sizable literature, which seems to tell us only that administrative discretion is abused in a variety of unpredictable ways; that is not enough to permit one to engage in precise institutional design.

Conclusions

This chapter has attempted to pull together and examine a number of bodies of work bearing on the appropriate design of institutional structures for the control of natural monopoly.

Considering the organizational-failures framework of Williamson (1973, 1975) as augmented by additional theoretical analysis and some relevant historical information, we can conclude that workable control devices must have buyers' agents and reasonably stable ownership structures, and they cannot rely entirely on explicit written contracts.

The literature on administrative and regulatory behavior is not so fertile. Simple generalizations of the producer-protection variety about regulatory behavior do not seem adequate, and neither a fully satisfactory alternative theoretical structure nor a comprehensive set of empirical studies has been produced. Our inability to predict how agencies will exercise their discretion argues for limiting such discretion by removing as much ambiguity as possible from agency mandates, but the literature on administrative behavior suggests little more than this.

Notes

1. This is an application of the argument in Coase, "Problem of Social Cost," that perfectly frictionless negotiation with well-defined property rights must serve to eliminate inefficient resource uses; see also Goldberg, "Expanded Theory of Contract."

2. An important factor here is the ability of the producer of a public good to exclude some from consuming or enjoying it; see Lee, "Discrimination and Efficiency," and the references he cites. Such exclusion is assumed impossible in the case of national defense.

3. The franchise bidding schemes discussed in chapter 5 represent arrangements with the intended effect of bringing market forces to bear here.

4. The principal-agency relationship in this context must be fundamentally different from that studied by such theorists as Ross, "Economic Theory of Agency." Because of the agency's special expertise, there cannot be an explicit agreed-upon reward structure, since the agent's performance is difficult for the principal(s) to evaluate precisely. This point relates to much of the discussion in chapter 2 as well.

5. General discussions of this period may be found in Clemens, *Economics and Public Utilities*, chs. 4, 15; Farris and Sampson, *Public Utilities*, pp. 62-63; Garfield and Lovejoy, *Public Utility Economics*, ch. 3; Glaeser, *Outlines of Public Utility Economics*, chs. 10, 13, and *Public Utilities*, chs. 3, 5, 8, 9; Jones, *Regulated Industries*, pp. 30-35; Nash, *Economics of Public Utilities*, ch. 3; Pegrum, *Public Regulation of Business*, pp. 624-44; Phillips, *Economics of Regulation*, pp. 84-88; Thompson and Smith, *Public Utility Economics*, chs. 8, 9; Troxel, *Economics of Public Utilities*, chs. 3, 18; Wilcox, *Municipal Franchises*, vols. 1-2; and Wilson, Herring, and Eutsler, *Public Utility Regulation*, ch. 2. The checkered early history of franchise regulation in New York City is described by Myers, *History of Public Franchises in New York City*, and Carman, *Street Surface Railway Franchises of New York City*.

6. Some clues as to the general experience in other countries are provided by Clough, *France*; Currie, "Rate Control on Canadian Utilities"; Cushman, *Independent Regulatory Commissions*; English, "Other Policies"; Meyer, *Gov-*

ernment Regulation; and Parris, *Government and Railways*. A comparison of Clough and Cushman, for instance, suggests that British railroad nationalization followed the effective breakdown of loose and erratic regulation, while French nationalization was a reaction to the failure of very tight and predictable control. A comprehensive history of control systems employed abroad would be of considerable interest.

7. On this episode, see Raffalovich, "L'avanc de l'heure legale"; Normand, "L'exploitation du gaz"; and Feugère, "L'augmentation du prix du vente du gaz."

8. Most actual service-at-cost arrangements were not quite this simple. Provisions were sometimes made for stabilization reserves to avoid excessive price fluctuations, and some contracts had sliding-scale provisions (see chapter 8) to provide efficiency incentives. For more on service-at-cost franchises, see Morgan, *Regulation*, pp. 190-91; Nash, *Economics of Public Utilities*, ch. 3; Clemens, *Economics and Public Utilities*, ch. 15; Thompson and Smith, *Public Utility Economics*, ch. 9; and Troxel, *Economics of Public Utilities*, ch. 18.

9. Most of the general discussions cited in n. 5, above, make reference to these problems. See also Beaulieu, "Le gaz et l'électricité à Paris," and "Les compagnies d'électricité a Paris"; Carman, *Street Surface Railway Franchises of New York City*, ch. 10; Clough, *France*, p. 177; Foster, "Public Utility Franchise in Missouri": Normand, "L'exploitation du gaz": and "Where Limited Franchises Lead."

10. See the general discussions of the franchise control period cited in n. 5, above, along with Wilcox, "Constructive Franchise Policy"; Foster, "Public Utility Franchise in Missouri"; and Clark, *Social Control of Business*, pp. 260-61.

11. A recent example of municipal takeover under a fixed-term franchise is provided by the *Otter Tail* case: *U.S.* v. *Otter Tail Power Co.*, 311 F.Supp. 54 (1971); *Otter Tail Power Co.* v. *United States*, 410 U.S. 366 (1973).

12. Municipal utility commissions in several cities before World War I are described in King, *Regulation of Municipal Utilities*. The state-local regulatory interface is discussed by Wilcox, *Municipal Franchises*, 2:744-45, and "Elements of a Constructive Franchise Policy"; King, "State versus Municipal Utility Commissions"; Morgan, *Regulation and Management*, pp. 188-233; Nash, *Economics of Public Utilities*, pp. 105-07; and Bauer, "Modernizing the Public Utility Franchise," and *Public Utility Franchise*.

13. The discussion that follows is not a complete survey. In particular, studies primarily concerned with the behavior of actors involved with public enterprises are discussed in chapter 6.

14. In an alternative life-cycle model, Shepherd, "Entry as a Substitute," and *Treatment of Market Power*, ch. 9, stresses changes in the economic aspects of regulated industries rather than shifts in regulatory behavior.

15. See Joskow, "Determination of the Allowed Rate of Return," and "Inflation and Environmental Concern"; Spence, "Monopoly, Quality, and Regulation"; Wendel, "Firm-Regulator Interaction"; Williamson, "Franchise Bidding"; Baron and Taggart, "Model of Regulation"; and Owen and Braeutigam, *Regulation Game.*

16. Most of this section has been concerned with the failure of administrators to pursue socially appropriate goals, but Bernstein's conclusion was also meant to apply to the sort of administrative failure referred to in chapter 2. He is supported in this regard by Noll, *Reforming Regulation*; Thomas, "Politics, Structure, and Personnel"; and many others.

5 Using Markets for Capital and Management

Outside the public utility context, it has become commonplace since Manne's (1965) analysis to observe that markets for capital funds and for managerial talent serve to constrain the ability of any firm's management to pursue goals other than shareholder wealth maximization. Even when equity ownership is dispersed, so that management is likely to be free from direct control by stockholders, mergers and tender offers initiated by outsiders can serve to displace inefficient managers, and the possibility of such actions can serve to discipline established managements. As recent studies by Smiley (1976) and Hull (1977) indicate, this market for corporate control does not work perfectly. Still it is natural, to an economist at least, to ask if markets for capital and management might be used to aid or accomplish control of natural monopolies. A number of investigators have considered this question, and this chapter presents and evaluates some of their affirmative answers.

Three general sorts of proposals are considered here. The first is franchise bidding, which, in various forms, seems to be the alternative to conventional regulation most discussed in the recent economics literature. In the simplest form of franchise bidding, firms would bid for the right to be the natural monopolist forever. The firm that offers to supply services at the lowest price is selected for this role, and it would then supply both capital and management. The idea here is that competition in markets for capital and management is made to replace uneconomic competition in the market for the natural monopoly's output.

The second set of proposals, automatic investment plans, rely only on the market for capital funds. Automatic investment plans seek to combat the tendency of a natural monopoly to restrict output and thereby to earn excess profits by allowing capital funds to flow automatically into or out of such a firm. Since the capital market can be expected to provide additional funds in response to excess profits and to withdraw funds in the face of losses, that market alone would tend to drive the natural monopoly toward a zero-profit point.

Finally, we consider two sets of proposals that rely primarily on the market for managerial talent. The first of these involves public ownership of the relevant tangible assets, with private management compensated under an operating franchise. Rival management teams would bid for this franchise, with the team offering to supply services at the lowest price declared the winner. The second set of management-market proposals would retain private ownership and something like conventional regulation. But obstacles to takeovers of utility firms would be lowered, thus more effectively using the market for corporate control to promote efficiency of operation.

Franchise Bidding

The franchise bidding approach to the control of natural monopoly seems to have originated in the nineteenth century, when it appeared in both theoretical discussions and practical applications. The earliest example of the former that I have been able to uncover is Mill's (1848, pp. 143-44) prescription for natural monopoly: "If it be not such as the government could beneficially undertake, it should be made over entire to the company or association which will perform it on the best terms for the public." Some years later, Chadwick (1859) published a long article extolling the virtues of this device. (Crain and Ekelund, 1976, provide a useful summary of Chadwick's relevant writings.) Two aspects of the Chadwick paper deserve mention. First, Chadwick would not limit application of franchise bidding to natural monopoly situations; he seems to view it as a cure for a number of different kinds of poor market performance. Second, he discusses enthusiastically and at length the use of franchise bidding in France around 1855 in connection with such diverse activities as water supply, omnibus service, and funerals.

Indeed, practice seems to have preceded theory here. Besides Chadwick's examples, from 1826 until 1851, many French railroad franchises were awarded to the firm offering to charge the lowest fare.[1] This practice was abolished by Napoleon III, who nonetheless, as Chadwick and Holcombe (1911, p. 745) report, apparently endorsed franchise bidding in other contexts.

Similarly Wilcox (1910, pp. 38-40) noted that competition had been frequently employed to determine franchise awards in the United States, though most often the winner was the firm promising the largest payment to the city. Posner (1972, p. 113) notes that competition of this sort has been employed in recent years in the awarding of cable television franchises. It is clear that bidding of this kind does not produce efficient pricing, since the winning firm is free to charge whatever price it likes in a monopoly situation. Nevertheless this may not be a totally unreasonable procedure in some cases. Customers pay monopoly prices during the franchise period, but the firm has clear incentives to produce efficiently, and product selection problems may be no more severe than under other forms of control. (If the bid is on the percentage of revenue to be given to the city, rather than on a lump sum or a fraction of profits, however, the winning bidder's most profitable price is above the uncontrolled monopoly level.) In theory, competitive bidding ensures that the city receives an estimate of capitalized monopoly profits, and it could use its receipts to undo at least the income or equity effects of monopoly pricing. For a number of reasons, however, Wilcox (1910, pp. 38-40) doubts that cities generally received such sums. (One problem Wilcox notes is that risk aversion tends to push bids well below the expected value of excess profit.)

The franchise bidding approach to the control of natural monopoly was introduced into the modern literature by Demsetz (1968), who rediscovered and extended Chadwick (1859). Demsetz's suggestion that firms be allowed to bid for relatively long-term franchises was soon endorsed by Stigler (1968, pp. 18-19). Posner (1972), in a discussion of social control of cable television monopolies, suggested that short-term franchises might be better. Wilcox and Shepherd (1975, p. 510) also seemed to favor some use of franchise bidding. This approach to control of natural monopoly has been criticized by a host of authors, of whom Williamson (1976) is probably the most thorough.[2]

Two aspects of franchise bidding as a control device must be distinguished: the likely behavior of the winning bidder during the franchise term and problems associated therewith, and the bidding process itself.

After the winner has been determined, franchise bidding becomes control by contract, of the sort formerly attempted widely in the United States. There are three central difficulties with franchise control, having to do with pricing, investment, and enforcement. First, if the contract is for a reasonably long period—long enough for significant changes in costs, demands, or technologies to be at all probable—either a formula for rate change must be built into the franchise, or some provision for regulation or renegotiation must be made. Given the bounded rationality of humans and the vast number of possible relevant future occurrences, the formula approach is likely to break down. But if regulation or renegotiation is chosen (that is, if the contract does not attempt to cover all contingencies), franchise bidding is robbed of its main desirable feature: reliance on input market competition to determine prices. Regulation or franchise renegotiation can be done effectively only by a buyers' agent; with the addition of such an agent, the system begins to resemble conventional regulation in important respects.

Second, the historical evidence indicates that as the end of a franchise term approaches, firms tend to underinvest in fixed assets and to cut back on maintenance. This underinvestment is especially acute when assets are to revert to the municipality or other authority at the end of the period, but the problem exists whenever there is some likelihood that the firm will lose all or part of its investment. It is clear that this problem is magnified by the use of short-term franchises.

There may, of course, exist contractual devices not employed during the period of franchise control that would maintain investment incentives until the end of the period. But the literature does not describe any. Posner (1972, p. 116) suggests that this problem can be solved by simply requiring the franchisee, if he loses the bidding at the end of his term, "at his successor's option, to sell his plant . . . to the latter at its original cost, as depreciated." But as Williamson

(1976, pp. 84-87) notes in his detailed critique of this proposal, the specialized nature and immobility of assets in public utility sectors mean that they are worth very little to a firm that loses the franchise to operate them. The successor firm might very well offer less than book value. (As Williamson notes, in the absence of detailed supervision, book value can itself be manipulated by the franchise holder.) The likelihood that this will occur will certainly inhibit the franchise holder from making investments toward the end of his contract. Since knowledge is even harder to value than machinery, Williamson (pp. 87-89) also indicates that investment in learning about the firm's specific problems and potentials will be similarly inhibited. It thus seems that, absent asset transfer schemes far superior to those that have been employed or discussed to date, the importance of specialized immobile assets implies that whenever franchises have only a limited period to run, investment decisions will be suboptimal. (See also Goldberg, 1976b, on this general problem.)

Third, as King (1912b, p. 206) noted near the end of the period of franchise control, "A franchise is not self-enforcing." An expert and informed buyers' agent must generally be in existence to enforce the franchise contract, in addition to participating in the evolution of that contract, under any long-term arrangement. Crain and Ekelund (1976) point out that Chadwick's early franchise bidding proposals assigned important functions to such an agent.

Two basic problems are associated with the bidding that would occur under these schemes. The first has to do with selection of the winning bid, and the second relates to the likely competitiveness of the bidding process.

The bid selection problem arises essentially because even if competitive bidding succeeds in eliminating the winner's excess profit and ensuring production efficiency, economic efficiency is not thereby ensured. Price structure and product selection issues cannot be avoided. This point is at the heart of Telser's (1969, 1971a, 1971b) critique of Demsetz (1968); Telser notes that zero excess profit does not imply marginal cost pricing. In his reply to Telser, Demsetz (1971, pp. 358-62) suggests that bidders be required to offer multipart tariffs (of the sort described in chapter 3's discussion of nonlinear pricing) that would then be evaluated by a buyers' cooperative. Plainly that cooperative would require the specialized knowledge that one normally associates with a somewhat idealized regulatory commission. In selecting among alternative rate structures, the cooperative would be making exactly the sort of decisions for which utility commissions are now responsible. The cooperative would of necessity be more or less political, and its managers would thus be likely to commit many of the actual and potential sins of regulatory commissions.[3]

Posner (1972, p. 115) has suggested that the pricing problem can be solved without resort to a commission-like entity by having bidders attempt to sign contingent contracts with potential customers at the prices and for the grades of service the former propose. These contracts would be binding only if the firm was selected as the winner. Posner proposes that the winner be the firm with the greatest dollar value of signed contracts by some specified date. As Williamson (1976, pp. 80-81) notes, it is not obvious that boundedly rational customers without specialized knowledge can in fact evaluate complex price-quality packages well. Further this scheme need not select the best bid according to any reasonable standards even if this problem is assumed away. Suppose, following Williamson (1976, p. 80), that proposal *A,* which involves high price and high quality, attracts 10 percent of potential customers, while nine nearly identical proposals, *B-J,* all of which offer low price and low quality, also get 10 percent each. Since *A*'s price is higher, it has the largest dollar value of contracts in hand and wins the bidding, even though 90 percent of buyers preferred a low price/low quality offering. Similarly suppose *A* and *B* are the only bidders; *A* offers a price of $1 to residential customers and $50 to business customers, while *B*'s prices are $1.01 and $2, respectively. If residential customers are more than twice as numerous as business customers, *A* wins in spite of what may be extreme discrimination against the latter group. (This last example would seem to indicate that even under reasonably competitive bidding, Posner's scheme does not always ensure that the winner does not receive substantial excess profit.)

A variety of additional bid selection problems could be mentioned. In considering expected total outlay, for instance, one ought to weigh the likelihood that the winning firm will breach its contract and thus impose negotiation or litigation costs on its customers. This suggests that bidders' reputations ought to affect bid selection, but it seems unlikely that business reputations can be well evaluated by unsophisticated consumers. Thus barring a noticeably better and more complete proposal than Posner's, it would seem that except in the very simplest cases, an expert buyers' agent would be required to evaluate rival bids. A commission-like entity is once again necessary in order to make franchise bidding work.

Further, evaluation of reputation by a commission or other buyers' agent is inevitably somewhat subjective. Since one tends to trust one's friends, obvious dangers of corruption emerge. See Lewis, 1898, for an example.

The second major problem with bidding for franchises is the difficulty of ensuring that bidding is competitive. Holcombe (1911, p. 745) does report that when the right to operate the Paris gas system was auctioned off in 1905, the city received thirteen bids; this at least suggests effective competition. (This was an operating franchise of the sort discussed below; the winning bidder did not buy the plant. The unhappy outcome of this contract was discussed in chapter 4.) On the other hand, Wilcox's (1910, pp. 38-40) review of experience with bidding for franchises leads him to doubt that real competition is likely to occur with any frequency. Wilcox discusses in particular New York City's experience with this device (more information is provided by Myers, 1900, ch. 8, and Wilcox, 1912). In most cases, bidders indicated the percentage of gross revenue they would give the city. In at least one instance, a bid of essentially 100 percent was received for a trolley franchise. Obviously the franchise was never intended to be exploited; the aim of the bid was presumably to block a rival. This experience relates to the suggestion of Peacock and Rowley (1972, p. 243) that a firm might bid to supply below cost if it felt that it had the political skill to arrange a favorable renegotiation of the franchise when its unfortunate position became known. (There are obvious parallels with defense procurement here; see, for instance, Scherer, 1964, and McCall, 1970.)

As Trebing (1974) has emphasized, current structures of many public utility industries make coordination among existing firms relatively easy, and those firms are the most likely bidders for franchises. If, for instance, bids are taken on the operation of a municipal electricity distribution system, bidders must have some expectations about the rates at which they can buy power. But if power supply is monopolized in an area, the power supplier has an obvious advantage in bidding.

The problem of imperfect bidding competition is likely to be most severe when a franchise has expired and the existing supplier is bidding against those who seek to replace him. There is apparently little historical evidence to draw on here. Although the literature contains numerous discussions of failures to renew limited-term franchises and of municipal purchase of assets, I have not found a reference to any case in which an existing supplier bid against other firms. Apparently franchises tended to be renewed unless the city (or other authority) was quite unhappy. In the latter cases, the franchise holder was evidently simply told to leave at the end of the contract.

Still the a priori arguments of Peacock and Rowley (1972, p. 242) and Williamson (1976, pp. 84-90) that effective competition is unlikely seem compelling here. In the first place, it seems virtually impossible to ensure that outsiders would pay for tangible assets exactly what they are worth to the existing supplier in their current use. Any discrepency between transfer price and value to the existing supplier creates an asymmetry in bidding that is likely to favor the current supplier. At the very least, the current supplier avoids the haggling costs associated with asset transfer if he wins. Second, the existing supplier is almost certain to be better informed about actual cost and demand conditions than his rivals are. He thus saves the cost of acquiring the information necessary to submit an intelligent bid, and he may be able to mislead or hinder his rivals. Third, the severe problems associated with pricing (or transferring) skills and knowledge that are specific to a single enterprise raise bidding parity issues, as well as the investment incentive difficulties noted above. Finally, any firm that managed to outbid an existing supplier would have to expect to go through a high-cost transition period during which its management team learned the firm-specific technical and personal aspects of their jobs.[4] These inevitable costs associated with managerial change give the existing supplier yet another advantage in bidding. It would seem that outsiders would be able to bid effectively against an existing supplier only in exceptional cases. The latter acquires important "first-mover advantages" in Williamson's (1975, ch. 2) terms.[5]

In summary, a priori argument and considerable historical experience combine to establish that franchise bidding is hardly a breakthrough in natural monopoly control technology. Under virtually any workable arrangement, some expert agency would be required to evaluate competing bids and to enforce the franchise contract. Further, if the franchise is relatively long term, detailed supervision and renegotiation of prices, more or less resembling conventional utility regulation, would be required. The similarity between franchise bidding and conventional regulation would necessarily increase with the length of the franchise term. The shorter the franchise, however, the more severe the problems associated with investment incentives and noncompetitive bidding behavior would become.

Posner (1972, p. 117) concludes his discussion of the promise of franchise bidding in cable television by stating merely that some experimentation seems called for. It is hard to object to experimentation in principle, but a number of experiments with franchise bidding have been conducted, and virtually no promising results have been obtained. Williamson's (1976, sect. 4) case study of a failure of franchise bidding in cable television is particularly to the point here. Further, the analysis above suggests that any additional experiments should be confined to the sort of situations recommended by Williamson (1976, p. 102), in which technology and demand are stable and well understood (minimizing uncertainty/complexity and imperfect bidding competition problems) and the assets supplied by the franchisee are relatively mobile (minimizing investment incentive and asset transfer problems).

Automatic Investment Schemes

The basic structure of automatic investment schemes is presented and discussed by Baumol (1965, pp. 109-113), who credits F.A. von Hayek with the original idea. Suppose a natural monopoly firm offers to buy or sell as many shares of its common stock as the market supplies or demands at a fixed price of, say, $20. All profits are divided among equity holders in proportion to the number of shares held. The firm's purchases and sales act to fix the share price at $20; market and book values of assets are equal. If the firm earns less than a competitive return on its capital, investors will earn less than a competitive return on their shares. (*Competitive return* here includes an appropriate allowance for risk.) They will then tend to sell shares to the firm and thus draw down its capital. If the firm earns excess profits, so will investors, and new capital will be supplied to the firm as investors buy shares from it. The idea here is to have the capital market drive the firm to a point at which zero economic profits are earned.

To my knowledge, no control device of this sort has ever been employed, and Baumol (1965, p. 108) does not advocate its use. On the other hand, Renshaw (1958, p. 343) does seriously propose a variant of this scheme. (I refer here to the second of his three proposals.) It differs from Baumol's plan mainly in that only a utility's customers would be allowed to purchase its stock. The firm would thus become a sort of cooperative. (The implications of such structures for the efficiency of risk bearing and for managerial behavior are discussed in chapter 6. Here managers are assumed to be concerned primarily with shareholder wealth maximization.) If only because Baumol's book and MacAvoy's (1970a) collection of readings, in which Renshaw's proposals are reprinted, seem to have been widely read (though probably by different audiences), it seems worthwhile to discuss briefly the basic properties of automatic investment plans.

First, Baumol (p. 109) notes that movement of capital into or out of the firm must be restricted to, say, one day per year, in order to permit rational planning and to have shareholders bear some risk. In fact, the long periods required to plan and build many public utility plants (consider nuclear power plants) may impose even more stringent limits here if rational planning is to be possible. Baumol (p. 110) also argues that with proper managerial compensation, it becomes reasonable to assume that management seeks to maximize profits between these "sale days." One can doubt the strength of managerial concern with profit under an arrangement of this sort, since the population of shareholders is likely to be unusually fluid, but let us accept the profit maximization assumption for purposes of discussion.

Then the capital market will generally serve to drive the firm to a point at which the maximum value of excess or economic profit obtainable from the capital stock on hand is zero.[6] The capital market thus ensures that revenues just cover costs on average, and the profit limitation function is performed automatically. But there are severe problems along the other three dimensions of efficient performance: production, pricing, and product selection. First, production is likely to be inefficient. Trebing (1960a, pp. 748-49) has argued that automatic investment plans are likely to increase equity costs by imposing unusual risks on shareholders. Further, if the firm hires labor to maximize profit and if the capital market drives excess profits to zero, the firm's choice of inputs will be inappropriate. Specifically it will overemploy capital, much as in the standard Averch-Johnson (1962) model of firm behavior under rate-of-return regulation. At all points, the firm restricts output to enhance profit by restricting its use of labor, so that the capital market drives it to a point at which labor is underutilized and thus capital is overutilized.

(Those willing to accept the assertion of overcapitalization on faith are invited to do so. For skeptics, this paragraph sketches its proof. Let us assume a standard two-input (labor and capital), one-output structure. Given any market-determined capital stock, the profit-maximizing firm will set the marginal revenue product of labor equal to the wage rate. This condition defines the firm's equilibrium position on the zero-profit locus in capital/labor space. It is easy to show that if net consumers' surplus is maximized subject to zero economic profit for the firm, a point on this same locus is reached at which the marginal revenue product of labor is less than the wage rate. (If the constraint is not binding, the marginal value product of labor is set equal to the wage rate.) Given diminishing returns to labor and downward sloping marginal revenue, the marginal revenue product of labor decreases as more labor is employed for a given capital stock. This means that if they employed the same capital stock, the efficient solution would call for more labor than the equilibrium point under automatic investment. But if profits are initially zero and labor is increased, profits will become negative, so that the efficient point must involve less capital as well as more labor.)

This control device leaves price structure and product selection issues entirely in the hands of the firm's management. There is no reason to think that acceptable decisions will be made along these dimensions. Indeed one can imagine the firm's employing ever more discriminatory rate structures as it vigorously attempts to squeeze excess profits from the market in spite of capital inflows. If this were done through efficient nonlinear pricing, as defined by Willig (1978), the efficiency costs might be tolerable, but if different prices were set for different services or to different customer classes (if the discriminatory Ramsey pricing scheme were employed to excess), these costs could be substantial. If pricing and product selection decisions were to be placed under some sort of regulatory supervision, however, much of the attractive simplicity of the automatic investment approach would vanish.

In short, automatic investment schemes do not appear to be good candidates for the control of natural monopolies. Baumol (1965, p. 109) would seem to be correct in his judgment that they offer little more than "an amusing exercise in economic analysis."

Operating Franchises

The operating franchise schemes that appear in the modern literature resemble franchise bidding plans except that ownership of tangible assets remains with some public authority or unit of government. With final responsibility for investment decisions removed from the operating firm, the adverse incentive effects of impending franchise termination can obviously be avoided. Perhaps just as obviously, new difficulties arise.

Demsetz (1968, p. 63) argues that it might be attractive to have bidding for operating franchises instead of for ordinary franchises. As Crain and Ekelund (1976) note, Demsetz was again anticipated by Chadwick, who advocated such an approach to control of railroads. (See also Clark, 1939, p. 375.)

A number of cases of private management of government-owned assets under conditions of legal monopoly have been reported. The initial lines of the Boston, New York, and Paris subways were leased to private operators. At about the same time, the right to operate the Philadelphia municipal gasworks was auctioned off, and a few years later the Paris gas system was similarly placed under private management.[7] In 1921, the Department of the Seine purchased the assets of the privately owned Paris bus and trolley system and turned them over to a private firm under a rather interesting operating franchise.[8]

The operating firm basically received a relatively low guaranteed return, a fraction of gross revenues, and a fraction of enterprise profit. The use of revenue or output bonuses of this sort to induce monopolists to produce at competitive output levels seems to have been discussed first (in English, at least) in theoretical terms more than a decade later by Robinson (1933, pp. 163-65). Under the Paris franchise, however, fares were fixed by the city, so the incentive effects of the revenue bonus were probably mitigated somewhat. The franchisee did control the frequency of service and speed, though, and the revenue bonus provided incentives to maintain these dimensions of product quality. The same basic arrangement was also imposed on French railroads in 1921 (see Morgan, 1923, pp. 331-37, and Huntington, 1922). One reason for the 1921 change in the ownership of the Paris bus and trolley system was poor performance under previous franchise arrangements. These had tied profits closely to traffic density, before 1910 by a tax on cars and thereafter by density-based fares.[9] These provisions led, predictably, to excessively full cars, slow speeds, infrequent service, and numerous complaints about service quality.

A substantial change was made in the Paris operating franchise in 1925. (Blake, 1927, describes this change but does not indicate why it occurred.) Basically the revenue and profit bonuses were replaced by a single payment related to R^2/C, where R is gross revenue and C is operating expense. If profit, π, is computed as $(R-C)$, this expression can be written as $R^2/(R-\pi)$. Calculus then shows that the payoff to the operating firm is an increasing function of both profit and revenue. The marginal payoff from an additional franc of profit is an increasing function of profit and a decreasing function of revenue. Similarly the payoff from additional revenue rises with revenue and falls with profit. It would be interesting to know why this formula appeared more attractive than separate revenue and profit bonuses and to learn what happened when it was imposed on the system.

One need not go back this far in time to find examples of operating franchises. Recent Italian experience with what seem to be arrangements of this sort is discussed by Treves (1970, pp. 133-37), and Locklin (1966, pp. 96-98) mentions that Georgia and North Carolina have leased railroads that they own. Still the combination of government or other public ownership and private operation seems uncommon in modern developed economies.

This rarity would not have surprised contemporary observers of many of the early arrangements of this sort. Lewis (1898), for instance, argued that the Philadelphia gasworks was leased mainly because the city was unable to raise funds for its improvement, while it could require the operating firm to do so. No special efficiency advantages were anticipated. Similarly Holcombe (1911, p. 734-44) argued that the operating franchise arrangement for the Paris gasworks had obvious disadvantages, and he doubted that it had any special advantages over the more conventional alternatives of public ownership and operation and private ownership under commission regulation. He notes (p. 742) that the previous franchise holder (which also owned the plant) had performed so poorly that further private provision of gas was a very unpopular alternative. On the other hand, municipal ownership and operation was viewed as politically impossible, leaving some sort of operating franchise arrangement as the only viable option. Finally, Wilcox's (1911, pp. 743-44) general review of experience with operating franchises led him to the negative assessment that public authorities had no lighter a regulatory burden than under private ownership because the franchisee's pursuit of its own gain needed to be controlled. A number of considerations suggest that this was not likely to have been a peculiar feature of the cases he considered.

From an analytical point of view, the main novelty in operating franchise structures (besides their bidding features) is the division of the usual managerial role under private ownership between the operating management (the winning bidder) and the relevant governmental entity. The latter supplies the major portion of the equity capital employed and takes ultimate responsibility for investment decisions. The government, and not the operating management, becomes in effect the agent of equity capital suppliers. The latter are, ultimately, the relevant set of taxpayers. If the government is also to serve as buyers' agent, which seems likely and is assumed in the following discussion, a variety of internal problems might appear, because the short-run objectives of equity suppliers and buyers may conflict.

Operating management is responsible only for short-run decisions. This sort of structure thus responds to Gray's (1976) call for public officials to make the major decisions in public utility industries, with private firms making only the minor ones. (Gray is a bit vague as to how this is to occur. He does not stress government ownership with private operation.)

Operating management can be presumed to serve its own interests under the term of the franchise agreement. This need not imply that it focuses entirely on maximizing the size of its bonus or compensation under that agreement. Unless its every act is carefully watched by the responsible government agency and unless that agency manages to duplicate the operating management's skills and knowledge, the latter will have an unusual amount of discretion during the franchise term. It might behave opportunistically, attempting to influence investment policy in order to enhance its bonus; unless the government agency probes and understands the details of the operation of the enterprise, the operating management is likely to possess major information impactedness advantages.

On the other hand, as the literature discussed by Scherer (1970, pp. 31-33) suggests, managements may have a variety of goals. Even if the bonus is carefully structured so that maximizing it enhances efficiency, there is no guarantee that operating management will in fact simply maximize its bonus. As Edwards (1977) and others have indicated, for instance, management may be willing to give up some compensation in order to acquire additional subordinates, the presence of whom makes top management feel and appear more important. Since the operating management is only indirectly responsible to equity suppliers, through its governmental control agency, the pressure against wasteful behavior of this and other sorts can be expected to be weaker than under private ownership.

One basic feature of operating franchises is clear: the performance of the whole enterprise after the franchisee has been determined depends on the decisions of both public officials and operating management. Close coordination between these dual managements is thus essential, but it will be difficult to maintain. The two groups' objectives differ, and neither can be expected to have all the information available to the other. Given bounded rationality, it is surely either impossible or unduly expensive and time-consuming in most cases to have exactly parallel structures and perfectly shared information. Further, in a small-numbers situation of this sort, the likely gains from opportunistic distortion of information flow may be substantial. The administrative machinery under operating franchises is thus subject to important frictions.

In order to maintain incentives, it will be necessary for net returns to both the government and operating management to depend on enterprise performance, presumably measured in terms of profit. Both the Paris gasworks and surface transit franchises discussed above had this feature. In an uncertain world, this means that both parties bear risk. As Drèze (1976) has shown in a related context, such risk sharing is generally necessary for efficient resource use. Moreover management salaries are a tiny fraction of the operating expenses of most sizable utilities, so that if the government's return were fixed and operating management were to bear all risks, the relative salary fluctuations produced by moderate shocks imposed on the enterprise by other sectors of the economy would be intolerably huge. (Under truly perfect capital markets, the management team might shed some of this risk by selling stock in its own performance. But since a reduction in risk would also diminish incentives, even a perfect market would not permit full risk avoidance. This is a standard moral-hazard problem; see Marshall, 1976, for a general discussion.) Thus both government and the operating management must bear some of the consequences of changes in cost and demand conditions that are beyond management's control.

The necessity for coordination and risk sharing has a number of implications for enterprise functioning under operating franchises that deserve discussion. These arise, as before, at both the operating and bidding levels.

If an operating franchise were of relatively short duration, management turnover costs would arise more frequently if bidding were truly competitive. Under an operating franchise structure, these costs would be compounded by the necessity of developing an acceptable close working arrangement with the controlling governmental entity. Under long-term arrangements, contractual terms would necessarily be incomplete because all contingencies would not be anticipated. This means, in Goldberg's (1976b) language, that the contract must be administered: the parties to it must themselves define and redefine their relationship over time. Thus the requisite coordination between public and private managements is substantial; they must be able to deal smoothly with situations not anticipated in the contract that connects them.

Contractual incompleteness implies that under an ordinary franchise contract of any duration, this definition and redefinition would come to resemble conventional regulation in important ways. Here, because of the presence of substantial government investment, the imperfection of markets for managerial skills, and the need for coordination and risk sharing, the closest analog seems to be single-source defense procurement under incentive contracting.[10] As there, no obvious market tests can be employed to determine fair compensation for given operating performance, while contractual incompleteness means that compensation cannot be determined by formula in all cases. Under conventional regulation, a market test can be employed to approximate fair compensation to equity suppliers. But managers are less easily evaluated than shares of common stock, and the market for management is accordingly much less easy to employ for this task than is the stock market under conventional regulation. There is little regulatory precedent because existing utility commissions have paid very little attention to management compensation.[11] The defense procurement analogy hardly suggests that long-term operating franchises would produce generally acceptable results. (For a particularly relevant and depressing discussion, see Burns's 1970 description of attempts to define reasonable profits in renegotiation litigation when much of the capital employed has been provided by the government.)

At the bidding level, competition by itself can at best ensure production efficiency and eliminate excess profit; price structure and product selection issues remain, presumably to be dealt with by the public half of the management team. And, as under bidding for ordinary franchises, competition is by no means certain to obtain at any stage. Asset valuation problems are eliminated, but strategic or coordinated bidding is no less likely. Similarly an established management, familiar with the particular enterprise and its environment, would have substantial advantages over those who might seek to displace it.

Moreover the apparent analogy with defense procurement suggests that bidding problems peculiar to operating franchises are likely to be encountered. Given that some sort of risk sharing or incentive contract is likely to prove desirable, competing bids might include not only some estimate of prices (or costs) but a proposed risk-sharing mechanism for determining managerial compensation. This would certainly complicate the problem of bid evaluation and require additional skills and resources of the relevant control agency. Even if this problem can be reduced somewhat by governmental dictation of the form of the risk-sharing formula, so that bids need only specify values of a few parameters, an even more serious problem would remain. As McCall (1970) has shown, the low bidder under incentive procurement contracting need not be the firm with the lowest expected costs. As long as there is some risk sharing, inefficient managements, with few attractive opportunities in competitive markets, have a strong incentive to enter low bids in order to obtain the contract, since the government will absorb some of the costs of their inefficiency. Thus the face value of competing bids under risk sharing may be an inadequate indicator of expected performance. This problem basically arises because boundedly rational humans cannot precisely evaluate managerial performance in complex situations; it is usually impossible to sort out the effects of managerial errors from those of unfavorable developments over which management had little or no control. Debates about cost overruns in defense procurement illustrate this point.

Recognition of the fact that bids may not be good predictors of performance suggests that the awarding authority might rely in part on bidders' experience, character, or reputation. But this consideration makes politically motivated or otherwise capricious bid selection likely. Lewis (1898), for instance, mentions the outcry that erupted when, because of reputation and experience, the most favorable bid for the Philadelphia gasworks lease was not selected. Under private ownership, the firm's immobile assets and the government's police power combine to provide a guarantee at least against plunder and flight. If one were to require similar financial hostages under an operating franchise, the importance of reputation might be diminished to some extent. This seems to have been done under the 1921 Paris transit franchise.[12]

Two potential advantages of operating franchises might be important under some circumstances. First, the direct focus on managerial compensation might provide a stronger positive incentive for superior efficiency than would exist under private ownership, where shareholders receive much of the benefit of superior management. Morgan (1923), for instance, was an early and vigorous advocate of this notion. On the other hand, the necessity for risk sharing serves to limit the power of this incentive, and freedom from any direct responsibility to shareholders may serve to entrench distinctly inept managements more firmly than under private ownership, where at least the threat of takeover exists. Second, vesting asset ownership in a governmental entity avoids the investment incentive problem that would otherwise plague operations under limited franchises and also removes the asset valuation difficulties that would otherwise inhibit competitive bidding to replace an existing franchise holder. This is not a strong positive point, of course, since it is relevant only when comparison is made with bidding for ordinary franchises.

There may be cases in which either or both of these advantages outweigh the problems discussed here. But it seems obvious that bidding for operating franchises is not an approach that can be recommended for any particular situation without careful study, particularly because of the coordination and control problems built into the dual management structure it requires. Like franchise bidding, operating franchises may sometimes be useful, but this device is hardly a panacea for the ills of natural monopoly situations. In particular, the analysis here suggests the general applicability of Wilcox's (1911, pp. 743-44) empirical observation that operating franchises do not reduce the tasks that must be performed by a governmental control agency.

Facilitating Utility Takeover

The suggestions discussed here do not propose replacing conventional utility regulation; rather they seek to improve it by enhancing the incentives for efficiency faced by regulated firms' managers. Shepherd (1973; 1975, ch. 9; 1976a) seems to be the most persistent advocate of this sort of reform. He argues that regulated firms' managements are insulated to an unusual extent from the discipline of the "market for corporate control" (Manne, 1965). Shepherd contends that takeovers are usually rare in public utility sectors because of legal barriers and commissions' generally protective attitudes toward existing managements. An obvious legal barrier is the Public Utilities Holding Company Act of 1935, which essentially forbids the common ownership of electric utilities that are not functionally integrated, thus preventing the experienced managements of well-run utilities from attempting to take over inefficient operations with which they are not directly connected. (For a general, critical discussion of the operation of this act, see Kahn, 1971, pp. 72-73.) Shepherd proposes that both legal and commission-established obstacles to takeovers be removed. This seems a difficult suggestion to oppose in general terms, and I have seen no such opposition in print. Still, several caveats should be noted.

First, the Public Utilities Holding Company Act was a response to real abuses during the 1920s and early 1930s. Some of these abuses may be adequately protected against by the Securities and Exchange Commission's (SEC) regulation of securities markets, but a thoroughly integrated structure can at least complicate the task of regulation. If a firm's common stock is all held by a holding company, for instance, stock market data cannot be usefully employed to determine its cost of capital funds.

Second, legislation may be required to remove commission-established obstacles to takeover. Exhortations to be less responsive to the wishes of established managements may not serve to change basic commission behavior patterns. Still there does seem little to be lost by taking from commissions the power to make case-by-case judgments on takeover attempts.

Third, because of the generally recognized importance of continuity of service in many public utility industries, which Goldberg (1976b, 1977) in particular has stressed, it might be necessary either to prescribe minimum service standards and liability rules in regulatory contracts, as Shepherd (1973, pp. 102-03) has suggested, or to legislate specific responsibility (but not experience) tests that must be passed by firms controlling utility operations. There are legitimate grounds for being more concerned with who is managing water supply than with who operates a grocery store in a competitive market. Since existing managements have generally been allowed to operate without passing any special tests, however, it is not obvious that takeovers should be inhibited by requiring their passage of potential new operators.

Fourth, the market for corporate control is not perfect. (For general discussions of this point, see Manne, 1965, Smiley, 1976, and Hull, 1977.) As Shepherd (1976a) acknowledges, incumbent managements generally have a number of important advantages over those who seek to displace them. As in other sectors, one can look to this market to correct instances of flagrantly inefficient operation.

The telephone industry in the United States poses special problems here, since AT&T's size, relative to other corporations in the economy, serves to make takeover of the bulk of the telephone industry virtually impossible. Shepherd's (1973, p. 102) proposal that 49 percent of the stock of all public utility subsidiaries of any firm be placed on the open market is designed to cope with this sort of difficulty by establishing an independent shareholder interest in such subsidiaries. Unless this interest is concentrated in a few hands, however, it is not clear how effective it could be in disciplining management. (This proposal would solve the problem of determining capital cost under integration though.) Manne (1965), for instance, concludes that proxy fights are a much less effective disciplinary device than takeover attempts.

Finally, under conventional regulation, profits are determined not just by the efficiency with which services are provided but by management's skill in dealing with regulators and with the political process in general. There may be instances in which economic efficiency is enhanced by greater skill in these activities, but it is not obvious that they are common. To the extent that takeovers occur because of superior political skills or resources rather than superior managerial abilities, stockholders benefit, but overall efficiency might well suffer. Existing utility managements have had considerable incentive in the past to develop political and bargaining capabilities, and it is not obvious that outsiders would generally be noticeably better at these activities.

Shepherd (1975, ch. 9; 1976a), Wilcox and Shepherd (1975, pp. 510-11), and Williamson (1971), among others, have argued that not only should impediments to takeovers of utility firms be removed, but regulators should take positive steps to make inefficient managements in utility sectors more visible. The most common suggestion is to require regulators to finance and publish periodic management audits of the firms under their supervision. Such audits are performed in other sectors by established management consulting firms, and regulatory commissions have begun to use them with some frequency in recent years. (For some evidence on this latter point, see Sargent, 1978.) Well-done management audits can serve to focus the attention of regulators, public opinion, shareholders, and potential new managements on instances of gross inefficiency. As Doades (1978) and Sargent (1978) note, however, management auditing is not easily done well. In particular, the utility's management, because it controls the flow of a good deal of critical information, plays an important role in the auditing process. Nevertheless although management audits cannot be expected to perform their information provision function perfectly, their more extensive use is difficult to oppose.

Conclusions

I have devoted considerable attention to control structures that rely on competition in the markets for capital and management for a number of reasons. First, the use of market competition as a control mechanism has great appeal to most economists. Second, because of this, there is considerable discussion of such structures in the recent literature. Finally, there is a great deal of relevant historical experience, though not all of it has been well documented.

Most of the implications of this chapter's investigations are negative. Automatic investment schemes, which rely entirely on the capital market, seem to have little or no promise. Neither bidding for ordinary franchises nor for operating franchises seems likely to outperform conventional regulation in most natural monopoly situations. Both approaches encounter problems of ensuring competitive bidding and efficient operation under franchise control. It seems clear that neither permits abolition of detailed public supervision; the markets for capital and management simply cannot adequately perform the control function unaided.

Facilitation of outside takeover of public utility firms seems likely to contribute to efficient production, and management audits may prove to be useful in this context. But this reform deals only with production efficiency; it thus has the potential for assisting regulators on only one of the four dimensions of efficient natural monopoly performance identified in chapter 3.

Notes

1. Lefranc, "French Railroads," and Clough, *France*, p. 178.
2. Williamson, "Franchise Bidding," also presents an interesting case study of franchise bidding in cable television. Other critics of franchise bidding include

Goldberg, "Regulation and Administered Contracts"; Peacock and Rowley, "Welfare Economics"; Sherman, *Economics of Industry,* ch. 23; Telser, "Regulation of Industry: A Note," and "Regulation of Industry: A Rejoinder"; and Trebing, "Realism and Relevance," "Chicago School," and "Market Structure."

3. Koller, "Why Regulate Utilities"? notes in particular that some provision might be necessary to prevent post-award discrimination against new customers not initially members of the cooperative.

4. Gouldner, *Patterns of Industrial Bureaucracy,* presents a case study of difficulties encountered by a new management attempting to change organizational style that bears on these issues, as does the analysis of Williamson, Wachter, and Harris, "Understanding the Employment Relation."

5. Of course, as Williamson, "Franchise Bidding," pp. 88-90, notes, one would expect the first set of bidders to recognize that the winner among them would be unlikely to be displaced by subsequent bidding. They might thus all offer to sell below cost for the first franchise period, confident of their ability to recoup losses by sales above cost later on. Such a pricing pattern is clearly inefficient.

6. Technically as long as the marginal product of capital is positive and demand is elastic, the firm will find it profitable to employ all capital supplied to it by the market.

7. On the various subways, see Brelay, "Le métropolitain"; Wilcox, *Municipal Franchises,* 2: 497-533; and "The Metropolitan Railway of Paris." Lewis, "Lease of the Philadelphia Gas Works," and Rowe, "Relation of the City of Philadelphia to the Gas Supply," describe the lease of the Philadelphia gasworks; as the latter notes, the city had acquired the plant in 1887 after a long struggle. The Paris leasing is described by Holcombe, "Régie Intéressée," and Normand, "L'exploitation du gaz."

8. The arrangement is described and discussed by Morgan, *Regulation and the Management of Public Utilities,* pp. 331-37, and in "Features of the New Paris Franchise" and "Has Paris Solved the 'Incentive' Problem in Railway-City Contracts?"

9. On this earlier experience, see Payen, "Les moyens transports"; Beaulieu, "Les divers systèmes"; "New Franchise Conditions in Paris"; and "Has Paris Solved the 'Incentive' Problem in Railway-City Contracts?"

10. Illuminating analyses of some relevant aspects of the defense procurement process are given by Scherer, *Weapons Acquisition Process*; Moore, "Incentive Contracts"; Williamson, "Economics of Defense Contracting"; Hall, "Defense Procurement"; Burns, "Tax Court"; and McCall, "Simple Economics of Incentive Contracting."

11. See, for instance, DeAllessi, "Economic Analysis of Government Ownership," p. 8, and Kahn, *Economics of Regulation,* 1:29, 2:99.

12. See "Features of the New Paris Franchise."

Public Ownership and Operation

Many early critics of public utility regulation in the United States attacked what Gray (1940, p. 8) termed "the delusion that private privilege can be reconciled with public interest by the alchemy of regulation" and argued for public ownership and operation of apparent natural monopoly enterprises. This strategy of natural monopoly control has been frequently, though not universally, employed in other countries (see Pryor, 1976, for some quantitative information).

Even in the United States, public ownership has long been important in public utility industries.[1] Water supply is an obvious example. Jones (1967, pp. 7-8) points out that the first three U.S. waterworks were built with private capital and that of the sixteen in existence by 1800, only one was publicly owned. By 1875, however, over half the U.S. water supply systems were publicly owned, and at least three-quarters of the population is now served by such systems. (See also Thompson and Smith, 1941, pp. 14-15.) In electricity, Nash (1925, p. 331) notes that the first municipal plant in the United States began operation shortly before the first privately owned central generating station. In 1976, about 22 percent of electricity generation in the United States was done by public enterprises (U.S. Department of Commerce 1977, p. 599). Pryor (1976, p. 11) reports that in 1960, 28 percent of the employees in utility sectors (electricity, gas, water, sanitation) in the United States worked for public enterprises. Comparable figures for Japan, West Germany, and Switzerland were 20 percent, 43 percent, and 60 percent, respectively.

There are a number of positive effects one might expect to obtain by a shift from private to public ownership of natural monopoly enterprises. (For general discussions, see Shepherd et al., 1976.) Three deserve mention.

First, one might hope that public firms would serve as especially vigorous competitors of private firms and thus act to improve the performance of the latter. Hellman (1972) in fact argues that competition of this sort was of some value in the electric utility industry, at least prior to 1940. But in natural monopoly sectors, by definition, such direct competition is wasteful. Further, experience abroad with public enterprises in other sectors suggests that they cannot be relied upon to display the aggressiveness necessary to function effectively as spurs to competition (see, for instance, Sheahan, 1976). For these reasons, it seems doubtful that the likelihood of increased competition can serve as a significant argument for public ownership and operation in natural monopoly sectors.

Second, it has sometimes been argued that public enterprises can productively serve as yardsticks with which the performance of private firms in the same sectors can be assessed (see, for instance, Gray, 1956). In an interesting reversal of this argument, Beaulieu (1901b) worried about inefficiency and political control of municipal gasworks and argued that private firms should be vigorously used as standards with which to evaluate them. In any case, most observers now seem to feel that the difficulty of comparing public and private enterprises is usually sufficiently great as to eliminate the yardstick function of either.[2] Though some attempts at such comparisons are considered below, we will not deal further with the yardstick potential of public enterprise.

Finally, public enterprises might be expected to behave in socially desirable ways because they are not concerned with the pursuit of private gain. That is, they might be expected to yield direct efficiency (or other) gains in their operations. This expectation is the focus of the discussion that follows.

The following section considers the structural alternatives that fall under the general classification of public enterprise. The next section considers theoretical and empirical analyses of the implications of public ownership for enterprise conduct and performance.

Structural Alternatives

Publicly owned enterprises can be divided into two classes: government enterprises and cooperatives. The former are attached, more or less closely, to some government with broader responsibilities. The latter are not; they are directly customer controlled.

Government enterprises take a wide variety of forms. Units of the executive branch of various governments, such as the U.S. Post Office prior to 1971, have acted as monopoly suppliers of goods and services for centuries. Many recent proposals and discussions focus on the public corporation as an alternative form. Though owned and operated by a government, these are separate legal entities, to some extent independent of day-to-day executive or legislative control. This structure is usually thought of as having been first systematically considered and employed in Great Britain in the 1930s, though many earlier examples doubtless exist. Since the 1930s, the public corporation seems to have become the preferred form of government enterprise in Western nations, and a large number of different types have been established in many countries.[3] Postal service in the United States, for instance, was transferred from a cabinet department to a public corporation in 1971. In 1933, the Tennessee Valley Authority (TVA) was set up as a public corporation (see Wilcox and Shepherd, 1975, pp. 556-61). The internal structures of public corporations vary considerably, as do their formal relationships with the governments to which they are attached.

Whatever the formal structure, government enterprises have common elements in both their ownership and control structures. In a pure government enterprise, the government involved is the only equity capital supplier (Caves, 1977, p. 112). The government directly, and the corresponding set of taxpayers indirectly, bears the risks normally borne by stockholders under private ownership. Depending on pricing policy, of course, customers may also bear noticeable risk, and many examples of mixed public/private ownership exist, with shared risk bearing. But in almost all government-controlled enterprises, a government bears a substantial part of what would be the stockholder's risk under private ownership.

Two interesting exceptions to this generalization deserve brief mention. First, Bauer (1950, ch. 11) has proposed, as part of a rather radical transformation of regulation that would involve continuous rate review, that private equity holders' control over utility management be effectively eliminated. He would have all interests affected by such a firm, including stockholders, represented on the board of directors. Under this proposal, private ownership is preserved de jure, but de facto management would not act solely as the agent of equity suppliers. With continuous rate review, however, most risk seems likely to be shifted from stockholders to customers, so that the former would probably be more like bondholders in practice. If not, one would expect equity capital to be unusually expensive, since stockholders would bear unusual risk about managerial goals and objectives. Second, Sheahan (1976, pp. 151-52) notes that since 1970 new investments in the French telephone system have been financed to some extent by selling equity-like securities to private investors. The latter, through special financing companies, retain title to the assets involved, and their returns depend (according to various formulas) on telephone activity. This is an odd sort of ownership, though, since the government (through an executive branch department) retains all planning and operating responsibility and is the ultimate recipient of operating surpluses or deficits. Lalumière (1975) describes this set-up in some detail and argues that it is an unnecessarily expensive way to raise capital; it is employed primarily because the government was unwilling to have the necessary borrowing show in its own accounts.

A second common feature of government enterprise is that the same government entity that serves as an equity holder generally acts as the buyers' agent as well. Some government enterprises in the United States are subjected to regulation by commissions associated with other branches of government, but the degree of effective control seems generally low.[4] It is useful to distinguish between the government enterprise's managers and its regulators or controllers. The former are responsible for the day-to-day operation of the enterprise, the latter for general oversight and verification that appropriate objectives are pursued. If the enterprise is part of the executive branch, this distinction is somewhat blurred, though generally one can think of career civil servants as managers and their politically appointed superiors as controllers. This distinction is quite clear in the case of public corporations. (On control of such enterprises in Britain, see, for instance, Robson, 1962, and Foster, 1971.) Indeed one of the virtues of the latter form is generally held to be the increased autonomy it provides managers. In much of the discussion of the public corporation form in the 1930s in Britain, however, it was clearly recognized that there was a trade-off between managerial autonomy, which was held to promote operating efficiency, and managerial accountability or effective governmental control, held to be necessary to ensure pursuit of appropriate objectives. (See, for instance, Gordon, 1938, O'Brien, 1938, and Robson, 1937.) Shepherd (1976b, pp. 41-45) provides a good general discussion of this trade-off.

Just as regulatory agencies can be more or less independent of executive control and legislative review, regardless of their nominal status, so too can the degree and form of control of both executive branch departments and public corporations vary considerably. Maass (1951) provides a classic example of a part of the executive branch—the U.S. Army Corps of Engineers—virtually free of control by the chief executive. Breyer (1971), Noll (1971b), and others have argued that empirically it is difficult to discern any systematic differences between the behavior of regulatory agencies that are and are not nominally independent of the executive branch, and it seems similarly unlikely that one can determine the nature and effectiveness of control over a public enterprise's managers simply by knowing whether the enterprise is organized as a public corporation. It is difficult to argue, for instance, that the conduct and performance of the U.S. Postal Service are drastically different from those of its predecessor, the U.S. Post Office, in spite of their rather different structures.[5]

At the conceptual level, managers of government enterprises, along with their controllers, are expected to serve as the agents of both equity capital and of buyers. This dual role is clearest in the case of those with oversight responsibilities, and it stems at least in part from their association with the equity-holding government. Some of the early British discussions of the public corporation seemed to hope and, sometimes, to expect that management would also take on both roles. As Pegrum (1940, p. 342) put it, in the absence of effective control, the management of public corporations is called upon to be both "actor and judge." If one accepts the controller-manager dichotomy, at least in the abstract, it becomes clear that at least some of the questions that one might ask about regulated industries can also be asked about government enterprises. One might wonder, for instance, what goals controllers and managers are likely to pursue, and what the performance implications of alternative control structures are.

Government enterprises, like regulatory commissions, are often called upon to assist in the pursuit of social goals not directly related to economic efficiency. At least in the traditional utility sectors, though, efficiency considerations are rarely explicitly excluded. Further, there seems to be a general presumption that government enterprises in these sectors should aim to break even, though the strength of this presumption varies. Although government utility enterprises have sometimes served as important revenue sources, it seems more common for them to incur substantial and persistent deficits, only part of which can be associated with conscious subsidies by the governments involved. Shepherd (1975, ch. 9; 1976c) has argued that profit limitation in the case of government enterprises usually amounts to setting a floor on profit (or a ceiling on the deficit), as opposed to the profit ceilings associated with regulation of private enterprises. (Shepherd, 1975, pp. 250-04, goes on to make a theoretical argument that this difference should lead to greater risk taking by government enterprises, all else equal. I know of no systematic attempt to test this conclusion, however.) This point should not be overstated, however; government enterprise in practice seems to operate with a wide range of rates of return, as the experience summarized by Sheahan (1976) and Shepherd (1976c) illustrates.

Many of the early discussions of public corporations seem to have expected them to be managed by the same sort of hard-working, competent idealists whom the Progressives expected to staff regulatory commissions in the United States. In contrast, most proposals for cooperative structures, in which a natural monopoly would be owned and directly controlled by its customers, with little or no outside government intervention, seem to ignore the role of management almost entirely. Thus Renshaw (1958) seems to feel that moving to total or partial customer ownership would automatically improve utility performance. Similarly Sherman's (1967a, 1967b, 1970) discussions of monopolies owned by "clubs" of their customers describe those clubs as both deciding on cost-sharing arrangements and either directly managing the enterprise or indirectly ensuring its operating efficiency.

In reality, the requirement for special skills implies a need for professional management in all but the very simplest cooperative ventures. Since customers are both equity suppliers and buyers, management must play the dual role of buyers' and equity suppliers' agent. As with a government enterprise, or a regulatory commission, a cooperative's management must be granted some autonomy and discretion. If nothing else, management's informational advantages over its customer-employers serves to render the latter incapable of perfect control. As Trebing (1960b, p. 748) points out in a critique of Renshaw (1958), imperfect control coupled with managers' pursuit of their self-interest is a potential problem for cooperatives, as it is for other structures.

Experience with cooperative ownership structures in natural monopoly sectors is not extensive. Apparently such enterprises are more common in the United States than elsewhere.[6] (Konopnicki, 1971, and San Pedro, 1971, mention sizable urban electric cooperatives in Argentina, but I have been unable to uncover any detailed information about their structure or operations.) Nebraska's public power system, which has provided all electricity in the state since 1946, comes under this heading, as it is not directly part of state government.[7] Similarly the public utility districts of Washington and Oregon are best thought of as cooperatives. These are legally municipal corporations (though not subject to municipal control), with the power to issue revenue bonds but only minimal power to tax, that own and operate electric, water, and (in at least one case) sewer utilities. Their boards of directors are popularly elected and not subject to commission regulation.[8]

Normally when one thinks of cooperatives in this country, rural telephone and electric coops come to mind. These served about 700,000 and 6.6 million residential customers in 1975, respectively.[9] They are a product of the 1930s and have obtained subsidized loans from the federal government since then. In recent years, because of a shortage of loanable funds at the Rural Electrification Administration (REA), some of the larger electric cooperatives have successfully tapped the private debt market.[10] The boards of directors of electric cooperatives are elected by the consumer members alone and set rates that are usually at least nominally subject to review by state regulatory commissions and by the REA. Their rate structures have generally been based on both cost of service and value of service (demand responsiveness to price) considerations.[11]

Conduct and Performance

As a classification, public ownership and operation includes a wide variety of apparently disparate institutional structures. It would be useful if the literature on administrative behavior permitted one to predict confidently the performance implications of structural differences. Unfortunately neither the study of administrative behavior in general nor the analysis of public enterprise in particular has yet advanced to the point where such predictions are possible.

The literature on regulatory behavior suggests that although commissions in principle are buyers' agents, their members are as likely as other people to pursue their self-interest subject to the constraints they face. The literature does not permit strong statements as to the precise nature or determinants of either regulators' objectives or the constraints under which they operate.

Under public ownership, the management and control structure of the enterprise serves as the agent of both buyers and equity capital suppliers. This merging of roles can hardly be expected to have a dramatic impact on the forces affecting the actors involved. Just as Stigler (1971) contemplates commissions' capture by regulated firms, Pegrum (1940) worries that public corporations will neglect their role as buyers' agents and be captured by the pursuit of profit. Lindsay's (1976) argument that managers subject to external control tend to distort outputs to overproduce those things that are easily measured would seem to apply to public enterprise (as he asserts) as well as to regulated private firms. Similarly the effects of concern for political support under regulation analyzed by Posner (1971, 1974), Peltzman (1976), and others ought also to be present under public ownership. Indeed Caves (1977, pp. 112-13), Tulkens (1976), and others have suggested that managers and controllers of public enterprises can be modeled as maximizing effective political support, subject to the constraint that the enterprise be financially viable. In general, the effective limits that Jaffe (1954) so clearly associated with conventional regulation would seem to apply no less directly to public ownership structures, whether of the government enterprise or cooperative variety.

All this is not to argue that ownership structure has no performance implications but rather that one should expect quantitative, not qualitative, differences between public and private enterprises as a general rule. There have been both theoretical and empirical studies of these differences.

Very little empirical work has been done on cooperatives. In particular, the politics and economics of rural electric and telephone cooperatives have been little studied, though one might expect that the experiences of these enterprises would be illuminating. Zank and Bakken (1959, esp. chs. 4-5) do provide considerable quantitative information about rural electric cooperatives in Wisconsin. They describe the mechanism by which, in effect, equity shares are divided among members, but they say very little about rate making other than a note (p. 130) to the effect that for most of these enterprises, rates were first set by the REA, which was concerned primarily with repayment of the initial construction loan. They say nothing about the implications for rate structure decisions of the fact that business customers to not have a vote on these matters. Zank and Bakken (pp. 10-14) document the cost problems implied by customer homogeneity (leading to sharp variation in demand over time), but they do not discuss the cost-sharing problems that customer diversity would imply or describe the actual role of management.

Theoretical considerations suggest some problems likely to be encountered in cooperative structures. Sherman (1970), for instance, provides a lucid discussion of (and an attempt at a partial solution to) the problem of arranging appropriate risk bearing by a cooperative's customer-owners. No matter how the latter share the risks involved, some inefficiency in risk bearing is inevitable, since this group cannot trade its equity with others in the economy. The risk involved thus cannot be spread as widely as would otherwise be possible and would generally be desirable. Indeed under the arrangements described by Zank and Bakken (1959, chs. 4-5) customers cannot even trade ownership shares with one another. (Sherman, 1970, proposes to facilitate such trading.) If this sort of trade cannot occur, inefficient risk bearing is virtually guaranteed. The importance of this general problem is, of course, directly proportional to the riskiness of the cooperative enterprise; for some it may not be of great moment, while in other situations it may suffice to rule out cooperative ownership. (It is worth noting that if there is some probability of default, debt holders also bear risk. Thus by making loans at subsidized rates even with some uncertainty about eventual repayment, the REA has shifted some of the risk of rural electric and telephone cooperatives from their customer-owners onto the federal government, in effect spreading it over a large population of taxpayers.)

Another set of issues involves the control of cooperatives' managers. Given managers' informational advantages, direct control by cooperative members, voting as shareholders at annual meetings, can be expected to be weak in all but the simplest ventures. Since any owner's investment in the knowledge necessary to evaluate managerial performance can be expected to confer benefits on all other owners, a public-good problem is present that can be expected to inhibit direct owner control when there are few members. Since managers, like the rest of us, have some tendency to pursue their own interests, exceptionally weak control can be expected to lead to exceptionally poor performance, though the nature and severity of the problems posed by managerial freedom will depend on the precise objectives that managers pursue.

Cooperatives need not rely entirely on shareholder meetings for managerial supervision, of course. They might hire outside experts to oversee the enterprise management, or they might elect a board of more or less amateur controllers from their own number. In the first case, the overseers would presumably resemble the managers they regulate in terms of background and expertise, and probably they would come to identify more closely with management than with the cooperative's membership. Even if capture of this sort does not occur, the behavior of such a board would tend to differ in degree but not in kind from that of a regulatory commission, particularly an elected one. Control by a board of amateurs from among the cooperative's membership may mitigate these problems somewhat, but it would likely encounter difficulties of ensuring that sufficient skills and resources were applied to the control function. If the enterprise is at all complex, managerial sloth or X-inefficiency, in Leibenstein's (1966) terminology, is difficult for outsiders to detect. Yet under cooperative ownership, it, along with politically motivated pricing, seems a principal danger.

One might expect to see measurable, though probably not dramatic, conduct and performance differences between government enterprises and cooperatives. In the latter structures, for instance, there is at least in principle greater freedom to allocate risk bearing among the individuals involved, though this freedom may not be frequently exercised. Since one bears risk in a government enterprise largely in one's role as a taxpayer, shifts in risk bearing are difficult to arrange. In the usual case, one must either change residence or engage in costly political activity to induce a shift in patterns of risk bearing. There appear to be no studies comparing the efficiency of risk bearing under these alternative structures, however.

A variety of more or less plausible behavioral hypotheses relating cooperatives to government enterprises can easily be produced. The greater ease of subsidizing a failing government enterprise from tax revenues might lead it to be less cost conscious than a cooperative with otherwise similar problems, for instance. On the other hand, the greater ease with which government enterprise profits could be used to lower tax rates or to subsidize unrelated activities might lead to more vigorous profit seeking (and cost cutting) in some situations.

Unfortunately there seem to be no comparative studies that would shed light on these or other similar conjectures.

Most of the discussion of public ownership does not distinguish explicitly among alternative forms, although a government enterprise is generally implicitly assumed. The stress is on comparing public and private enterprise, and the most common guiding hypothesis is that managerial freedom to pursue self-interest, at the expense of economic efficiency, is greater under public ownership.

Following Williamson (1967) and Wilson (1971, 1974), one might reach this hypothesis by arguing that the greater ambiguity attaching to managerial tasks under public ownership should increase management's freedom of action. Another route to the same point is the property rights approach, the application of which to this context is surveyed by DeAlessi (1974b). The notion here is that a crucial difference between private and public enterprise is the greater difficulty of transferring one's equity holding in the latter. This, it is argued, tends to loosen the constraints imposed on managers by ultimate equity suppliers, thus reducing the incentive to lower costs or to adopt profit-enhancing pricing patterns. Greater managerial flexibility might be devoted to ensuring political support, as Peltzman (1971) contends, or to increasing perquisites and minimizing effort, as DeAlessi (1974b) argues. In the latter case, but not in the former, one would expect to find X-inefficiency. Thus, for instance, DeAlessi (1974b) worries about the lack of incentive for public corporation managers to be hard bargainers with labor unions. (Gordon, 1938, ch. 6, expressed the same worry earlier.)

When the standard of comparison is regulated private enterprise, however, the theoretical case for noticeable performance differences becomes less clear. If regulation is at all effective, it serves to limit profits and thus inevitably to reduce management's incentive to seek profit. Regulatory constraints may thus play a role under private ownership similar to that played by freedom from capital market discipline under public ownership. Similarly regulators' mandates are not typically less vague than the assigned tasks of public enterprise managers. Further, under conditions of legal monopoly, regulators may have considerable freedom to pursue such goals as political support or leisure time; it may not matter much for ultimate performance whether regulators (or controllers under public ownership) or enterprise managers are engaged in such behavior. Still the comparative question is empirical, and some relevant evidence is considered below.

On a different level, Pegram (1965, pp. 697-98) argues that one can expect to see excessive use of capital, of the sort that Averch and Johnson (1962) associate with conventional regulation, in public enterprise. The basic notion is that most capital funds are raised for such enterprises by borrowing, and the cost of debt is the only cost of capital seen by management. (Both Gordon, 1938, ch. 6, and Pegrum, 1940, note problems that the highly levered capitalizations of most public corporations might cause.) There is no market measure of the cost of equity, since risk bearing is generally imposed rather than purchased. Moreover if debt is raised by municipal bond issues in the United States, the federal income tax subsidy lowers the private cost of debt below the social cost. Thus the public enterprise manager is likely to see a cost of capital funds well below the true social cost. Any attempt at cost minimization using a capital cost that is too low from a social point of view leads naturally to overuse of capital. This effect is likely to be enhanced in a political environment to the extent that highly visible dimensions of performance, such as freedom from blackouts, are capital intensive.

In order to test hypotheses that relate performance under private ownership with that under government enterprise structures, comparative studies are necessary. A number of quantitative studies of this sort have been done. Davies (1971, 1977), for instance, finds that Australia's private airline is more efficient in production than its publicly owned rival. Pashigian's (1976) study of the shift to public ownership of urban transit in the 1960s provides a number of interesting observations, among them a tendency for public firms to show lower profit rates than private enterprises do. The bulk of the quantitative comparative literature seems to focus on differences between municipal and private electric utilities in the United States; DeAlessi (1974b, pp. 22-37) provides a useful survey.[1][2] These studies provide some evidence consistent with the hypothesis of greater managerial discretion under public ownership, along with other evidence that is either ambiguous or difficult to rationalize in terms of this hypothesis.

DeAlessi (1974a), for instance, finds some evidence for longer managerial tenure in municipal utilities, after correcting for enterprise scale. He contends that this is consistent with the notion that public enterprise managers have more freedom to act so as to enhance their security. Neuberg (1977), however, argues that this finding is also consistent with a superiority of those managers over their private counterparts. If greater security is offered, he notes, then all else equal, a given managerial position is more attractive; by offering greater security, municipal utilities can attract better managers without having to pay higher salaries. The evidence cannot discriminate between these views.

More interesting comparisons focus on performance differences along the four dimensions of production efficiency, price structure, product selection, and profit limitation. Unfortunately comparisons of productive efficiency are greatly complicated in the present context by the various tax exemptions from which municipal utilities benefit; one might expect them to show lower costs even if they are actually somewhat less efficient than private firms. (On the various difficulties involved in comparing municipal and private electric utilities, see Trebing, 1976a, pp. 107-08.) Both Meyer (1975) and Neuberg (1977) find that municipal utilities have significantly lower costs than private firms do, but they do not address this issue. Peltzman (1971) finds that municipal utilities charge lower prices on average, but he argues (pp. 135-36) that the difference can be entirely accounted for by tax exemptions. In terms of differential incentives to bargain, DeAlessi's (1975) finding that, holding various factors constant, municipal utilities tend to sell power to other enterprises at lower wholesale rates than private utilities do suggests that the former bargain less vigorously. His analysis may also suggest a greater degree of effective political influence by business when a utility is government owned, however. This interpretation is strengthened by his failure to find any difference in the rates paid by public and private firms for purchased power; bargaining toughness clearly should matter here. DeAlessi (1974b, pp. 35-36) discusses an unpublished study that suggests that municipal firms are slower than private utilities to adopt cost-saving innovations. On balance, it seems safe to say that the literature does not support assertions of dramatic efficiency differences between municipally owned and private electric utilities. While consistent with a number of conflicting theories, this negative finding is of some interest in its own right.

Concerning the tendency to earn excess profits, DeAlessi (1974b, pp. 33-35) mentions some research suggesting that municipal utilities earn lower and more variable (in cross-section) profit rates than private electric firms do. This finding is consistent with Moore's (1971) that private utilities charged approximately profit-maximizing prices in the early 1960s, while the rates of municipal utilities were significantly below profit-maximizing levels. Though these studies hardly settle the point, they do suggest that profit limitation may be somewhat more successfully achieved under municipal than private ownership. This is consistent with the generally hypothesized greater concern for profit in the latter case.

Peltzman (1971) tests a variety of specific hypotheses about rate structures, all based on the general notion that concern for political support should have a stronger effect on municipal utilities; DeAlessi (1974b, pp. 23-31) carefully examines and confronts Peltzman's results with other evidence. The main conclusions that emerge seem to be that municipal firms tend to group buyers into broader classes, treat them more uniformly, and make less use of declining block tariffs within customer classes. DeAlessi later (1977) provides corroborating evidence on the relatively less frequent use of peak-load pricing, as well as declining block pricing, by municipal utilities. These results suggest less intensive pursuit of profit by municipals, as does Peltzman's (1971) finding of greater price rigidity in municipal utilities. On the other hand, for a given level of profit, one can discriminate too little as well as too much; thus these findings do not imply greater or lesser economic efficiency of municipal rate structures.

In an interesting study not covered by DeAlessi's (1974b) survey, Mann (1974) attempts to test directly for differences in political sensitivity between private and public electric utilities. He examines the effects of voter turnout and majority party dominance on residential electric rates. The former variable has no effect; the latter is found to lower the prices charged by municipal firms but to raise private utilities' rates, though the latter effect is less clearly significant. As Mann indicates, it is hard to see why the extent of majority party dominance should have systematic but opposite-signed effects on rates under the different structures.

Finally DeAlessi (1974b, pp. 28-29) mentions some evidence suggesting that municipal utilities' pricing is more favorable to commercial and industrial users than that of private firms. This conclusion is reminiscent of the capture theories of regulation that emphasize the disproportionate political power of small groups with intense interests.

In summary, although there do seem to be systematic differences between privately and municipally owned electric utilities, they are not dramatic ones. In efficiency and profitability, the observed differences may be within the range of uncertainty induced by the different tax statuses and accounting conventions of the two sorts of enterprises. There is weak evidence for lower average profitability under municipal ownership. The differences in pricing patterns of municipal and private firms seem to be explicable in terms of greater concern for political support and less concern for profits under municipal ownership, but the differences are not huge. On product selection, Moore (1971, pp. 373-74) notes that the ratio of peak demand to capacity was lower, though not significantly, under municipal ownership than for private firms. This suggests, though very weakly, a higher level of reliability (or a stronger tendency to overuse capital) in municipal electrics.

The comparative work discussed so far has been quantitative and econometric. There exist many comparisons between public and private enterprises, between different public enterprises, and between different periods in the life of a single public enterprise that are more impressionistic. Thus Sheahan (1976) easily shows that telephone service in France, under public ownership, is much worse than in the United States, under private ownership and also that it is much worse in France than in most other nations with public ownership. Similarly Sheahan (1976) and Shepherd (1976c) indicate clearly that the French and British nationalized electricity systems, respectively, have been more innovative, particularly in adopting efficiency-enhancing pricing systems, than both U.S. privately owned commission-regulated electric utilities and the government-owned TVA. (On the other hand, Sheahan, 1976, pp. 148-49, does note the extreme persistence and, by the standards of U.S. utilities, heavy-handedness of the French nationalized electric system's lobbying for nuclear power.) Pryke (1971) provides a detailed study of performance trends in the nationalized industries in Britain. He and Shepherd (1976c) both argue that performance improved markedly in the second postwar decade, although no dramatic structural changes in these enterprises occurred. Pryke points to management shake-ups, more severe financial pressures, and closer public scrutiny as leading to productivity improvement.

Two major conclusions seem to emerge from the case study literature. First, a wide range of performance outcomes—clear successes and dismal failures—have been observed under public ownership. General praise or condemnation is clearly not justified. Second, although it is not entirely clear what makes the difference in all cases, on the basis of extensive experience in Western Europe both Sheahan

(1976, 1977) and Shepherd (1976b, 1976c) point to the importance of the effective control of enterprise management. Good government enterprises are generally subject to effective, though not stifling, control by the relevant arm of the executive. It is clear that one cannot gauge the effectiveness of control merely by looking at an organization chart any more than one can judge the effectiveness of regulation by reading the governing statute. (Robson, 1962, and especially Foster, 1971, provide interesting discussions of the complexity of the actual control process in Britain.) Shepherd (1976b, pp. 41-45) explicitly notes the parallel between the two situations. Just as chapter 4 argued that we do not know enough to design regulatory structures that will effectively pursue preset objectives, Shepherd contends that we are not able to design control systems for public enterprises that will perform well reliably. Managers of government enterprises are apparently not dramatically more likely to be selfless public servants than are regulators or private utility executives. Indeed Sheahan (1977) argues that neglect of this fact was the source of many of the early postwar difficulties with nationalized industries in the United Kingdom; only when the need for effective control of enterprise managements was recognized and acted upon did performance improve. In light of Shepherd's (1976b) analysis, however, effective control or accountability is hard to guarantee. We do not know how to obtain the tightest control consistent with given managerial autonomy, nor do we know what point on the trade-off locus to aim for in individual cases.

Conclusions

Public ownership is an important device for controlling natural monopolies. A large number of diverse public ownership structures have been employed in public utility sectors and elsewhere. However, little evidence exists that can serve to inform choice among these structures or between them and other control devices. There are a large number of studies relating the conduct and performance of municipally owned electric utilities to those of privately owned firms in that industry, but the variety of public ownership structures and devices for managerial control that might be employed and the different economic characteristics of the industries in which public ownership might be applied suggest that considerable caution should be exercised in generalizing from these. Perhaps their most comforting finding is that conduct and performance differences between municipal and private electric utilities are not dramatic, but even this statement may not be applicable generally. Public enterprises sometimes perform extraordinarily well by any standards; sometimes they are terrible. The nature of public enterprise management's accountability seems an important determinant of performance, but we are not able to say much more than this.

Indeed Kahn (1971, p. 328) argues that the mixed experience with public enterprise in the postwar period has had a lot to do with the waning of enthusiasm for government ownership of public utility firms in the United States. One cannot confidently predict that a shift to government ownership will generally improve performance; as Kahn puts it, experience has demonstrated "that there is no easy solution in changing the institutional form." As he notes, and as I have sought to indicate, many of the problems that are usually associated with conventional utility regulation arise, though often in somewhat different shapes, under public ownership. This supports the argument of chapter 4 that a number of problems are intrinsic to natural monopoly situations and do not seem to have easy solutions. For instance, enterprise managers must be subjected to appropriate control by outsiders, whether equity is publicly or privately held. On the basis of postwar experience with public enterprises in various industries, Shepherd (1976b, p. 35), who argues that government enterprise can be a useful device elsewhere in an economy, concludes that "the strictly economic case for public enterprise in utility sectors . . . is relatively weak."

On the other hand, natural monopoly industries have different basic economic characteristics along some dimensions. Some such industries may accordingly be much better suited than others for the application of public enterprise. Studies of municipal electric utilities seem to indicate that these enterprises pursue profit less vigorously than their privately owned counterparts do. If this finding generalizes, it would imply that abuse of natural monopoly positions, which would generally be indicated by persistent excess profits, is less likely under public than private ownership, though it raises questions about productive efficiency, pricing, and product selection aspects of performance. This suggests that public ownership and operation is likely to prove superior in situations in which the potential for monopoly abuse is relatively great, while the possibility for major undetected pricing and operating inefficiency is relatively small.

Clemens (1950, p. 549), for instance, argues that water supply systems are well suited to government operation. In making this case, he notes that these systems have simple and stable technologies and that water supply is a matter of great public importance. The first attribute suggests tight limits on the extent to which operating management can use superior information to avoid real accountability to and control by political officials. Because water is a necessity (with inelastic demand), the potential for monopoly abuse is great. These are hardly controversial observations, of course.[13] And since colonial times, there has been a marked trend toward government ownership of waterworks in the United States. Whether this reflects an institutional survival of the fittest or other forces is not clear.

Similarly one might suspect that other basic public utility functions, such as retail distribution of electricity, would satisfy these same conditions. However, the early trend toward municipal ownership of electricity distribution systems reversed in the 1920s, and the relative importance of municipal electrics has declined since. Some of this decline may have been caused by pressures put on municipal utilities by nearby private power suppliers; some may reflect operating difficulties experienced.[14] Further, the real gains (as opposed to the tax savings) from municipal ownership here are most likely modest, if they exist at all. It is clear that a close examination of particular cases is required before any sort of public ownership option can be recommended, and it should also be clear that the choice among the options of this sort that are available cannot be confidently made on the basis of current knowledge.

Notes

1. For general discussion of public ownership and operation of legal (and likely natural) monopoly enterprises in the United States, see Clemens, *Economics and Public Utilities*, ch. 23; Farris and Sampson, *Public Utilities*, chs. 17-23; Shepherd, "British and United States Experience"; and Wilçox and Shepherd, *Public Policies*, chs. 21-22.

2. See, for instance, Trebing, "What's Wrong with Commission Regulation? Part I"; Farris and Sampson, *Public Utilities*, p. 293; and Wilcox and Shepherd, *Public Policies*, pp. 528-30. Note also the discussion in chapter 8 of the difficulty of employing efficiency assessments in the regulation of private firms.

3. For description of a host of public corporation structures, see Ashley and Smails, *Canadian Crown Corporations*; Centre Européen de l'Enterprise Public, *Les Enterprises Publiques*; Hirschfeld, "Role of Public Enterprise in the French Economy"; Musolf, *Public Ownership and Accountability*; Wilcox and Shepherd, *Public Policies*, chs. 19-23; and various chapters in Friedman and Garner, *Government Enterprise*, and Shepherd et al., *Public Enterprise*. Useful references on the British experience are Robson, *Nationalized Industry*; Pryke, *Public Enterprise*; and Shepherd, *Economic Performance under Public Ownership*, and "British and United States Experience."

4. See, for example, Clemens, *Economics and Public Utilities*, ch. 23, and Mann and Seifried, "Pricing," p. 78. Beigie, "Telecommunication," and Stromberg, "Public Corporation in Sweden," mention independent regulation of public corporations in Canada and Sweden, respectively, but they do not indicate the effectiveness of that regulation.

5. See, for instance, "Still Trying to Make the Post Office Work."

6. This is the opinion of P. Derrick of the International Cooperative Alliance (London), expressed in a personal communication (April 14, 1976).

7. Some history of the Nebraska system is given by Firth, *Public Power in Nebraska*. More recent information is provided by "Public Power in Nebraska" and Nebraska Legislative Council, *Nebraska Blue Book*.

8. See Washington Public Utility Districts' Association, *Laws of the Public Utility Districts*, and *What Is a P.U.D.?*

9. These numbers are based on Rural Electrification Administration, *Rural Telephone Borrowers*, table 8, and *Rural Electric Borrowers*, table 17; they refer only to cooperatives with REA loans outstanding and thus provide lower bounds.

10. See "A Big Money Tap for Rural Electric Co-ops."

11. This sentence and the preceding one are based on D.E. Smith, staff economist, National Rural Electric Cooperative Association (Washington), personal communication (April 26, 1976). Only the rates of cooperatives with outstanding REA loans are subject to review by that agency.

12. For general background on municipal electric utilities, see, for instance, Clemens, *Economics and Public Utilities*, ch. 23; Farris and Sampson, *Public Utilities*, pp. 270-71; and Wilcox and Shepherd, *Public Policies*, pp. 554-55.

13. For broadly similar discussions, see Thompson and Smith, *Public Utility Economics*, pp. 603-04, and Wilcox and Shepherd, *Public Policies*, pp. 554-55.

14. For a general discussion of such pressures, see Kahn, *Economics of Regulation*, 2:316-23. An interesting example is provided by the *Otter Tail* case: *U.S.* v. *Otter Tail Power Co.*, 311 F.Supp. 54 (1971); *Otter Tail Power Co.* v. *U.S.*, 410 U.S. 366 (1973). On trends in public ownership of electricity distribution systems, see the references cited in note 12, above.

7

Regulatory Reform: Greater Sensitivity

Assumptions and Problems

This chapter and the next deal with control structures involving private ownership and operation of natural monopoly enterprises. If nothing else, the prevalence of such structures in the United States and the traditional national distaste for public enterprise would justify such an analysis. This case is strengthened by the agnostic general conclusions of chapter 6 regarding public enterprise. Also since chapter 5 indicated that bidding schemes involving frequent transfer of specialized, long-lived assets between private firms were not particularly attractive, it is assumed here and in chapter 8 that the natural monopoly enterprise can expect to retain its plant and equipment for a long period. This need not imply that the firm's management is immune to displacement by takeover or proxy fight, however, or that the firm can count on retaining a monopoly position indefinitely. Under arrangements of this sort, the need for a buyers' agent is clear, and one is assumed to exist. For ease of expression, it is generally referred to as a commission, though this usage should not be understood as an endorsement of the particulars of current regulatory arrangements.

The main concern of this chapter and the next is with rules that can be laid down for commission behavior that are likely to enhance economic efficiency. They may be adopted voluntarily by real regulatory commissions in some instances, but legislation may be necessary in many cases. Commissions might not voluntarily limit themselves to pursuit of economic efficiency as long as they operate in political environments under vague mandates. The intention here is not to make particular legislative proposals, though, since differences among natural monopoly industries may have substantial effects on the performance implications of alternative control arrangements.

Consistent with chapter 2's conclusion that economic efficiency should be the goal of natural monopoly control, the emphasis in this chapter is on devices for making regulation more sensitive and responsive to economic changes. (The kind of political sensitivity sought by Cutler and Johnson, 1975, and others is not an objective here.) There seem to be two rather different relevant criticisms of conventional public utility regulation. First, in the short run, the detailed procedural restrictions imposed upon regulators and the rate-setting techniques they have developed are held to mean that price adjustments arrived at through rate cases lag cost and demand shifts by often unacceptable intervals.[1] Decisions that might have promoted efficient resource use in some test year have no obvious implications for current performance if that test year has long since ended and conditions have changed. Second, in the long run, regulation has been criticized for hanging on past its time and, in particular, for attempting to shield regulated firms from the evolutionary forces generated in the rest of the economy. (This long-run rigidity is stressed by Shepherd, 1973, 1975, ch. 9; see also Kahn, 1971, ch. 1, and, for the classic example of the ICC, Huntington, 1952, and Hilton, 1972.)

In considering proposals that respond to these and related criticisms, a basic trade-off between sensitivity to change and productive efficiency appears. The problem is clearest and has received most attention in the context of price setting under current regulatory arrangements.[2] If rates are held fixed for long periods, they will become increasingly inappropriate as cost and demand shift, and they will thus reduce overall economic efficiency. But during periods when its prices are fixed, a regulated firm's management has clear incentives to reduce costs, since cost reductions translate directly into profit increases.

On the other hand, if prices are adjusted sensitively in response to cost and demand changes visible to regulators, the pricing, profit limitation, and product selection conditions for efficiency can be more or less continuously satisfied. But under such conditions, productive efficiency is likely to suffer; costs are likely to be inflated by both Leibenstein's (1966) X-inefficiency and by Averch and Johnson's (1962) overcapitalization. The former is likely because the tendency to pass costs along in rate changes reduces the incentive to work hard trying to keep costs down. Overcapitalization effects of the AJ variety intensify with frequent rate revision because rate-of-return regulation rewards capital use precisely when rates are revised. As Bailey (1973, ch. 7) shows, if the next rate case is many years away, the present value of rate base inflation is lower than if it is to occur next week. The empirical importance of AJ effects is not clear, but the tendency for frequent cost-based price increases at least to reduce the rewards to diligent and efficient management seems apparent.

As Kahn (1970, pp. 26-35) notes, conventional utility regulation does not involve close monitoring or control of firms' operating decisions. It is not obvious that this is inappropriate. Because of regulators' bounded rationality and because the firm's management is in control of key information sources (information impactedness), neither monitoring nor control is likely to be perfect. But tight and misdirected constraints on managerial behavior can create sizable efficiency losses. If constraints are so tight as to dictate most managerial decisions, the commission has assumed the managerial function without having management's information sources, and the firm's management is at best superfluous. Thus the commission is inherently unable to impose production efficiency directly with any precision. If the incentives for efficiency that face a regulated firm's management are inadequate, there is little the commission can do effectively to supplement them; the only feasible remedy is to change managerial incentives.

The general sensitivity-production efficiency trade-off arises for some of the same reasons discussed in chapters 2 and 4. Some decision-making authority must be delegated to an actor with objectives that likely differ from those of the delegator(s), and that actor's performance cannot be easily evaluated. In the present case the actor is a profit-seeking management; in the earlier discussions it was a self-interested administrator. If regulators react sensitively to perceived changes in demand and cost conditions, the regulated firm's incentives to take appropriate actions are correspondingly diminished. On the other hand, policies that put the greatest pressure on management to maintain productive efficiency tend to have built-in rigidities that give rise to potential problems along other performance dimensions. This sort of trade-off clearly arises in other regulatory contexts besides the choice of the period between rate cases. (For general discussions, see Massel, 1961, on the performance implications of regulatory efficiency and Williamson, 1971. For an implicit recognition of the problem, in the context of a proposal involving extreme regulatory sensitivity to change, see Bauer, 1950.)

The notion that in any natural monopoly situation there exists some fixed function giving the maximum sensitivity or responsiveness to economic change consistent with any particular degree of efficiency in production seems useful to keep in mind. It certainly does not follow that all possible regulatory structures must lie on this frontier. Some may be absolutely better than others along both dimensions, and it is an important task of analysis to determine when this is the case. But barring such dominance, this notion suggests that many reform proposals can be viewed, roughly, as trying to move regulatory practice toward one end or the other of the spectrum of possibilities. The optimal location along that spectrum must depend on particular characteristics of an industry and its environment. The more slowly the latter is expected to change, for instance, the closer to the efficiency end of the spectrum one would expect the optimal point to lie. Of course the optimal response in any particular case depends on the nature of the trade-off, on just how much efficiency must be sacrificed for any particular increase in sensitivity. One can thus interpret Trebing (1976b) as arguing, among other things, that utility regulation in the 1970s has generally moved too far toward the sensitivity end of the trade-off locus, sacrificing too much efficiency for the clear increase in sensitivity it has attained.

The next section considers proposals to enhance regulatory flexibility in both the short and long runs by replacing conventional procedures with some form of excess profits taxation. We then turn to proposals to enhance long-run sensitivity to economic change by relaxing restrictions on entry into regulated markets and take up automatic adjustment clauses, which provide for price change by formula when some or all costs change. The discussion focuses on clauses that pass through all changes in the elements of cost they cover, thus providing maximum sensitivity. This chapter concludes with a brief considera-tion of several alternative proposals for increasing the flexibility of regulation, especially its ability to deal with the challenges posed by inflation.

Chapter 8 focuses primarily on proposals that aim to increase firms' incentives for efficiency. (The division of material between this chapter and chapter 8 is somewhat arbitrary.) It deals with the conscious use of regulatory lag as a policy tool; considers types of automatic adjustment clauses designed to enhance incentives for production efficiency; discusses the use of periodic efficiency measurements, along with rewards and punishments based on those measurements, the use of taxation and subsidy schemes as control devices, and recent proposals to fix rate structures more or less automatically; and summarizes the implications of the analysis in that chapter and this one.

Excess Profits Recapture

In a provocative and thorough critique of public utility regulation, Posner (1969) proposed that the traditional regulatory apparatus be abolished and replaced by a system of excess-profits taxation.[3] Later (1970, 1972) he seems to have dropped this proposal in favor of franchise bidding, but it nonetheless merits consideration, especially in light of chapter 5's generally negative assessment of franchise bidding. Excess profits taxation would provide natural monopoly firms with complete freedom to respond sensitively to cost and demand shifts, and incentives to produce efficiently would be present. As long as the tax takes only a fraction of true excess or economic profit, the firm has every incentive to maximize total excess profit and thus to minimize cost. Under such a scheme, a well-placed and well-run natural monopoly would likely retain some excess profit on average, and the condition of zero average excess profit would thus not be met in general. Still taxation would at least recapture some of those profits for the public at large. (Recall the discussion in chapter 5 of bidding for franchises by offering lump sum payments to the relevant government.)

Moreover the control process would be sensitive to the sort of long-run changes in economic conditions Shepherd emphasizes (1973, 1975, ch. 9). When an enterprise no longer held a natural monopoly position of any importance, it would no longer be able to earn noticeable excess profits, and it would thus automatically cease to be subject to the special tax. The tendency of regulation to hang on past its time and to attempt to protect regulated firms would be eliminated. This last attribute of control by excess profits taxation might give it a considerable advantage over conventional rate-of-return regulation under certain conditions, but some important offsetting disadvantages are also present.

First, in order to remove protectionist tendencies and to eliminate the need for detailed supervision by commissions, all entry restrictions into natural monopoly industries would have to be done away with. This move is not necessarily wise, but even if it were, there would remain the problem of how to tax new entrants. Presumably excess-profits taxes would be applied only to natural monopoly activities. But if an entrant produced other goods or services as well, total profits would have to be divided into those subject to the tax and those not taxable. In order to determine whether excess profits were earned, total assets would also have to be allocated between the covered and noncovered activities. Such divisions are inevitably somewhat arbitrary and subject to protracted dispute. The same problem would arise if a firm initially judged to be a natural monopoly entered new activities after the tax scheme were adopted.

Second, even if all of a firm's activities are subject to excess profits taxation, the determination of the fraction of its earnings that are excess is not simple. In fact, the difficulties are precisely those of determining a regulated firm's cost of capital. Under any reasonable definition, excess profits must be the difference between actual and normal or competitive earnings. The latter quantity can be determined only by calculating the firm's assets (rate base) and multiplying by its cost of capital (fair rate of return). Experience in the United States with excess profits taxation, as outlined by Lent (1951), does nothing to dispel this impression of intrinsic complexity. Lent points out that only in World War I was such taxation concerned primarily with excess profit in the economic sense; in World War II and the Korean conflict, the main goal was to tax profits directly attributable to the war. In all three, a prewar base period was used to determine normal profits. This device would not be available in the natural monopoly context, especially not if excess profits taxation were employed for any substantial length of time. Thus if excess profits taxation is to be employed with any care, the determination of excess profits must come to resemble very closely the process of fixing a fair return on capital under conventional regulation. In practice, excess profits taxation would thus likely embody many of the undesirable rigidities of conventional regulation.

Third, control by excess profits taxation leaves product selection and price structure decisions entirely in the monopolist's hands. It is not obvious that such a firm will choose the qualities of its products in especially undesirable ways. Pricing is likely to be a serious problem, however. As Posner (1969) acknowledges, a natural monopoly free to select its own rate structure and subject to control only by excess profits taxation will tend to engage in extensive price discrimination in order to increase profits. This propensity does not disturb Posner, since he seems to feel that price discrimination always increases the efficiency of resource use. But he is not generally correct; his feeling reflects a confusion often encountered in certain strands of the literature.

There are two general types of price discrimination in which a monopoly can profitably indulge. (These correspond, respectively, to the second- and third-degree discrimination that Pigou, 1920, pp. 240-56, describes.) In the first, the average price per unit a customer pays depends on the quantity he purchases of various products, not on other attributes such as his age. This sort of discrimination generally increases both firm profits and economic efficiency. Under the second type of discrimination, each customer pays a constant price per unit, regardless of quantity purchased, but that price differs from customer to customer depending on other attributes. Or, more generally, since different customers concentrate their purchases on different products, the difference between price and marginal cost varies among products depending on demand conditions, with those products for which demand is least responsive to price generally carrying the highest mark-ups. If nonlinear pricing is ruled out, discrimination of this sort generally minimizes the efficiency loss associated with a given level of profits for the enterprise. But it does not follow that efficiency is enhanced if this sort of discrimination raises profits above the level that would be earned by a nondiscriminating monopoly; as Yamey (1974) has shown, efficiency enhancement requires strong assumptions. If a natural monopoly pursues such Ramsey-type discrimination beyond the point necessary to cover costs, sizable efficiency losses can result. Of course, if the commission reviews pricing (and, possibly, product selection) decisions in order to protect against such losses, control by excess profits taxation comes to resemble conventional regulation even more closely.

Scherer (1970, p. 413) and Trebing (1976a) have argued that excess profits taxes can produce an incentive for overcapitalization much like the Averch-Johnson (1962) effect. If such an effect is present, product selection and pricing decisions may be distorted in major ways. But the theoretical case for overcapitalization is not straightforward here, since an excess profits tax would presumably be applied on top of the general corporate income tax, which may act to inhibit the use of capital. It seems entirely possible that the addition of an excess profits tax would further enhance the incentive to substitute other inputs for capital whenever possible.[4]

Excess profits taxation does not emerge from this analyses as an especially attractive approach to natural monopoly control; it is not as simple a device as it might appear, and it leaves uncontrolled decisions that can have substantial adverse effects on efficiency.

Some of the short-run flexibility promised by excess profits taxation can be obtained within the framework of conventional regulation by the device of interim rate increases with profit recapture provisions. This device has in fact been employed by various regulatory commissions as a response to the rapid inflation that began in the late 1960s.[5] Basically firms are allowed to change prices without going through a formal rate case. (The interim price changes might be made on the basis of some automatic adjustment formula, for instance.) But if a subsequent audit finds that earnings exceeded those allowed under the applicable fair rate of return, refunds must be made to customers who were overcharged.

This approach is advocated in the U.S. Congress (1975), where it is noted that the refunds must be made with interest. If this is not done, utilities might rationally use overcharges as a cheap source of capital. Hardies (1974) notes a New Hampshire law that provides for negative refunds if interim rates are later found to be too low. He expresses concern that with mobile populations, either positive or negative refunds could produce arbitrary transfers among utility customers. Finally, in 1975, the New Jersey Supreme Court required some sort of recapture provision as part of the automatic adjustment plan applied to telephone companies in that state.[6]

In principle, this sort of recapture amounts to excess profits taxation at a 100 percent rate, with immediate redistribution of the proceeds to buyers. If the regulated firm is earning near the allowed rate of return, the efficiency implications of such a high rate of taxation would be extreme; incentives for cost reduction would be reduced to zero. If negative refunds are also required, the plan amounts to fixing the firm's rate of return regardless of managerial performance. To provide some incentives for efficiency, occasionally it might be better to allow the firm to retain some excess profits or to earn less than its fair rate of return. (Sliding scale devices discussed in chapter 8 provide one way of doing this.) But if this is done, interim price changes cannot be simply rubber-stamped by the commission. Some crude tests (perhaps those built into an automatic adjustment clause) must be applied to ensure that the probability of outrageous excess profits being received is suitably low.

Relaxing Entry Restrictions

A central feature of conventional utility regulation is the restriction of entry. Regulatory commissions generally possess and exercise the power to restrict the activities of firms desiring to compete with existing suppliers under the commissions' control. Friedman (1962, p. 29) and others have advocated the abolition of such powers. As Kahn (1971, p. 146) puts it, the key question is, "If competitors want to enter, how natural can monopoly be?" In the classic textbook case of natural monopoly, with a single product and unit costs that always fall with increases in output (all else constant), competition is not viable. In this case, a true natural monopoly does not need protection from entry. If competitors want to enter a market occupied by a regulated monopoly, this provides at least a suggestion that monopoly is the creation of regulation, not of technology. In the textbook world, entry restrictions perform no economic function other than the protection of such artificial market dominance; commission enforcement of entry restrictions suggests capture of the regulators by existing suppliers. (It does not establish capture, though; as Eckert, 1973, and Noll, 1971a, note, entry restriction may be valued by regulators because it simplifies their jobs by limiting the number of firms to be supervised.)

As Kahn's (1971, pp. 146-52) examination of the issues surrounding competitive entry in telecommunications shows clearly, the real world is much more complex than that of the usual textbook discussion. A central difference is that regulated firms generally produce multiple products. As Kahn notes and

Posner (1971) stresses, entry control in a multiproduct setting enables the regulatory authority (or the regulated firm) to engage in cross-subsidization. That is, the prices of some products are held substantially above the costs of the existing supplier in order to permit other products to be sold below cost. Absent entry restrictions, it might well be possible for so-called cream-skimming entrants to invade the high-margin markets profitably even though their costs exceed those of the existing supplier. It might seem to follow that if cross-subsidization is not desirable on economic efficiency grounds, neither are the entry restrictions that facilitate it.

Goldberg (1977) argues that entry restrictions might nevertheless serve buyers' interests by enhancing the regulated firm's incentives to invest and to develop and employ new technology. But these same purposes would be served by entry restrictions elsewhere in the economy as well. It is not obvious why their net benefits should be positive in regulated sectors and negative elsewhere. Indeed it is usually argued that the threat of new entry is generally a strong positive force for efficiency. Many managerial errors, such as investment in obsolete technology, take some time to undo. If such errors are made by monopoly enterprises free from the threat of entry, profits may be reduced somewhat. But if they are committed by firms operating in markets with unrestricted entry, they may induce more efficient and aggressive new rivals to appear, and new entrants can slash profits dramatically.

The discussion so far suggests the desirability of removing all entry restrictions in regulated sectors. But the recent sustainability literature indicates that such a sweeping prescription cannot be rigorously defended.[7] In a multiple product setting, this literature indicates the possibility that entry restrictions may be necessary for efficiency. That is, it seems possible that in some cases of true natural monopoly, where production by a single enterprise is required for efficiency, firms producing a subset of the products involved may nevertheless find entry profitable. In such cases, when natural monopoly is not sustainable, permitting inefficient but profitable entry would serve to raise average costs.

As Joskow and Noll (1978) emphasize, it is important to understand that the sustainability literature does not justify prohibition of entry in all regulated industries. It argues instead for a careful case-by-case approach. Entry restriction can be defended on efficiency grounds only if (1) the industry involved really is a natural monopoly and if (2) its technology is such that no set of marginal-cost-based prices exists that produces zero economic profits and is immune to entry. In many situations, point 1 is difficult to establish with certainty; it is hard to imagine proving point 2 beyond a shadow of doubt in any real industry. Even under the rather restrictive assumptions about entry it has employed, the sustainability literature finds no simple tests for point 2; detailed knowledge of the entire multiple-product cost function is necessary.

The sustainability literature indicates that entirely removing commissions' power to restrict competitive entry might not be desirable, but it does not imply that this power should be retained in its present form. It would seem desirable at least to shift the burden of proof onto those wishing to bar new competition and to require them to make a case for nonsustainability of efficient pricing. That is, since entry restrictions are either unnecessary (if the existing supplier is efficient) or harmful (since they lessen the incentives for efficiency), unless the existing supplier's cost function has certain properties, it would appear desirable to permit entry in all cases unless the existing firm can establish that those properties are reasonably certain to be present. (Requiring absolute proof would likely be equivalent here to permitting all proposed entry.) At the very least, this shift would put the burden of proof on the interested party with the best relevant information.

If that burden were not met, and entry were nonetheless barred in some case, one would expect appeal of the commission's decision to the courts. If the commission were bound by statute to base its decision on the presence or absence of certain cost conditions, the courts would be able (perhaps with some expert assistance) to determine in a nonarbitrary way whether the commission had done its job. It is hard to see how a commission decision that new entry is not justified by public convenience or necessity or some other similarly vague phrase can be effectively reviewed.

Not too much can be expected from this sort of reform. In most situations that involve natural monopoly, it is hard to imagine the threat of new entry being especially strong.[8] Relaxing entry restrictions should serve to reduce both the possible scope of cross-subsidization and management's freedom to be inefficient, but it is not obvious that either would be reduced dramatically.

Automatic Adjustment Clauses

The basic aim of automatic adjustment clauses is to have prices reflect fairly quickly, without the need for extensive formal proceedings, cost changes beyond a regulated firm's control. As Schwartz (1976) and others have noted, to the extent that the variability of prices is increased by such adjustments, risk is shifted from equity suppliers to buyers. Although such shifts are not obviously desirable, some of the risk involved is created by the rigidities of the regulatory process itself. A more serious problem is that it is virtually impossible in practice to limit coverage to cost changes that are truly beyond the firm's control. Since some managerial errors will thus necessarily be covered to some extent by automatic price increases, there is an inevitable reduction in the incentive to produce efficiently.

Automatic adjustment clauses allow for periodic rate changes by formula, and they usually operate with some lag. They differ along two main dimensions. They can be limited, applying only to a subset of cost components, or comprehensive, attempting to consider most or all elements of cost. Similarly they can be total or partial. In the first case, the clause allows rate changes to reflect the total amount of the relevant cost changes; partial plans allow only a fraction of covered cost changes to be passed on to buyers in any single period. Total adjustment clauses provide the maximum sensitivity to economic changes, and the rest of this section will focus on such plans. Adoption of partial clauses is generally justified on grounds of superior efficiency incentives; they are accordingly discussed in the next chapter.

Fuel adjustment clauses, which allow automatic price changes when fuel costs change, are limited and generally total schemes. They have been in use in the United States since 1917. Nash (1925, p. 254) describes them as "in common use" in electric utilities in the mid-1920s. Fuel adjustment clauses are currently used in over forty states, and their operation accounted for about two-thirds of electricity rate increases in 1974.[9] These devices obviously serve to make regulation more responsive to cost shifts, but they have a number of critics, who make two main points.

First, Schwartz (1976) and others have argued that fuel costs are not always in fact beyond a utility's control; the delivered cost of fuel to a large user may be determined by a bargaining process. (See also U.S. Congress, 1975.) Thus the total nature of fuel adjustment clauses can have a serious effect on actual costs by reducing the incentive to try to hold fuel prices down. Schiffel (1975) argues that this problem is mitigated to some extent by the lag with which these clauses generally operate. Because this argument depends in large part on managements' tendencies toward Leibenstein's (1966) X-inefficiency under various arrangements, the actual effect of fuel adjustment clauses on fuel costs remains unknown.

Second, Joskow and MacAvoy (1975) and Trebing (1976b) note that the limited nature of fuel adjustment clauses gives utilities an incentive to employ excessively fuel-intensive technologies. Under such clauses, the more fuel intensive the production process, the less risk is borne by shareholders, since the clause insulates them from the impact on profits of changes in fuel costs but not in other cost components. The empirical importance of this distortion seems never to have been estimated. Schiffel (1975) notes its existence but argues that it is offset by the AJ effect's pressure toward more capital-intensive technologies. Many utilities in the 1970s, however, may have had allowed rates of return below their costs of capital. As Myers (1976) notes, under such circumstances the AJ effect operates in reverse, rewarding undercapitalization and thus adding to the input choice distortion likely to be produced by fuel adjustment clauses.

Adjustment clauses that are comprehensive and total can be expected to minimize or eliminate the problem of input choice bias but to reduce overall incentives for efficiency further. Although Kendrick (1975, p. 303) reports that comprehensive adjustment clauses have been used in Dallas since 1918, comprehensive and total adjustment clauses are generally thought of as recent developments having arisen in response to the current episode of rapid inflation. (See, for instance, Joskow, 1974, and Joskow and MacAvoy, 1975.)

The clearest example of a comprehensive and total adjustment clause was applied to the Public Service Company of New Mexico in 1975.[10] Under the New Mexico plan, rates are automatically adjusted on a quarterly basis (with a built-in lag of about six months) by the amount necessary to bring the rate of return on equity to the nearest point of a fixed band. All operating cost changes are thus fully reflected in prices whenever the rate of return is outside this band. This plan, like most other recent ones, is not fully comprehensive, since it covers only operating costs; changes in capital costs may be recognized only after formal proceedings. (West and Eubank, 1975, advocate automatic recognition of changes in capital costs. A sliding scale plan employed in New Jersey in the 1940s had this feature; see, for instance, Harbeson, 1944.) An independent study of the effects of the New Mexico plan on operating and capital costs was being conducted in 1978 at the request of the New Mexico Public Service Commission, but the results of it are not yet available. Although this scheme has attracted a number of critics, such as Schwartz (1976) and Trebing (1976b), the problem of measuring productive efficiency would seem to make it unlikely that the current study will be able to reach definitive conclusions.

Another widely discussed comprehensive adjustment clause was applied to telephone companies in New Jersey in 1974.[11] The New Jersey plan provides for essentially total adjustment on an annual basis as long as the adjustment would not raise the rate of return above a fixed limit. (From the observed increase in wage and salary cost, the formula subtracts an industry average productivity gain, so that only the difference is applied to adjust rates. But on the margin, since the productivity term is beyond the firm's control, changes in labor costs are fully reflected in rates.) Increases in excess of the various bounds are not reflected in rates at all unless a formal proceeding is held. But for moderate cost increases, the plan is essentially total.

Automatic adjustment plans typically provide for simple proportionate changes in rates. Since changes in relative costs of different inputs often translate into nonproportional changes in the marginal costs of different outputs, this provision is not necessarily appropriate. Thus the pricing and product selection problems are not dealt with fully by these clauses. Their main function is to automate the profit limitation function of regulation to keep revenues close to costs in a period of price changes. Their weakness is clearly along the fourth dimension of efficient performance: production cost may not be minimized. Limited clauses provide incentives to use an inappropriate mix of inputs; comprehensive clauses reduce incentives to control costs in general.

Since these plans inevitably operate with lags, some profit increase always results from cost reduction, but much less than would occur if rates were fixed for long periods. As risk is shifted from shareholders to buyers, so are the consequences of managerial error and inertia since management performance is not easily measured. Under total and comprehensive adjustment clauses, the commission, as the buyers' agent, essentially signs a cost-plus contract for the provision of utility services that holds until the next rate case. Revenues are then adjusted upward dollar for dollar to cover cost changes at the margin, and the incentive problem arises with particular force. (On cost-plus contracts and their incentive implications, see, for instance, Scherer, 1964, and Cross, 1970.) If this is done, most of the risk is shifted to buyers, and they bear most of the consequences of managerial decisions. Since the firm's rate of return is fixed in principle under total and comprehensive adjustment, management has no economic incentive to control costs. Given the political problems associated with service breakdowns, one might expect management to seek excessive reliability. Or the firm might concentrate on distorting the information available, to increase real profit even though accounting profit is fixed.

The case for comprehensive rather than limited adjustment clauses seems clear. Although the importance of the input choice distortions produced by the latter is not clear, there is no obvious reason to set up positive incentives for inefficiency if this can be avoided. In exceptionally high-risk situations, a case might be made for total adjustment clauses, but such situations do not arise with much frequency. In most circumstances, some sensitivity ought to be sacrificed in the interest of efficiency, and partial rather than total clauses should be employed. This argument is similar to the one that in defense procurement, cost-plus contracts should be reserved for exceptionally risky situations, with the contractor bearing some risk (by incentive contracts) in most cases. Indeed most comprehensive adjustment clauses that have been employed provide for less than total adjustment under at least some circumstances in order to provide efficiency incentives. (Recall that even the New Mexico plan yields no adjustment at all if the company's rate of return is within a certain range, though adjustment is total if the rate of return is outside that range.)

Other Proposals

Four proposals that are designed to increase regulatory sensitivity to economic changes are sunset laws, operating ratio regulation, use of future test periods, and use of replacement cost in computing rate bases.

Sunset Laws

If entry into some activity previously dominated by a natural monopoly supplier can be permitted without raising costs (because the natural monopoly was only temporary) to the point where market competition provides effective price control, or if competition from other industries makes demand for a temporary or permanent natural monopoly's output highly responsive to price, the case for detailed commission supervision vanishes. As Shepherd (1973; 1975, ch. 9) has stressed, it would be efficient for regulation to vanish then also. Since regulators generally value their jobs and since regulatory control of entry can be valuable to established suppliers, it is not likely that this will happen automatically in most cases.

Lowi (1969, pp. 297-310) and others have advocated in this context sunset laws, which would require legislative reconsideration of all regulatory programs on a periodic basis. Unless a commission's powers were reestablished by new legislation at these times, they would vanish. Behn (1977) notes the recent popularity of this sort of proposal, which has not been confined to regulatory programs, but he also points out some problems. The main one is that the legislative decision-making apparatus is subject to bounded rationality, among other weaknesses. While reexamination of regulatory mandates might occasionally result in deregulation, it seems optimistic to hope for periodic careful redefinition of the scope of regulated natural monopoly; this would require a noticeable increase in legislative decision making if consideration of other issues is not to suffer. Even deregulation is unlikely if it is opposed by organized special interests. Absent effective opposition to such interests, the legislature's easiest course is to approve the existing set-up in its entirety. Since we do not have much experience with sunset laws, it is hard to be confident that Behn is correct when he argues that they will not lead to much regulatory reform, but his prediction seems the most plausible one at the moment. Other approaches to producing the appropriate periodic redefinitions of the scope of regulation should be devised and examined.

Operating Ratio Regulation

Slesinger (1971) has argued that the complexities of rate base and rate of return determination serve to build an unacceptable delay into regulatory proceedings. He suggests a process of continuous review of utility operations, using as a key measure the ratio of profit to sales.[12] Interim rate increases would be granted on the basis of changes in this ratio. There are two basic problems with this suggestion. First, the ratio of profit to sales has no real economic meaning, as Kahn (1971, pp. 54-56) and Stelzer (1969) have stressed. It does not yield a measure of the return to equity capital suppliers, and the latter is the inescapably key variable. Second, the New Mexico plan would seem to indicate that interim rate increases can be as easily based on the observed rate of return on capital employed. The first problem implies that operating ratio regulation is, at best, suitable only for use over very short periods, while the second indicates that it has no special advantage there. In short, this approach does not have much merit.

Future Test Periods

A number of commissions have moved to the employment of future test periods in the 1970s.[13] They set prices at least in part on the basis of estimates of cost and demand conditions for the period during which they are to be effective. This procedure has much to recommend it, given the obvious problems associated with basing prices on conditions in the more or less distant past, but it also has some problems. If the future is easily forecast, the effect of using future test periods is to move toward a guaranteed rate of return; risk is shifted from shareholders to buyers. To the extent that use of future test periods moves regulation toward a long-term, cost-plus arrangement, incentives to hold down costs are reduced. If the future is hard to forecast, prices may turn out to be inappropriate. In particular, the regulated firm's informational advantage over the commission might be expected to lead to biased forecasts that would justify excessively high prices. If noticeable forecast errors, honest or not, are expected to occur with reasonable probability, some sort of profit recapture device— probably designed with an eye to its effects on the regulated firm's incentives to produce efficiently—would appear necessary.

Replacement Cost Rate Base

Under inflation, conventional accounting techniques yield biased measures of firms' rates of return.[14] A key problem is that the historical cost of tangible assets, which is the basis of conventional accounting, becomes less and less meaningful over time. This problem affects both the measurement of net assets and (by depreciation charges) net income. Generally the result is that the accounting rate of return is above the true rate of return, with the bias increasing with the longevity of the firm's assets. Utility enterprises, with relatively long-lived assets, can thus show accounting rates of return that are significantly above their true or economic rates of return.

A simple mathematical investigation of this accounting bias will illustrate this problem. Suppose that all prices are rising steadily at $i\%$ per year. Let the real cash flow from each dollar of new investment decrease exponentially at $d\%$ per year and be such that the rate of return in constant dollars is r^*. Suppose the firm's real growth rate is $g\%$ per year. If all these trends have persisted for a long time, the firm's accounting rate of return based on original cost depreciation, r, can be shown to be given by

$$r = r^* + i\frac{r^* + d}{g + d}.\tag{7.2}$$

If assets depreciate rapidly, so that d is very large, the accounting measure overstates the true rate of return by exactly the rate of inflation. In the usual case where r^* exceeds g, the bias is worse for small values of d, that is, for longer-lived assets.

The consequence is that if the rate base is computed using the original cost of assets and if the allowed rate of return is computed without adjustment for inflation, revenues will be inadequate to cover total real costs, even though the accounting rate of return may appear respectable. In principle there are two ways around this problem: either the rate base or the rate of return can be adjusted for inflation. A number of commissions have recently moved in the first direction by adopting rate base determination procedures based in part on the replacement cost, rather than the original acquisition cost, of tangible assets.[15] As Kahn (1970, pp. 109-16) argues, there are serious operational problems with this approach. Its only apparent virtue is that a commission can provide adequate earnings with a lower allowed rate of return. If controversy focuses on that number, the commission thus exposes itself to less criticism. But there is little to be said in economic terms for adjusting the rate base rather than the rate of return; what matters is the level of earnings, not the formalism by which they were derived.[16]

But the discussion of inflation bias does not point up a real problem with conventional regulation. As Solomon (1970) has emphasized, conventional accounting measures of the rate of return may diverge systematically from an enterprise's real (or economic or discounted-cash-flow) rate of return for a number of reasons; inflation is only one source of bias. This poses no deep problems for determination of a regulated firm's cost of capital since securities market data are central to that process. But it does make it difficult to tell if a firm is in fact covering its cost of capital funds. (Under inflation, for instance, conventionally computed book value can deviate persistently from market value even if costs are exactly covered.) Systematic reform of utility accounting procedures would facilitate the process of profit limitation by revealing the actual level of profit with more precision.[17] But such reform encounters serious theoretical and operational difficulties, and it can hardly be expected to solve all of the problems of regulation; better data can but need not produce better regulation.

Notes

1. This point, particularly as it relates to profit limitation, was discussed in chapter 3. See, among others, Hyman, "Rate Cases"; Joskow, "Inflation and Environmental Concern"; Joskow and MacAvoy, "Regulation"; and Myers, "Rate of Return Regulation."

2. This paragraph anticipates some of the discussion of regulatory lag in chapter 8. On the basic issues involved, see Clark, *Social Control*, pp. 341-42, and Baumol, "Reasonable Rules."

3. See also the comments by Comanor, "Should Natural Monopolies Be Regulated?"; Shepherd, "Regulation and Its Alternatives"; and Swidler, "Comments on the Case for Deregulation," along with Posner, "Natural Monopoly and Its Regulation," for his reply.

4. For interested readers, this footnote sketches an analysis of the effect of excess profits taxation on input choice. Consider a standard two-input, one-output firm, with L and K the amounts of labor and capital employed. Let w be the wage rate and r the cost of capital funds. Let t be the rate of the corporate income tax, which applies to pretax profits (in the accounting sense) of $(R - wL)$, where R is sales revenue. Suppose that earnings in excess of sK are subject to an additional tax at rate x. Thus s is the maximum rate of return that can be earned before excess profits taxation applies. If the firm actually pays some excess profits tax, its aftertax economic profit can be written as

$$\pi = R(1 - t - x) - wL(1 - t - x) - K(r - sx). \qquad (7.1)$$

If L and K are chosen to maximize π, the ratio of the marginal product of capital to that of labor is a decreasing function of x, so that increases in the rate of excess profits taxation tend to encourage the use of capital if and only if s exceeds $r/(1 - t)$. It is usual in Averch-Johnson models to assume that s exceeds r, and if there were no corporate income tax (that is, if $t = 0$), this would suffice to support the Scherer-Trebing conclusion. But if t is positive, this conclusion follows only if s exceeds r by a sufficient margin. If $t = 0.5$, for instance, s must be twice r. If excess profits taxation were applied to a large number of firms by a commission with limited resources concerned that it only apply the tax to profits that are truly excess, such a large value of s might be chosen, but this seems far from certain.

5. For general discussions, see Hardies, "Inflation Dilemma"; Joskow, "Inflation and Environmental Concern"; and U.S. Congress, *Fuel Adjustment Clauses.*

6. *In re Board's Investigation of Telephone Companies,* 66 N.J.: 476 (1975).

7. See Faulhaber, "Cross-subsidization"; Panzar and Willig, "Free Entry"; and Baumol, Bailey, and Willig, "Weak Invisible Hand Theorems."

8. See Klass and Shepherd, *Regulation and Entry*, especially the final chapter, for evidence on this point.

9. For general background on fuel adjustment clauses, see Kendrick, "Efficiency Incentives"; Schiffel, "Electric Utility Regulation"; U.S. Congress, *Fuel Adjustment Clauses*; and Schwartz, "Regulatory Change."

10. *Re Public Service Company of New Mexico*, 8 PUR 4th 113 (1975). For a brief description, see "A Utility's Experience in Rate-Setting."

11. *Re Adjustment Clauses in Telephone Rate Schedules*, 3 PUR 4th 298 (1974). The legality of this plan was later upheld by the New Jersey Supreme

Court, *In re Board's Investigation.* For discussions, see Backman and Kirsten, "Comprehensive Adjustment Clause"; DePodwin Associates, *Regulation of Utility Performance*; Hardies, "Inflation Dilemma"; and Kendrick, "Efficiency Incentives."

12. See also Welch, "Constant Surveillance," and DePodwin Associates, *Regulation of Utility Performance.*

13. See Joskow, "Inflation and Environmental Concern"; Myers, "Rate of Return Regulation"; and, especially, Hardies, "Inflation Dilemma."

14. The literature on this general point has grown at least as rapidly as the price level. See, for instance, Goldschmidt and Admon, *Profit Measurement During Inflation*, and Hendricksen, *Accounting Theory*, ch. 7, and the references they cite.

15. See Spiro, "Alternative Methods of Inflation Adjustment"; "Recent Cases on Measures of Value"; and, for somewhat earlier information, Wilcox and Shepherd, *Public Policies*, pp. 372-73.

16. Spiro, "Alternative Methods of Inflation Adjustment," dissents from the general view here.

17. On accounting biases and accounting reform, see also Myers, "Application of Finance Theory," and "Rate of Return Regulation"; Stauffer, "Measurement of Corporate Rates of Return"; Goldschmidt and Aron, *Profit Measurement During Inflation*; and Hendricksen, *Accounting Theory*, ch. 7.

8

Regulatory Reform: Greater Efficiency

Conscious Regulatory Lag

If the prices at which a regulated firm can sell are fixed, at any levels, over a relatively long period, the firm is directly rewarded on a dollar-for-dollar basis for cost reduction activities. On the other hand, if prices are continually adjusted to reflect cost changes, no such incentive is present. (Massel, 1961, notes the incentive effect of regulatory lag as an example to show that improvement in commission efficiency can have an adverse ultimate impact; see also Kahn, 1971, pp. 59-60.) This observation led Baumol (1967, pp. 114-15), Williamson (1971), Myers (1972), and others to advocate the use of price rigidity as a regulatory tool. The inevitable lag between cost changes and movements in regulated prices was to be institutionalized and consciously adjusted.[1]

As Joskow (1974) notes, intervals between rate cases (for electric power companies at least) were quite long during the early and mid-1960s, though this resulted not from adoption of the above proposal but from stable or declining costs of production coupled with regulatory passivity. The proposal to institutionalize regulatory lag, with prices fixed for long periods, has not been heard much in recent years; the events of the 1970s have made its primary weakness obvious. If the environment is changing rapidly, any set of constant prices quickly becomes inappropriate.

In periods of relatively stable input prices and rapid productivity advance, commissions' refusal to force lower rates can permit regulated firms to retain substantial excess profits. This situation may be descriptive of the period immediately preceding the current brisk inflation, at least for some utilities. On the other hand, in an inflationary period, commission refusal to respond to utility rate increase requests for long periods can lead to severely depressed earnings. This corresponds to the experience of the 1970s, though the actual lags were apparently the result of administrative breakdown, not conscious policy. (Joskow, 1974, makes this point clearly.) Although the 1960s produced proposals for increasing or formalizing what were generally long lags, the 1970s gave rise to suggestions responsive to commissions' general efforts to reduce what now seem to be excessive regulatory lags.

The basic idea behind the proposal to institutionalize the regulatory lag between cost and price changes is sound; unless control is rigid enough to permit some profit fluctuation, no economic incentives for production efficiency are present under private ownership. The problem is that the optimal degree of

119

rigidity to be maintained during any period must depend on expectations about the stability of cost and demand conditions during that period. If extreme stability is expected, prices can be fixed. But if formal regulatory proceedings (rate cases) are to be relatively widely spaced, some provision for interim price change will be necessary in most cases. Comprehensive and total adjustment clauses provide maximum price sensitivity, along with minimum efficiency incentives. In between such clauses, on the one hand, and the simple fixed-price regulatory lag proposals, on the other hand, a whole spectrum of devices might be employed to permit some price variation between formal proceedings.

It is worth devoting some discussion to the general nature and application of such devices. The basic suggestion is that commissions fix a formula for determining price changes that is to operate until modified by formal proceedings. The simplest such formula would have prices remain constant. It is likely to be impossible to devise a formula that can be expected to work indefinitely. (For general arguments, see Macneil, 1974, Goldberg, 1976b, and Williamson, 1976.) Thus periodic reassessment of adjustment formulas is as necessary as readjustment of rates without such formulas; the hope is that it will not need to occur as often.

The commission might either announce the date of the next proceeding at the conclusion of each revision of the formula, or it might allow that date to be determined by observed performance. If the time until the next review is fixed, there is a danger that more rapid than anticipated changes in costs or demands will cause serious problems before that time is reached. Further the firm might find it profitable to inflate its costs (by making unnecessary investments, for instance) just before a scheduled proceeding in order to build a case for a large rate increase. Some proposals for the use of regulatory lag call for proceedings to be held whenever the firm's rate of return falls outside some fixed range. As the rate of return nears the top of the range, however, the firm may seek to increase its costs to avoid a rate case that will likely lead to price cuts; and if the rate of return is near the bottom of the range, it may also pad costs to strengthen the case for a sizable price rise. (On these incentive problems, see Kahn, 1971, pp. 59-60.) It may be most sensible to adopt a third approach that avoids these perverse incentives; a commission could choose the time for the next proceeding more or less randomly, giving the regulated firm only minimal advance notice. (Klevorick, 1973, 1974, and Ziemba, 1974, provide theoretical analyses of random regulatory lag.) A common denominator of all three approaches is that the commission assumes complete control of the scheduling of formal proceedings; firm-initiated requests for hearings would be considered only under truly exceptional circumstances.

In any case, the formula to hold between proceedings should be designed as a compromise, appropriate for the expected stability of the firm's environment, between two conflicting goals. First, it should be sensitive enough so that totally inappropriate price and profit levels do not persist. Second, it should be rigid enough so that incentives for cost reduction are substantial. Note that the more sensitive (less rigid) the formula, the more risk is shifted onto the firm's customers. This should serve to lower the firm's market cost of capital funds. But it will not reduce the true social cost of those funds unless a real reduction in overall risk, not merely a shift of part of that risk, is achieved.

There seem to be two classes of potentially relevant formulas that have been proposed or employed besides the total adjustment clauses discussed in chapter 7. Neither deals with rate structure or product selection issues; these would presumably be addressed only in the periodic formal proceedings. The first class attempts to minimize input choice bias by treating all cost changes more or less symmetrically. The second class is a variant of the sliding scale plan and retains primary focus on the return to equity.

Comprehensive Partial Adjustment Formulas

As Bailey (1973, ch. 4) shows, all regulatory approaches that do not treat inputs symmetrically give incentives for inefficient production by rewarding firms for selecting the wrong mix of inputs. The Averch-Johnson (1962) effect is a special case of this. Even though the empirical importance of the various inefficiencies that can arise in this way is in doubt, there is at least a good case in theory for treating inputs symmetrically.

In a static context, the most commonly discussed symmetric regulatory constraint would compute allowable revenue as some markup over total cost. As Cross (1970), Sherman (1974, p. 395), and others have noted, however, regulation of this pure cost-plus variety gives profit-maximizing firms a positive incentive to inflate all costs and thus clearly permits managers to indulge in inefficient behavior without adverse effects on stockholders. This incentive is easily illustrated. Suppose there is only a single product; let P be the allowed price and C be average or unit cost. Markup regulation would set $P = \gamma C$, where γ is some constant greater than one. But then profit per unit of sales is $(P - C) = (\gamma - 1)C$, which rises with increases in cost. Markup regulation thus not only allows X-inefficiency (Leibenstein, 1966); it positively encourages it.

Cross (1970) proposes an interesting remedy for this problem.[2] Instead of a markup or cost-plus formula, he advocates a rule closely resembling incentive contracts used in defense procurement. In a static, single-product context, price would be given by a formula of the following sort:

$$P = \alpha + \beta C, \tag{8.1}$$

where α and β are positive constants, with β less than 1. These constants would be chosen so that P and C were approximately equal in some (past or future) test period. The key to the device's incentive feature is that the multiplier of unit cost, β, is less than 1. Because of this, profit per unit of sales, $(P - C) = \alpha + (\beta - 1)C$, falls with C.[3] (This cannot be achieved by setting γ less than 1 in the preceding paragraph, as this would force the firm to take continual losses.) This eliminates the profit payoff from cost padding that exists under markup regulation, and it thus penalizes equity suppliers for management inefficiency. If α and β are held constant over some period of time, price automatically changes in the direction of unit cost, but by a smaller percentage amount. Equation 8.1 thus represents what chapter 7 defined as a comprehensive and partial adjustment clause.

Cross (1970) recognizes that the basic formula (8.1) will produce unreasonable prices after a relatively short time if either input prices or productivity change rapidly. As he sensibly contends that whatever formula is adopted, it should stay in effect for long periods in order to enhance efficiency incentives, he recommends that equation 8.1 be applied to deflated values of P and C. These would be computed using some measure of the general price level in the economy, such as the implicit deflator for gross national product. If $\bar{P}$ is such a measure or index, the formula becomes

$$(P/\bar{P}) = \alpha + \beta(C/\bar{P}). \tag{8.2}$$

Further, he suggests that α might be systematically reduced when technical progress occurs in order to avoid excess profits.

In order to see the implications of this equation more clearly and to relate the Cross formulas to other proposals, it is useful to work with percentage changes. Let ΔX be shorthand for "percentage change in X" for any variable X. Then, when P and C are equal, the modified formula—8.2—with variable α would determine price changes according to

$$\Delta P = (1 - \beta)(\Delta \bar{P} + \Delta \alpha) + (\beta)\Delta C. \tag{8.3}$$

(In this notation, the New Mexico plan discussed in chapter 7 would be described by the equation $\Delta P = \Delta C$.) If α is constant, P stays equal to C as long as the latter rises at the same rate as the general price level. If costs increase more rapidly, the rate of growth of P is less than that of C (recall that β is less than 1), and costs are not covered. If α is reduced when the firm's productivity increases, excess profits that might arise because ΔC is less than $\Delta \bar{P}$ could be avoided, but the firm's incentive to strive for more efficient production is clearly reduced.

In order to apply any of these formulas to firms with multiple outputs, some index of total real output would be required. That is, equation 8.2 cannot be used with P equal to total revenue and C equal to total cost, for then changes in output mix can cause price changes even with unit cost constant. In the New Mexico plan, total kilowatt-hour sales serve as a real output index; P can then be computed by dividing total revenue by total kilowatt-hours sold. This may serve as an adequate first approximation, but in other industries, such as telephone service, an adequate output index must be more complex (see Kendrick, 1975, for a discussion).

In 1974, Illinois Bell Telephone Company proposed to its state commission an adjustment formula similar to equation 8.3 but with more direct incentives for productivity improvement.[4] Though this proposal was rejected by the commission, it is nevertheless of considerable interest. As in the Cross formulas, any given percentage change in unit cost generally produces a smaller relative change in prices. The difference is that the firm receives a positive reward for increased productivity.

Suppose that a firm produces a single output; let Q be the unit volume of production. Suppose further that this firm uses only one input; let I be the amount employed and W its unit cost. A natural measure of productivity in this simple case is $Z = Q/I$. In a multiple product setting, a similar measure can be computed, using appropriate indexes of real output and real inputs employed in place of Q and I, respectively. With Z thus defined, we have $C = WI/Q = W/Z$, so that productivity can also be computed by using unit cost (obtained by dividing total cost by a real output index) and input price indexes. This last relation yields

$$\Delta C = \Delta W - \Delta Z. \qquad (8.4)$$

With Z computed in either fashion, the Illinois Bell proposal would determine price changes roughly as follows:[5]

$$\Delta P = \alpha \Delta Z + \beta \Delta C, \qquad (8.5)$$

where, as before, α and β are positive constants with β less than 1.

Under this approach, costs are covered only if productivity increases sufficiently rapidly. To see this, substitute 8.4 into 8.5 to obtain

$$\Delta P = (\alpha - \beta)\Delta Z + \beta \Delta W. \qquad (8.6)$$

Since β is less than 1, input price changes are not fully covered unless productivity rises fast enough. Under the Illinois Bell proposal, $\alpha = 1.5$ and $\beta = 0.5$, so that the coefficient of ΔZ is unity. Then a 10 percent rise in the prices of all the firm's inputs results in a 10 percent output price increase only if productivity rises by 5 percent. If this happens, costs rise by only 5 percent—from equation 8.4—so that excess profits would be created if none had existed initially. In this example, a productivity increase of 2.5 percent maintains $\Delta P = \Delta C (= 7.5\%)$, so that a situation of zero excess profits is preserved.

One problem with this proposal is that profits can be strongly affected by input price changes beyond the firm's control. Logically α and β ought to be chosen so that $\Delta P = \Delta C$ if input costs and productivity change at expected rates. Let the expected average value of ΔZ over the relevant period be ΔZ^*, and define ΔW^* similarly. Using equations 8.4 and 8.6, if $\Delta P = \Delta C$ when $\Delta Z = \Delta Z^*$ and $\Delta W = \Delta W^*$, then

$$\alpha = (1 - \beta)(\Delta W^* - \Delta Z^*)/\Delta Z^*. \qquad (8.7)$$

Substituting into equation 8.6, the formula for price change becomes

$$\Delta P = \Delta C + (1 - \beta)[\Delta W^*(\Delta Z/\Delta Z^*) - \Delta W]. \qquad (8.8)$$

Since β is between 0 and 1, equation 8.8 shows that prices can fail to keep pace with costs either because ΔZ is too small or because ΔW is too large.

If one feels that input costs are in large measure beyond the control of most regulated firms, this feature of the Illinois Bell plan is unattractive. Renshaw (1978) has recently proposed a simple modification that avoids this problem. Under the same assumptions that underlie equation 8.5, Renshaw's adjustment formula can be written as

$$\Delta P = \Delta C + \beta(\Delta Z - \Delta Z^*), \qquad (8.9)$$

where β is a positive constant less than 1, as before. Here prices keep pace with costs exactly if and only if productivity increases match expectations; changes in input prices are automatically passed through to buyers.

The choice between formula 8.8 and formula 8.9 ought to depend on the extent to which the regulated firm considered can affect the prices it pays for its inputs of fuel, labor, and other goods and services, as well as on the range of uncertainty that surrounds the price level in general. If the utility has substantial potential ability to bargain down the prices it pays for important inputs, in order to preserve incentives for hard bargaining, profits should suffer if ΔW is well above ΔW^*. On the other hand, no firm has perfect control over its input costs; the actual value of ΔW observed will depend at least to some extent on the general rate of inflation, $\Delta \overline{P}$, and other uncertain future variables beyond the firm's control. If important variables of this sort are subject to great uncertainty, large differences between ΔW and ΔW^* might be expected to arise for reasons having nothing to do with the vigor of the firm's bargaining efforts. In this case, such differences ought logically to have a relatively small effect on the difference between ΔP and ΔC.

Under either the original Illinois Bell proposal or Renshaw's modification, more information is needed than under the Cross approach, at least with constant α. Given an index of real output, total cost can be used to compute ΔC in formula 8.3, and ΔP can be obtained from published sources. In order to compute ΔZ, however, either an index of real inputs employed or an index of input prices must also be prepared on a regular basis.

Finally, an exceedingly simple proposal by Jones (1976) deserves presentation.[6] He would index utility prices without regard to productivity changes or to changes in individual input prices. He would set

$$\Delta P = \Delta \bar{P}. \qquad (8.10)$$

By adjusting for changes in the general price level, this proposal would certainly lengthen the time between regulatory proceedings under inflation. It is symmetric in its treatment of the firm's inputs. It provides strong efficiency incentives between formal proceedings since prices are unaffected by the firm's own cost changes, so that these are exactly reflected in profits. But this feature also represents the plan's main drawback. If input cost trends for the firm or industry considered diverge from those elsewhere because of factors beyond the firm's or industry's control (for example, because natural gas is suddenly deregulated or an effective uranium cartel forms), failure to allow for that divergence will render prices inappropriate sooner than will the other formulas.

A few general remarks are in order at this point. First, even apart from choice of parameters like α and β, there is no universally ideal comprehensive partial adjustment clause. As the comparison of equations 8.8 and 8.9 indicated, the best formula in any particular situation depends on the nature of expectations about the future, especially on the extent of the firm's control over various quantities and on the uncertainty attached to important uncontrollable variables. In some situations, costs of acquiring information (for various indexes, for instance) may be important elements in the decision process. Though the aim of this general approach is to protect the firm from changes beyond its control while rewarding it for diligent and efficient management, it should be obvious that no formula, simple or complex, can hope to do this with any precision in all circumstances. Protection will sometimes be imperfect and rewards sometimes undeserved under any scheme of this sort.

Second, although it is easiest to think of the various plans in terms of period-by-period percentage changes in price and even though they are sometimes presented in this form, this may not be the best way to apply them. If price is well above cost, one might want to grant smaller price increases and larger price decreases, all else equal, than if price is below cost. This means that one might want to look at levels of various quantities, not just percentage changes.

One approach to doing this is illustrated by the following formula:

$$\Delta P = (\alpha)[(C - P)/P]$$
$$+ (1 - \alpha)\langle \Delta C + \beta(\Delta Z - \Delta Z^*) \qquad (8.11)$$
$$+ \gamma[\Delta W^* + \delta(\Delta \bar{P} - \Delta \bar{P}^*) - \Delta W]\rangle,$$

where α, β, γ, and δ are constants between zero and one. The term multiplying α (which can be computed using total revenue and total cost, including the cost of equity capital) is the percentage change in price necessary to make excess profit zero. Part of this change is made in each period, so there is a tendency to drive revenue toward total cost, regardless of what else happens. The first part of the term multiplying $(1 - \alpha)$ is just the Renshaw adjustment. The second term is designed to give the firm some benefit from rises in its input prices that are less than expected. The notion is that the expected rate of growth of W is the initial expectation, ΔW^*, modified by the addition of a fraction, δ, of the difference between the actual rate of inflation, ΔP, and the expected rate, ΔP^*, on which the calculation of ΔW^* must have been based in part. I do not contend that this is an ideal formula. Its linearity, among other things, might be troublesome. I present it merely to indicate the range of possibilities. A simpler approach might be to employ one of the other formulas given above but to specify that prices will not be raised (or lowered) if the firm's rate of return is above (or below) some fixed number. Bounds of this sort are inevitably somewhat arbitrary, however, as are the discontinuities they introduce.

Finally it is important to note that the general approach discussed here presents substantial challenges to regulators. If they can unilaterally decree that formula 8.10 will be employed so that prices will be simply tied to the economy-wide inflation rate, the scope for strategic behavior by regulated firms is minimized. But in any real proceeding, the choice of an adjustment formula itself is likely to be a matter of dispute between the parties involved. If that selection process results in alternatives to formula 8.10 of the sort discussed here, parameter values must be selected, potentially complex indexing formulas devised and implemented, and expectations of various sorts quantified. Given the utility's information advantage over its regulators, it is in position to influence all these choices to its own advantage. In the terms of Williamson's (1973; 1975, ch. 2) framework, there is a severe information impactedness problem here, and one must expect the regulated firm to behave opportunistically. This does not mean, of course, that the firm will always be able to guarantee itself the expectation of significant excess profits if a commission attempts the approach considered in this section. But it will likely have the resources and incentives to make a serious attempt to do so, and even an able and zealous commission will not be able to detect and counteract opportunistic behavior of this sort by a regulated firm with great precision. Thus although adjustment clauses of the type considered here should be carefully tailored to the exact situation to which they are to be applied, such tailoring is likely to be very difficult to accomplish. To do even a barely acceptable job will likely require considerably more analytical input than is needed to handle a traditional rate case well.

Variants of the Sliding Scale

The first sliding scale plans were employed in England, beginning in the middle of the nineteenth century, to regulate gas companies.[7] The key element in these early plans was a formula (or table) giving the maximum dividend the firm could pay on its stock as a declining function of the price of gas. Generally this device came to be replaced by a provision that prices be changed mechanically to move the regulated firm's rate of return toward some fixed allowed rate, but usually to permit only partial adjustment in order to provide efficiency incentives. Various stabilization devices were employed to avoid excessive price fluctuations. The most common one seems to have been a reserve fund, into which the company deposited cash during good years and from which it made withdrawals during bad ones. The size of the fund's balance would then affect the magnitude of the price change to be granted at any time, with larger balances generally calling for smaller price increases or larger decreases. A variety of plans of this sort were employed in the United States and abroad, with mixed results.

In the United States, the most famous sliding scale scheme was used to regulate electricity prices in the District of Columbia from 1924 through 1955.[8] Initially prices were to be automatically raised to permit the supplier to earn a rate of return of 7.5 percent whenever the observed rate of return was less than this figure. If it was greater, rates were to be reduced so as to eliminate half the difference between the observed rate and 7.5 percent. Subsequent changes in the plan, described by Trebing (1963), preserved this partial adjustment feature. During the 1920s and 1930s, demand for electricity in Washington, D.C., grew rapidly and may have been very responsive to price. In any case, the sliding scale plan produced low prices and high profits during this period, but it broke down in the inflation of the 1950s.

A somewhat more complex plan was applied with great fanfare to the New Jersey Power and Light Company, beginning in 1944.[9] Perhaps its most novel feature was the specification of a formula, based on price-earnings ratios of selected utility stocks, that produced updated estimates of the firm's cost of capital automatically. Multiplication of the rate base by this number produced the basic return. The difference between the firm's actual operating income and the basic return was termed its additional return, which might be positive or negative in any period. The plan set up a stabilizing reserve fund. As long as the balance in the fund was between 1.5 percent and 4.5 percent of the firm's rate base, the firm's additional return was to be added to the fund (or subtracted if additional return was negative) and prices were to be held fixed. When the fund exceeded 4.5 percent of the utility's rate base and additional return was positive, prices were to be cut, with the size of the decrease depending on the balance in the fund and on the ratio of additional return to the rate base. Similarly if the fund's balance was below the lower bound and additional return was negative, price increases would automatically occur. This elaborate plan governed rates for only four years; it was dropped in 1949 at the utility's request.[10]

In a recent report to the Federal Communications Commission, H.J. DePodwin Associates (1974) propose yet another sliding scale plan, with the cost of equity also computed by formula. This would be done every three years or so, and a range of acceptable returns around this best estimate would be fixed. Using an index of the firm's real output, the upper and lower bounds on this range would be translated into upper and lower bounds on profit per unit of output. Both the return to equity and the profit-output ratio would be computed annually and compared to the corresponding ranges. Only if the profit-output ratio were above its range would rate reductions be considered. If both ratios were below their lower limits, rates would be increased to bring the return on equity to an acceptable level. This level would be the lower bound of the allowable range if the commission determined that the utility had made no effort to improve efficiency, and it would be the estimated cost of equity (the middle of the range) if such efforts were found. Since it is hard to imagine a firm's ever being unable to document efforts to cut costs, it seems likely that in practice the acceptable level would most often be the cost of equity.

The basic reason for focusing on the ratio of profit to output as the signal for rate cuts seems to be to avoid the Averch-Johnson (1962) effects associated with a rate of return ceiling. But since the maximum profit-output ratio is to be derived mechanically from just such a ceiling, the actual incentive effects are unclear. It is also not obvious how the width of the acceptable band of returns is to be justified or why small changes in performance that place a firm outside that band are to trigger possibly substantial price changes.

It might be worthwhile to outline a sliding scale plan that is simpler than the last two discussed and yet seems to have most of the virtues of its genus. Let the regulated firm's cost of capital, r^*, be fixed by formula or by hearings at regular intervals. Suppose that in some year the firm's actual rate of return is r or is forecast at current prices to be r. If r and r^* are widely divergent, prices are clearly far out of line and major changes are called for to avoid breakdown. If they are close, prices should change only moderately to preserve efficiency incentives. (This is, after all, the sort of price movement one would expect under competition.)

If rates are to be changed to yield a rate of return r', the simplest sort of partial adjustment rule would be linear:

$$r' = \beta(r^* - r) + r, \tag{8.12}$$

with β some constant between 0 and 1. This resembles the original Washington plan in that a constant fraction of profit excess or shortfall is eliminated each period. But the arguments above suggest that β ought to be an increasing function of the absolute difference between r and r^*. This means that adjustment should be nonlinear or progressive, and such adjustment was in fact part of the Washington plan after 1933 (see Trebing (1963, n. 19)). There are a variety of ways that the appropriate sort of smooth nonlinearity can be built into formula 8.12.

Here is a simple example. Suppose that β is determined by the following function of the absolute value of the difference between r and r^*:

$$\beta = [1 - e^{-\gamma |r^* - r|}], \tag{8.13}$$

with γ some positive constant. Unless $r^* = r$, β is positive, and it is always less than one. If $\gamma = 10$, for instance, $\beta = 0.10$ when the gap between r and r^* is one percentage point, while β rises to 0.63 when the gap widens to five percentage points. Efficiency incentives are always present under this sort of nonlinear adjustment, more rapid adjustment is made when prices are farther away from costs, and the discontinuities in behavior associated with fixed bands are avoided.

In his classic analysis of sliding scale plans, Bussing (1936) emphasizes the intrinsic difficulty of distinguishing between "earned and gratuitous super-normal income."[11] Utility performance along any dimension is determined by managerial skill and diligence and by factors totally beyond management's control. Just like the plans discussed in the preceding section, no sliding scale scheme can be expected to apportion performance changes accurately over time between managerial and external causes. Either sort of plan will from time to time permit ineptly run firms to enjoy windfall profits and punish efficient managements with inadequate earnings. The longer any particular adjustment formula is retained, the more likely such outcomes are to occur.

There are some important differences between sliding scale and comprehensive partial adjustment plans. First, sliding scale plans typically require less information. A firm's rate of return on assets or equity is regularly estimated (with more or less accuracy) by its accounting system, while the indexes of real output and other quantities used in symmetric schemes necessitate additional computation. (Also, it may not be simple to derive or agree on sound and practical index formulas.) The other side of this coin is that sliding scale plans in principle are capable of less accuracy in meting out appropriate rewards and punishments; productivity improvement cannot be directly rewarded unless it is measured.

Second, sliding scale plans focus on levels of total cost and total revenue, not just on rates of change. They thus do not permit profits to explode upward or downward as some comprehensive plans may. This feature can be added to comprehensive plans, but not without also adding either complexity or arbitrary bounds on various quantities.

Third, sliding scale plans present a more limited range of options than comprehensive clauses do. Given the target rate of return, the only issue is the form of the adjustment mechanism that moves the actual rate of return toward the target. This feature might serve to ease the burden on regulatory proceedings concerned with adjustment mechanisms. It is still true, however, that sliding scale plans require tailoring to the particular circumstances considered. The more variation in cost and demand conditions because of factors beyond the firm's control, the more rapid adjustment toward the target rate of return should be. Moving to nonlinear adjustment may mitigate but cannot solve the problems of tailoring plans to individual cases. Even if formula 8.13 is selected, a value of γ must be chosen, for instance.

Finally, sliding scale plans do not treat inputs symmetrically. They focus continually on the rate of return to capital. This is likely to give rise to more severe Averch-Johnson (1962) overcapitalization problems than under conventional regulation, which considers the rate of return only during formal proceedings, or comprehensive adjustment clauses.

Periodic Efficiency Assessments

It is unrealistic to treat any automatic adjustment rule as if it were to hold in perpetuity. (Davis, 1944, emphasizes this point in his discussion of the New Jersey plan.) Adjustment clauses of the sort discussed above and in chapter 7 are clearly incomplete contracts; they do not and cannot ensure acceptable performance under all possible conditions. They can serve a useful purpose by rendering formal proceedings less frequent while providing some incentive for efficient production, but such proceedings will be required from time to time for modification of the controlling formula, as well as to deal with price structure and product selection issues.

Formal proceedings provide opportunities for assessing and rewarding managerial performance. This point has not been lost on diligent regulatory commissions. Nash (1925, p. 110) reports that in the early 1920s, the Wisconsin and Illinois commissions had developed elaborate schemes for grading the efficiency of utilities under their jurisdictions. The modern literature seems to concentrate on two approaches to utility performance assessment.[12] The first employs statistical techniques to compare an individual firm's efficiency with that of other firms in its industry. The second attempts direct assessment of a firm's management, often through the device of a management audit.

Most discussions of the first of these approaches begin with Iulo's (1961) multiple regression analysis of the unit costs of a cross-section sample of electric utilities, which explicitly attempted to identify efficient and inefficient firms. (See also Shepherd, 1966b.) As a number of writers have noted, however, not only are there technical problems with some of Iulo's procedures, but there are weaknesses in his basic approach.[13] It is likely to be hard to apply to other sectors. Further, all interfirm comparisons based on a limited number of quantitative variables must omit some potentially relevant factors, and they are vulnerable to challenges by interested parties on these grounds. It is not dramatically easier to separate out statistically the effects of management alone on performance in cross-section comparisons of many firms than it is to devise automatic adjustment clauses to do this for a single firm over time. In any case, though it is often cited, Iulo's effort does not seem to have inspired either potential imitators or regulators.

The second approach to assessing and rewarding efficiency depends much more heavily on the judgment of the commission and of the management auditors it may employ. As Kahn (1971, p. 63) notes, commissions have traditionally made efficiency determinations based on judgmental factors from time to time, and some such determinations have explicitly affected firms' allowed earnings. As Doades (1978) and Sargent (1978) point out, commissions in recent years have come to employ management auditing as part of this process. Actions of this sort, if not capricious, can probably be expected to enhance productive efficiency, at least in the long run.

From an institutional design point of view, however, heavy reliance on commissions' judgments of managerial efficiency has several shortcomings. First, as Auerbach (1972), Noll (1971a), and others have observed, regulators tend to avoid making potentially controversial judgments in public. Were legislation to require periodic efficiency assessments, there might be a tendency to evade its spirit by finding that almost all regulated firms were almost always slightly above average in efficiency.

Second, by its very nature, a judgmental approach to efficiency assessment is bound to be affected by nonquantifiable factors. It is not clear that management auditing is sufficiently well developed that the final assessment can be independent of the consulting firm chosen to conduct the audit. The discussions of management auditing of utility firms by Doades (1978) and Sargent (1978) point up the delicacy of the auditing process and the importance of managerial attitudes and actions. In short, even if nontrivial assessments can be required, it is not obvious that capriciousness can be ensured against.

Finally judgmental assessments yield adjectives, not numbers. Even if an auditor can argue, for instance, that a change in management practices can save a particular firm a million dollars, this does not imply, let alone quantify, management inefficiency. Consulting firms are in the business of detecting potential cost savings in unregulated sectors as well. A finding that some utility can cut costs by some apparently sizable figure may be simply a tribute to the auditor's skill, not to management's negligence. Judgment, expressed in words, is required to interpret any such quantitative findings. The auditor, placed between a firm and its commission and perhaps interested in further utility auditing work, is subject to conflicting pressures on its choice of adjectives from both sides.

There are likely to be cases in which the auditor's professional standards would require that inescapably strong conclusions be drawn. But the temptation to avoid such conclusions must be strong. It is surely not sensible to attempt to legislate a correspondence between the auditor's adjectives and the rewards or punishments to be imposed on regulated firms. But without some such constraint, and even with it, it is hard to be confident that regulators' and auditors' propensities for conflict avoidance would not lead the process to translate sizable efficiency differences into tiny pecuniary differentials. It may be possible for published management audits reliably to point out exceptionally inept management, but it seems unrealistic to hope for much more.

If it is decided, in any case, that formal commission proceedings, perhaps informed by management audits, should be used to pass judgment on firms' managements, such proceedings must occur periodically. Surely one would not want to reward or punish today's managerial performance in perpetuity; the prospect of subsequent detailed review must be present as both carrot and stick.

Interim rewards and punishments might be meted out in basically three ways. First, the commission might raise or lower the firm's maximum or average allowed rate of return relative to its cost of capital. (Alternatively the pricing rule might be targeted on an average stock price above or below book value by some fixed percentage.) Second, the parameters of whatever price adjustment or profit recapture rule that is to hold until the next proceeding might be modified. Finally, the management team might be rewarded directly.

Primary stress probably should be placed on the first and third of these devices. The appropriate degree of rate flexibility, with rigid rates at one extreme and total comprehensive adjustment clauses at the other, ought logically to be primarily determined by the nature and magnitude of expected risks in the interval between formal proceedings. Morgan (1923) and others have placed great stress on the desirability of rewarding management directly. On the other hand, as Kahn (1971, p. 62) observes, higher profits typically benefit managers both directly and indirectly. As a practical matter, the discussion of operating franchises in chapter 5 suggests that it might be difficult to fix managerial rewards in any systematic fashion without angering either stockholders or managements. Appropriate managerial compensation is, after all, the share-holders' decision, at least in principle.

Finally, Shepherd (1975, ch. 9) and Wilcox and Shepherd (1975, p. 510) have suggested that profit ceilings might be related by commissions to firms' performance of designated tasks or achievement of specified results. They term this device "if-then" regulation. In some instances, this approach might provide a commission with useful and powerful leverage, but it is hard to build it into a general regulatory structure; exactly how appropriate tasks and compensation for performing them are to be determined must be left somewhat vague. A sophisticated commission is required to make quantitative judgments of this sort with confidence and accuracy.

Control by Taxation and Subsidy

The basic principle that output bonuses can be used to improve a monopoly's performance seems to have been first analyzed in print by J. Robinson (1933, pp. 163-65), who credits E.A.G. Robinson with the idea. She notes that if a monopolist is given a bonus per unit of output equal to the difference between marginal cost and marginal revenue at the competitive output level, that level will be chosen to maximize the firm's profit. The taxing authority could break even by requiring the firm to make a fixed dollar payment. Robinson (p. 165) concludes, however, that changes in demands and costs and imperfect knowledge of these quantities imply that "there is not likely to be much scope for applying [this scheme] in actual cases." (See also Baumol, 1965, pp. 108-09, for a discussion of this approach, which reaches the same conclusion.)

Domar (1974) has recently proposed an iterative version of this scheme that requires less knowledge of demand. Domar's main concern is with the compensation of a monopolistic firm's management under government ownership, but he notes that his device might have broader application. Domar deals with a bonus related to revenue, while Robinson analyzed a subsidy tied to physical units of output.[14] In a single-product model, Domar shows that under certain assumptions, if the regulator can accurately estimate the price elasticity of demand at each output level actually observed, he can vary the bonus formula according to a particular rule and eventually induce competitive output. By imposing fixed, lump-sum taxes, the regulator can avoid making net payments.

This approach to natural monopoly control would leave pricing entirely in the hands of the firm. It would provide strong incentives for cost minimization, though only as long as the firm's management treated the tax-subsidy scheme as beyond its control. Product selection issues would still presumably require explicit commission attention.

Still it would be premature at this stage to advocate experimentation with this approach as a replacement for conventional regulation, for a number of reasons. First, as Domar (1974, pp. 7-8) notes, the situation becomes very complicated when the firm produces many products and the demand for some depends on the prices of others. No iterative scheme for this case has been devised to my knowledge, but it is the typical case in natural monopoly industries.

Second, even with only one output and a fixed demand curve (unaffected by changes in GNP, for instance), the procedure will not perform well unless the demand elasticity estimates are of high quality. If demand is insufficiently responsive to price or the demand curve is of the wrong shape, the procedure will not work at all. (Technically demand must be elastic and elasticity must be nonincreasing in output to guarantee convergence. The restriction to elastic demand curves is particularly bothersome in the context of public utility sectors, though it seems that an output subsidy might be workable in principle even with inelastic demand.) Even if the process does work in the sense of ensuring competitive output in the limit after enough iterations, rapid convergence to that output level is not ensured. This can be a serious problem in the real world of shifting demand and cost curves.

Third, as Domar (1974, p. 13) recognizes, if management anticipates the changes in the bonus rule (and in the fixed tax) that the iterative procedure requires the commission to make, the entire process becomes indeterminate. A sophisticated firm, having read Domar's article, knows how its response to today's bonus formula determines the formula it will face tomorrow. But if it takes this knowledge into account in determining today's action, the assumptions that underlie the whole procedure are violated. Domar's scheme depends on the firm's passively and myopically responding to the commission, and this may be unlikely.

Fourth, both the Robinson (1933) and Domar (1974) plans aim for marginal cost pricing. But this is generally too simple a rule for natural monopoly situations. It typically results in a deficit that must be covered. That is, it does not ensure that zero excess profit is earned on average. The tax-subsidy approach does not provide for the discrimination that is generally needed to do this. While it might be possible to modify the scheme to take care of this problem, it does not seem likely that the required modifications are simple. Finally, in the U.S. context, the net payments or receipts that the commission would make or receive from time to time because of forecast errors might cause legal problems.

In short, in its present state of development, the tax-subsidy approach to natural monopoly control, like automatic investment schemes, cannot be considered a serious candidate for employment in any real situation. Unlike automatic investment schemes, however, further theoretical analysis might produce plans that deserve field testing.[15]

Rate Structure Policies

Two proposals for rationalizing rate structure determination have recently appeared. The first, advanced by Baumol, Bailey, and Willig (1977), has its origins in the sustainability literature. The second is embodied in recently enacted (November, 1978) federal legislation that restricts state commissions' powers to determine electricity rate structures. It derives from concern for energy use and environmental degradation.

Baumol, Bailey, and Willig (1977), hereafter referred to as BBW, show under certain assumptions about costs and entry behavior that Ramsey-optimal prices, discussed in chapter 3, are sustainable. That is, if a natural monopoly charges such prices and just breaks even, no outside firm will be able to enter and to earn positive profits. They then suggest that entry restrictions be removed from natural monopoly industries and the firms involved be free to select their own rate structures, subject only to limits on overall profits. The monopolists would not be allowed to revise prices later if actual or potential extrants appeared, however. The idea is that the firm would have to protect itself in advance against any possible entry, to do so it would select Ramsey prices, and Ramsey prices have desirable economic efficiency properties. The threat of entry is to be used to force the firm to choose an efficient rate structure. Like franchise bidding schemes, this is an elegant proposal that is likely to encounter serious problems in applications, though the problems have different sources. (See Joskow and Noll, 1978, on some of the points that follow.)

First, the main appeal of the proposal lies in its automatic nature: the natural monopoly firm is supposedly motivated to use all the information at its disposal to set appropriate prices, and the commission need not deal directly with rate structure questions. But this automatic mechanism is a delicate one; if the BBW assumptions are not satisfied, it may not work well. On the one hand, costs may be such that some prices that are not Ramsey optimal are nevertheless sustainable. Given an effective profit ceiling, the regulated firm has no strong reason to prefer efficient pricing in such cases, and inefficient rate structures may occur by default. If, as seems likely, the theoretical development of the sustainability literature is based on assumptions that make entry more attractive than it would be in practice, this might occur frequently. (See Shepherd, 1976a, and Joskow and Noll, 1978.) On the other hand, BBW find that even under their assumptions about entry, strong assumptions on cost functions are required to show that Ramsey prices are sustainable. If the latter assumptions are not satisfied, the only sustainable set of prices may not be efficient, or no set of prices may be sustainable. In the first case this plan would induce inappropriate rate structures, and in the second it would permit inefficient entry. If the commission learns enough about the natural monopoly's cost structure, it can, of course, deal with these problems, but then it can also deal directly with rate structure decisions.

Second, it is hard to see how in the real world, where costs and demands change over time and where firms have informational advantages over commissions, price changes in response to actual or threatened entry can be prevented. Obvious and dramatic cases of predatory reaction can probably be detected, but if a commission has systematically avoided rate structure issues, even this may be too strong an assumption. In any real market, a potential entrant must expect the existing supplier to be able to react to it by making at least some price changes, which can be defended on the basis of cost data if necessary. This will tend further to discourage entry, weakening the forces for efficient pricing and, incidentally, for efficient production.

Finally, Ramsey pricing is not necessarily the optimal goal. Recent theoretical work indicates that nonlinear pricing, which typically involves bulk discounts that are steeper than the corresponding cost declines, is generally superior on efficiency grounds to Ramsey pricing. (See especially Willig, 1978.) But the BBW analysis does not deal with nonlinear pricing; the model assumes that it does not occur. Banning nonlinear pricing would likely be inefficient, and permitting it would rob the BBW proposal of its elegant theoretical basis.

In short, the BBW approach does not seem particularly attractive. Under certain assumptions about the nature of costs and the expectations of entrants, it does provide a simple way of avoiding the complexities of regulatory price-setting in a multiple product context. But the assumptions are strong, and if they do not hold, the BBW plan can lead to clearly undesirable outcomes.

The second proposal to rationalize rate structures has as its intellectual basis the literature on peak-load pricing. As Joskow (1977) notes, however, the recent enthusiasm for peak-load pricing of electricity in the United States has less to do with that literature's ability to persuade noneconomists than with a set of political and administrative considerations bound up with energy policy and environmental concerns. In any case, a bill to require state regulatory commissions to consider peak-load pricing of electricity (along with other pricing schemes) has recently been enacted. Given that many states have already moved some distance toward such pricing (Joskow, 1977), the recent legislation may not have great impact.

The intelligent application of peak-load pricing principles can produce a sizable step toward economic efficiency. These principles have been applied effectively abroad; their systematic use in the United States is long overdue. But other applications of marginal cost pricing principles are also potentially important, and electricity is not the only regulated sector that could use rate structure reform. Since the details of the ultimate federal program in this area are not yet clear, a detailed discussion is inappropriate. Nevertheless some comments deserve to be made about the key features of the recent legislation.[16]

First, state regulatory commissions are required to investigate the marginal cost of providing electricity at various times of day, in various seasons, to various customer groups. The procedures adopted to determine these costs are subject to federal review. This idea is excellent and suitable for application to other sectors. Any rational rate structure policy must be based on marginal costs, and a requirement that such costs be sensibly estimated goes at least part way toward imposing rationality.

Second, state commissions are required to consider adopting prices that vary seasonally and by the time of day if these are cost effective in light of additional metering costs that may be involved. There is a provision for federal review of states' rate structure policies. Again, this is a sensible requirement; it forces commissions to deal with the right questions. Metering costs can be important, and not all peak-load pricing schemes that can be devised by theorists make sense in application. But many do, and it is certainly a move in the right direction to require commissions to deal with this fact.

Third, this legislation, and a good deal of recent discussion of electricity prices, display a marked hostility to nonlinear pricing, in its traditional incarnation as declining-block rates for electricity. (Under such rates, one pays some price per kilowatt-hour for the first block of consumption, a lower price for the next block, and so on; the average cost of electricity paid by any customer thus declines with the amount used after the second block has been entered.) There seems to be a general feeling, unsupported by rigorous analysis, that such rates unduly encourage electricity consumption, leading to excessive use of scarce fuels and to increased air pollution. Further, declining-block rates tend to reduce utilities' revenue per kilowatt-hour sold when demand grows, because of regulatory lag. (See Joskow, 1974, on these points.) Finally, recent increases in the cost of electricity seem to have led some observers to the conclusion that unit costs no longer fall with output in this industry, so that marginal cost pricing will suffice to generate adequate revenues. This seems to reflect, at least in part, a confusion between changes in cost over time, as input prices change, and changes in cost that would be produced by output changes, input prices held constant. The latter are relevant for pricing, though the former are directly observed. Even if average costs always decline with increased output, all else equal, observed average costs can rise sharply over time as input prices increase.

This hostility to declining block structures is disturbing in light of the discussion of nonlinear pricing in chapter 3. In the first place, not all customer-specific costs are proportional to the amount of electricity demanded. Some, such as the cost of metering equipment, are likely to be more or less independent of demand, so that even a pure marginal cost rate structure would likely provide for a decrease in the average price of power as a customer's demand rises. Second, and more importantly, if at least parts of the electric power industry retain natural monopoly status, pure marginal cost pricing is unlikely to provide sufficient revenue to cover all costs. Nonlinear pricing is likely to be an efficient way to raise the necessary additional revenue, and it is hard to make a general case for ruling out its employment for this purpose.

There is no conflict between nonlinear (or declining-block) rate structures and marginal cost pricing principles. Under any sensible natural monopoly price policy, marginal cost provides a floor below which price cannot go (see Baumol, 1967, on this point). The real issue is how deviations between price and marginal cost, if they are necessary, should be structured in order to secure an appropriate level of profits on average. It would be unfortunate if the recent legislation served to inhibit unduly the use of nonlinear pricing policies in electricity or elsewhere.

Finally, federal review of state commission policies serves to push regulation to another level. Unless those in charge of such reviews are skillful and diligent, inefficient or unduly protective commission decisions may be allowed to pass. States may "consider" all the right factors to comply with the law but ignore them when making decisions. Diligence without skill and, inevitably, without detailed knowledge of local conditions may inject considerable arbitrariness into the process.

Conclusions on Regulatory Reform

Of the many changes in commission regulation of natural monopoly firms discussed here, some showed little operational promise: replacement of regulation by excess profits taxation, use of operating ratios for interim rate changes, control by taxation and revenue or output subsidy, and the BBW proposal to place price structure decisions entirely in the firms' hands.[17] But a number of the schemes appear to have some potential value.

Relaxation of entry restrictions, by shifting the burden of proof onto those who would bar entry in particular cases, should make regulation more sensitive to changes in market conditions and put more pressure on existing firms to produce efficiently. One cannot expect this reform to cause major changes in performance, however. Similarly although sunset laws, under which regulatory mandates would be subjected to periodic legislative review, promise much in the way of increased flexibility in principle, there are reasons to doubt that they will have 'great impact in practice. Regulation can be made potentially, if not actually, more precise by systematic reform of utility accounting, so that accounting data provide better estimates of actual rates of return. Periodic assessments by commissions, perhaps aided by management audits, of regulated firms' efficiencies might permit the imposition of rewards and punishments that would enhance efficiency incentives. (This process can also serve to facilitate the takeover of exceptionally poorly run enterprises.) But one should not expect that these assessments will be regularly made with great precision.

Much of the discussion has been devoted to consideration of devices for adapting conventional regulation to inflationary conditions: interim rate increases (with profit recapture provisions), use of future test years, computing the rate base in terms of replacement cost, and a variety of automatic price adjustment clauses. None of these is without problems, but all of them may be useful in some situations. Regulators face a trade-off between incentives for productive efficiency and the sensitivity of regulation to economic change. All of the devices listed above can be thought of as ways of affecting the position of the system along this locus.

This is especially clear in the case of automatic adjustment clauses. In principle, the most attractive of these involve comprehensive partial adjustment. Partial adjustment serves to preserve efficiency incentives, while a comprehensive focus on all cost elements serves to avoid building in incentives to select inappropriate mixes of inputs. But sliding scale or other plans may be better suited for some particular applications.

It should be clear that automatic price adjustment can be either forward or backward looking; that is, it can be used to set prices for some fixed period no matter what happens, as in conventional adjustment clauses, or it can be used to evaluate the positive or negative overcharge in some past period, as in recapture provisions. The speed and form of adjustment are capable of considerable variation. Depending on the appropriate trade-off between sensitivity and productive efficiency and considering operational problems, any of a number of particular schemes might be usefully employed in individual cases.

It is important to realize, however, that schemes for dealing with inflation are at best partial reforms. Legislation might well force a commission to automate regulation partially by selecting an adjustment clause of one sort or another. But it would generally be inappropriate to legislate the precise form of the clause to be employed in all cases, let alone the parameters involved. These decisions must depend on the magnitude and nature of uncertainties about the future. It is hard to see how these issues can be assessed mechanically. Thus although automatic adjustment clauses and other related devices can be useful tools for improving regulation, they do not lend themselves well to inclusion in the basic design of control structures. There is no real substitute here for commission judgment in selecting appropriate devices; one cannot legislate the particular approaches or formulas to be adopted with any confidence. Further, it is worth noting that even after an automatic adjustment plan is selected, the commission must act as buyers' agent between formal hearings in order to enforce the terms of the plan (for some relevant experience under the Washington plan, see Elgen, 1940).

Most of the proposals considered in these two chapters dealt only with two of the four dimensions of performance: productive efficiency and profit limitation. None considered product selection issues, so there appears to be no alternative to having these dealt with by commissions on a case-by-case basis. The two proposals considered in the preceding section focused on the pricing dimension of performance. Federal legislation mandating consideration of peak-load pricing of electricity seems a useful reform. It illustrates the possibility of prescribing general rules for regulatory behavior in this area. But it also illustrates that these rules must be drafted with considerable care and enforced with considerable skill if adverse results are to be ensured against.

In short, regulatory commissions can adopt a number of proposals that are likely to enhance economic efficiency. The general nature of some of these can be easily prescribed. Prices should be based on marginal costs, for instance, and automatic adjustment clauses should weigh carefully the trade-off between sensitivity and productive efficiency. But it does not seem to be desirable, even if it is possible, to eliminate completely commission discretion in any broad area; there are apparently no formulas that can be confidently written into legislation for universal application. The attractive proposals considered in these two chapters are tactics that might be employed by commissions; they are not strategies for control process design. Under private ownership, if controls are imposed, they must involve a commission charged with acting as the buyers' agent and with some freedom to make its own decisions as to how that role should be played.

Notes

1. Theoretical analyses of regulatory lag are provided by Baumol and Klevorick, "Input Choices"; Bailey, *Economic Theory*, ch. 7; Klevorick, "Be-

havior of a Firm Subject to Stochastic Regulatory Review"; and Wendel, "Firm-Regulator Interaction." See also Ziemba, "Behavior of a Firm: Comment," and Klevorick, "Behavior of a Firm: Correction." Joskow, "Pricing Decisions of Regulated Firms," presents an interesting model of the determinants of part of the regulatory lag under traditional arrangements.

2. See also Jaffee, "Incentive Pricing"; Cross, "Incentive Pricing"; and Kennedy, "Incentive Pricing."

3. Formally, this only suffices to show that total profit is decreasing in C at the point $P = C$. In general, increases in C raise total profit if and only if $(\beta - 1)/\beta > E[(P - C)/P]$, where E is the absolute value of the price elasticity of demand. If $\alpha = 0$ and $\beta = \gamma > 1$, as under markup regulation, this condition is satisifed for P sufficiently close to C. If β is less than 1, however, increases in C can be profitable only if the firm is taking substantial losses. McCall, "Incentive Contracting," provides more on the formal properties of incentive contracts of this basic sort. Some of Hall's discussion is also relevant here. Hall, "Defense Procurement."

4. This proposal is discussed by Latimer, "Cost and Efficiency Revenue Adjustment Clause"; Hardies, "Inflation Dilemma"; and Kendrick, "Efficiency Incentives." It is not fully symmetric or comprehensive because changes in the cost of equity capital are not covered.

5. This simplified formula assumes that all costs are included in C and that revenues equal costs; Kendrick, "Efficiency Incentives," provides a more complete description. It should also be noted that the price change to go into effect was to be the smaller of the one given by the formula and the change necessary to bring the utility's rate of return to a fixed upper bound.

6. Ram-Mohan, Salas, and Whinston, "Automatic Price Adjustment," propose yet another adjustment formula, but its complexity renders it unsuitable for presentation here and, probably, for use in real applications.

7. For general discussions and mixed evaluations of various sliding scale plans, see Morgan, *Regulation and the Management of Public Utilities*, ch. 5, and Bussing, *Public Utility Regulation*. Wrightington, "Sliding Scale Method," provides a contemporary account of one early plan. See also Glaeser, *Outlines of Public Utility Economics*, pp. 299-310; Thompson and Smith, *Public Utility Economics*, ch. 9; Troxel, *Economics of Public Utilities*, pp. 403-17; Clemens, *Economics and Public Utilities*, pp. 346-53; and Trebing, "Towards an Incentive System." Some of these writers reserve the term *sliding scale* for the early dividend-price plans, describing all more sophisticated variants as *service at cost plans*.

8. The Washington plan is discussed by all of the authors cited in n. 7 above except Morgan and Wrightington. Elgen, "Profit Sharing," provides a defense of the plan based on first-hand experience with its operation, and Trebing, "Towards an Incentive System," gives an overall history and evaluation.

9. Discussions of the plan soon after its adoption were provided by Davis,

"Regulation by Formula"; Foster, "New Jersey Adjustment Plan"; Foster and Davis, "Structure and Mechanics of the New Jersey Adjustment Plan"; and Harbeson, " 'New Jersey Plan.' " See also Clemens, *Economics and Public Utilities*, pp. 346-53, and Troxel, *Economics of Public Utilities*, pp. 403-17.

10. See Backman and Kirsten, 'Comprehensive Adjustment Clause," and *Re New Jersey Power and Light Company*, 95 PUR NS 467 (N.J. 1952).

11. See also Clark, *Social Control*, pp. 246-47; Kahn, *Economics of Regulation*, 2:62; and Wilson, Herring, and Eutsler, *Public Utility Regulation*, ch. 2.

12. For general discussions of these approaches, see Doades, "Mentality of Management Audits"; Sargent, "Fishbowl Planning in Management Audits"; Shepherd, *Treatment of Market Power*, ch. 9; Trebing, "Towards an Incentive System"; Wilcox and Shepherd, *Public Policies*, pp. 368-88; and Williamson, "Administrative Controls." See also Clark, *Social Control*, pp. 328-32.

13. For details, see Shepherd, *Teatment of Market Power*, ch. 9; Trebing, "Towards an Incentive System"; Wilcox and Shepherd, *Public Policies*, pp. 368-88; and Kahn, *Economics of Regulation*, p. 63.

14. In a later paper, Domar, "Effects of a Managerial Bonus," analyzed the impact of revenue subsidies on product quality. For an example of the use of such subsidies in an operating franchise, see chapter 5.

15. Sherman (1974, pp. 393-95; 1976) has discussed the use of labor subsidies and capital taxes to offset the Averch-Johnson effect ("Behavior of the Firm") associated with conventional regulation. It would seem that if regulators knew enough to implement his scheme, however, they could simply prescribe the details of an efficient production plan; Sherman's proposal requires too much information to be workable.

16. On this legislation and the debate surrounding its enactment, see "A New Federal Hand on Electricity Rates" and, especially, American Enterprise Institute, *Electric Utility Rate Reform*.

17. One additional proposal should be mentioned. Weintraub, "Rate Making," has suggested that in order to encourage adoption of new techniques, utilities be permitted to retain abandoned equipment in their rate bases. The possibilities for abuse and intensification of AJ effects seem obvious, but the basic notion may deserve further study.

9 Conclusions and Implications

Efficiency as the Control Objective

The problem posed by natural monopoly is fundamentally economic. The defining characteristic of natural monopoly is the necessity to have production done by a single enterprise if costs are to be minimized. In the absence of special controls, natural monopoly situations generally tend toward single-seller dominance. If the product or set of products involved does not have good substitutes, uncontrolled monopoly implies substantial efficiency losses. It also implies high profits, which represent a transfer of wealth from buyers to the seller. Efficiency losses are the more basic problem, if only because policies designed to eliminate them also generally reduce or eliminate excess profits, while profit limitation alone can reduce efficiency.

The only appropriate objective of natural monopoly control is economic or allocative efficiency; the argument is one of expediency, not of principle. If natural monopoly control were or could be part of an ideal government administrative apparatus, it could deal effectively with all the government's objectives as developed in the political process. But the degree of coordination and central control that this would require cannot be attained.

Targeting the control process on the single goal of economic efficiency reflects both administrative feasibility and the nature of the problem addressed. If those charged with the control function are instructed or encouraged to consider other goals as well, effective administrative or judicial review of their actions becomes all but impossible because there can be no clear standard for appropriate trade-offs among the many conflicting and imprecise goals that governments nominally pursue. This ambiguity makes it more likely that decisions will reflect the values and objectives of the administrators involved or those of other special interests than any defensible conception of the public interest. Administrative feasibility indicates the desirability of a single control objective; the character of the natural monopoly problem indicates that the objective chosen should be economic efficiency. Moreover an increase in the efficiency of resource use increases society's options and capabilities in a general way, regardless of the more basic objectives on which private or public attention is focused at any moment.

The selection of economic or allocative efficiency as the objective of natural monopoly control has two important and direct implications for policy. First, the control process should be heavily influenced, if not dominated, by the relevant experts: economists. The arguments of Bernstein (1955, ch. 4) and others against regulation by experts have little force if regulators are to pursue a single, well-defined objective. Second, the relevant statutes should reflect the objective of the control process. Vague mandates, apparently concerned with ill-defined issues of fairness and reasonability, can serve only to justify efficiency-reducing actions; they surely do nothing to encourage decision making focused on economic efficiency.

There is a sense in which these arguments are essential to all the analysis in chapters 3-8. Unless one has a clear objective, there is no way to evaluate systematically and consistently either existing practice or proposals for change. The analysis presented here assumes that economic efficiency is the goal of natural monopoly control; this assumption makes possible a more or less coherent treatment of both practice and proposals. On the other hand, even if one does not agree that efficiency ought to be the only objective in this context, analyses of the efficiency implications of alternative policies should be of some interest unless one adopts the extreme position that it does not matter how society uses its scarce resources.

The major dimensions of efficient natural monopoly performance are pricing based on marginal cost, appropriate product selection, production efficiency, and excess profit on average zero. Attainment of efficient performance in any real industry is no simple task. Limiting natural monopoly control to the pursuit of economic efficiency would not make controllers' jobs easy or uninteresting by any standards.

The Imperfect Alternatives

One important approach to natural monopoly is to do nothing. If the imposition of special controls involves some cost, there must exist natural monopoly situations in which those costs exceed the potential benefits from control. Given the tendency of government programs and agencies to cling to life, the argument for leaving a natural monopoly alone is especially strong if that natural monopoly is temporary, since changes in demand may subsequently render special control unnecessary.

On the other hand, in some situations, a hands-off policy is either politically infeasible or economically unsound. In many of these cases in the United States, public utility regulation is employed as the control device, but it has generally failed to produce optimal performance. Profit limitation has not been consistently achieved, there are obvious problems in pricing and product selection, and there may be inefficiencies in production. But this is not much of an indictment. If controls are to be applied, the choice is not between conventional regulation and perfection but rather between conventional regulation and alternative human institutions. It is easier and more elegant to compare regulation to an ideal than to another imperfect structure, but it is much less helpful for policy decisions.

On the general issue of control system design, there are a number of transactional problems of the sort not much dealt with in conventional textbook microeconomics that are intrinsic to natural monopoly situations and that greatly complicate the task of control. These problems seem to imply that effective control arrangements must involve a buyers' agent with appropriate skills and resources, relatively long-lived supply arrangements, and incomplete reliance on written contracts. These, of course, are features of conventional utility regulation. Additionally the existing literature on administrative and regulatory behavior contains a number of interesting insights, hypotheses, and observations, but none are sufficiently developed to be relied upon for the design of effective administrative arrangements. The institutional inventor, upon whom Gray (1940) pinned his hopes, still lacks an adequate science base. In particular, we do not know how to ensure that the buyers' agent will play its role with vigor and skill. Perhaps the most firmly established result is that many detailed aspects of administrative structures are not major determinants of behavior.[1] Our inability to predict actual behavior from knowledge of institutional structure, broadly defined, suggests at least that the interests of effective administration are generally ill served by grants of excessive discretion; such freedom may be abused in a variety of unpredictable and often difficult-to-detect ways.

Both these points suggest that there are unlikely to be miracle cures for the shortcomings of conventional regulation. Given the severe transactional problems that must plague the natural monopoly control process and given that this process must be shaped at least in part by difficult-to-predict administrative behavior, one cannot hope for perfection. At best, one can hope that different control strategies will have different performance characteristics so that there is some possibility of sensibly matching control devices to economic attributes of the industries involved.

This rather pessimistic expectation is supported by the discussions of control structures that at least appeared to be basically different from conventional regulation. Automatic investment schemes seemed to have little promise. Bidding for operating or ordinary franchises did not emerge as an attractive alternative in general, and it seemed likely that in practice the resemblance to conventional regulation would come to exceed that commonly anticipated. The buyers' agent would often encounter severe problems in attempting to make input market competition effective and still provide continuity of performance. The markets for capital and for managerial talent cannot be relied upon very heavily to control most natural monopolies, though the role of such markets could be usefully expanded by facilitating takeovers of regulated firms.

The key theoretical feature of public enterprise is the merger it involves between the roles of buyers' agent and equity capital suppliers' agent. (These are performed by regulators and managers, respectively, under conventional regulatory arrangements.) One would not expect this merger to cause dramatic shifts in behavior, and the available evidence, though sketchy in many respects, suggests that it does not. Moreover a key factor in determining performance under public ownership and operation seems to be the control exercised over enterprise managers, and the problems of making that control effective and responsive to efficiency considerations seem no less great than the similar problems encountered under regulation. Public ownership and operation may be attractive in certain natural monopoly industries, but as a general rule, one would expect modest (and difficult to predict) differences from performance under regulation, not dramatic efficiency gains or losses.

Public ownership structures might contribute directly, by their existence or their intrinsic operating tendencies, to goals other than efficiency. If so, these advantages should be considered in the choice between public and private ownership. But even under public ownership, natural monopoly operation should aim for economic efficiency alone. Public enterprise managers and their overseers are no better able than utility regulators to make appropriate choices among competing objectives. Government enterprise does offer the possibility of subsidizing some activities from the public treasury, of course, and it is hard to object to such subsidies in principle. Like most other economists, however, I would argue that subsidies of this sort should be decided upon in the political process and be publicly announced. This may not be any easier to do under public ownership than under alternative arrangements; hiding subsidies (and the corresponding taxes) seems generally to have greater political appeal.[2]

As Kahn (1971, p. 328) notes, the choice between public and private ownership of natural monopoly enterprises is "inescapably one between imperfect institutions." The choice between conventional regulation and any imaginable alternative is of exactly this same variety.

Improving Utility Regulation

Public utility regulation, broadly defined, seems generally at least as well suited to the task of natural monopoly control as any of the alternatives considered above. This does not mean that the observed tactical elements of this broad control strategy are optimal in any sense, however; a number of changes deserve consideration.[3]

There is a general case for more participation by economists if economic efficiency is accepted as the objective of regulation. This is not a panacea, of course; not all economists are able and energetic. Similarly there is a general case for more narrowly focused statutory mandates. Noll (1971b) and a number of other authors have plausibly attributed at least some of the shortcomings of conventional regulation to the vague mandates under which it operates.

Much can be done within the existing statutory framework to move regulated sectors toward economic efficiency. It is certainly true that the quality of personnel matters in regulation, as it does in most other human institutions. Able regulators, dedicated to the goal of efficiency, can do much to improve performance. But conventional regulatory arrangements do not always attract or select such individuals; the literature on regulatory behavior makes this clear. In principle, one ought to attempt to design control devices that are likely to be operated effectively by persons without unusual ability and knowledge, rather than to rely on the appearance of exceptional individuals who will be able to produce good policy in spite of their situation.

Thus under regulation, as well as under alternative control strategies, legislation may often be necessary to improve performance. Just as expecting regulators to reform themselves idealizes the regulatory process, however, so looking for new laws that would tightly focus regulation on the pursuit of economic efficiency may involve somewhat unrealistic expectations about the legislative process. As Friendly (1962, ch. 7) and Davis (1969), among others, have argued, legislatures have obvious incentives to delegate complex and politically difficult decisions to administrators. The vagueness of regulatory mandates is not accidental. Expecting legislatures to limit the objectives and alternatives of their designated agents requires optimism, as such acts tend to make the legislature more vulnerable to criticism of the agent's actions. But laws of this sort are enacted from time to time; the recent federal legislation on electricity pricing may serve as a particularly relevant example. Moreover to rule out such legislation as politically impossible and to rely instead on the chance appearance of exceptional personalities is to a considerable extent to give up the possibility of lasting reform.

Legislation would seem to be required to facilitate utility takeovers to the appropriate degree, not only because of statutory barriers to such acts but also because of commissions' widely noted protective tendencies. If commissions retain the power to block takeovers on a case-by-case basis, too many may be blocked. Commission financing and publication of periodic management audits might both increase the susceptibility of regulated firms to desirable takeovers by more efficient management and provide a basis for explicit rewards and punishments keyed to managerial efficiency. The management audit process, however, is far from routine, and decisions as to appropriate rewards and punishments are difficult and require considerable judgment. A systematic reform of utility accounting, aimed at producing more accurate estimates of real, economic rates of return, would make more precise profit control possible. Legislation shifting the burden of proof onto those who oppose entry of new suppliers and requiring that their case be made in economic efficiency (or sustainability) terms might well facilitate a more rapid redefinition of the proper sphere of regulatory control. Other devices aimed at this end, such as sunset laws for commissions, show modest promise, but there do not appear to exist operational proposals that would ensure that regulation, like the ideal Marxist state, would automatically wither away when it was no longer necessary.

There are clear limits to the extent to which legislation can serve to automate the regulatory process and to remove commission discretion. As the discussion of the electricity pricing proposals indicated, general rules and principles for commission decision making can mandate a focus on relevant considerations and prescribe at least the language in which some decisions must be couched. Legislation of this sort could be usefully applied to other sectors and other sorts of decisions. But general rules cannot completely eliminate the need for commissions to exercise judgment; such rules must be drafted with care and precision lest they foreclose attractive alternatives or have other undesirable side-effects. Existing knowledge would appear to permit more confident prescription of operational principles for pricing or cost of capital determination than for product selection, for instance.

The limits on the extent to which regulation can sensibly be automated by prescriptive legislation are also illustrated by the discussion of price adjustment clauses. The appropriate trade-off between sensitivity to economic change and efficiency-enhancing rigidities cannot be made in general terms; it must reflect the nature and importance of uncertainties about the future in each particular case. A large number of apparently sensible devices have been proposed and employed in adapting conventional regulation to a world of rapidly changing prices, and the selection and application of these devices require judgment. Imaginative legislation might lay down guidelines and factors to be considered, of course, but it would not be easy to do this well on the basis of current knowledge; various operational properties of several alternatives are simply not clear enough in quantitative terms. Not only can the appropriate point on the efficiency-sensitivity trade-off locus not be sensibly prescribed by legislation that covers many different cases, so that some commission discretion to choose that point in each case must remain, but it is not even likely that commissions can be confidently instructed by economists or legislators as to how best to reach any particular point.

It thus seems that neither the choice of a particular automatic price adjustment clause nor a number of other tactical regulatory choices can be rendered routine if efficiency is to be served. Commission discretion can be reduced by desirable legislation of various sorts, but it cannot sensibly be eliminated. This further strengthens the argument that commissions' general mandates should focus on economic efficiency as the objective to be pursued. Only then can administrators or courts review nonroutine exercises of regulatory discretion in a nonarbitrary fashion. The inevitability of commission discretion also indicates that no reform can eliminate the importance of having commissioners with ability and suitable skills.

Research Needs

As an academic, I am bound by guild rules to close this work with a plea for further research. The case for additional research in this area is quite strong. We know something about the actual or likely performance of conventional regulation and various alternatives when the standard of comparison is the ideal of perfectly efficient resource use, but we know relatively little about the comparative performance, under different conditions, of alternative control strategies and tactics. And comparative performance is vital in policy selection.

It would be useful in this context to know more about the relation between administrative structure and behavior. We apparently cannot even describe structural conditions that will ensure that specific and narrowly defined tasks will be performed well. We are clearly not able to identify structural conditions under which administrative discretion will be exercised in acceptable ways. It does seem that some details of administrative structure do not have major effects on behavior, but negative information of this sort is not of great use in institutional design.

It is important to understand better the relation between intrinsic characteristics of natural monopoly industries and the comparative performance of alternative control devices. Bits of evidence and conjecture bearing on this relation are available, but much more theoretical and empirical work is required to produce a systematic treatment. The various control approaches discussed in this book differ along a number of dimensions, and some of their apparent strengths and weaknesses have been discussed. Depending on the technical and transactional attributes of individual natural monopoly sectors, different control approaches may be more or less attractive. Matching of this kind requires a thorough knowledge, with both empirical and theoretical dimensions, of alternative control strategies as well as of individual industries. But as Breyer (1977) has argued in a broader context, the matching of tools and tasks is an essential part of intelligent policy design.

In these and other areas, a systematic and integrated analysis of natural monopoly control experience in the United States and elsewhere would be informative. Bits and pieces of historical and comparative evidence are available. The value of more cross-country and intertemporal analysis of public ownership options is clear. Detailed case studies of particular experiments in natural monopoly control, such as Williamson's (1976) examination of an experiment with franchise bidding, are of potentially great value. Public enterprise and government control of privately owned natural monopoly firms have been around for centuries. The opportunity for productive research in the economic history of these institutions seems considerable.[4]

Finally, a large number of areas would benefit from further economic research of the traditional sort. More theoretical and empirical work on the use of nonlinear pricing might permit a drafting of intelligent operational rules for its use. The important study of multiproduct natural monopoly is really just beginning; the sustainability literature is likely to be only the first chapter. Additional theoretical and applied work on product selection or, more narrowly, reliability choice would be useful. It is not yet clear in detail how utility accounting systems can be made to yield more useful information on actual rates of return. The theoretical and empirical properties of various automatic price adjustment clauses and related devices in a dynamic world in which costs and demands are uncertain and X-inefficiency is a real possibility are not well understood. The theoretical literature on peak-load pricing and other applications of marginal cost pricing principles is well developed, but all operationally relevant problems have certainly not been solved. Finally, there is room for much more research on the implications of strategic behavior by the controlled enterprise, whether privately or publicly owned. It is simply not adequate to treat enterprise management as passive recipients of controllers' commands.

In sum, we know a good deal less than we should. Textbooks tell us that special controls of some sort may be desirable in natural monopoly situations. This book should make it clear that there is a great difference between statements of this sort and complete, defensible, operational policy prescriptions.

Notes

1. On this point, see in particular Noll, *Reforming Regulation*, Bernstein, "Regulatory Process," and "Independent Regulatory Agencies," and Breyer, "The Ash Council's Report."

2. Sheahan's discussion of French and Italian experience is particularly relevant here. Sheahan, "Experience with Public Enterprise," pp. 156-66.

3. Two that apparently do not deserve to be considered for implementation, as chapters 7 and 8 argued, are regulation by excess profits taxation or by use of revenue or output bonus schemes.

4. In particular, the writings of Chadwick, "Results of Different Principles," and other clues mentioned in previous chapters indicate that a study of the use of limited franchises in nineteenth- and early twentieth-century France would be of considerable interest.

Bibliography

American Enterprise Institute. 1977. *Electric Utility Rate Reform.* Washington, D.C., September.

Ashley, C.A., and R.G.H. Smails. 1965. *Canadian Crown Corporations.* Toronto: Macmillan of Canada.

Auerbach, C.A. 1972. "Pluralism and the Administrative Process." *Annals of the American Academy of Political and Social Science* (March):1-13.

Averch, H., and L.L. Johnson. 1962. "Behavior of the Firm under Regulatory Constraint." *American Economic Review* 52 (December):1052-69.

Backman, J., and J.B. Kirsten. 1974. "Comprehensive Adjustment Clause for Telephone Companies." *Public Utilities Fortnightly* 93 (28 March):21-26.

Bailey, E.E. 1972. "Peak Load Pricing under Regulatory Constraint." *Journal of Political Economy* 80 (July-August):662-79.

_____ . 1973. *Economic Theory of Regulatory Constraint.* Lexington, Mass.: D.C. Heath.

Bailey, E.E., and L.J. White. 1974. "Reversals in Peak and Offpeak Prices." *Bell Journal of Economics and Management Science* 5 (Spring):75-92.

Baron, D.P., and R.A. Taggart. 1977. "A Model of Regulation under Uncertainty and a Test of Regulatory Bias." *Bell Journal of Economics* 8 (Spring):151-67.

Bauer, J. 1939. "Modernizing the Public Utility Franchise." *Public Management* 21 (August):235-40.

_____ . 1946. *The Public Utility Franchise: Its Functions and Terms under State Regulation.* Chicago: Public Administration Service.

_____ . 1950. *Transforming Public Utility Regulation: A Definite Administrative Proposal.* New York: Harper.

Baumol, W.J. 1965. *Welfare Economics and the Theory of the State.* 2d ed. Cambridge: Harvard University Press.

_____ . 1967. "Reasonable Rules for Rate Regulation: Plausible Policies for an Imperfect World." In A. Phillips and O.E. Williamson, eds. *Prices: Issues in Theory, Practice, and Public Policy.* Philadelphia: University of Pennsylvania Press.

_____ . 1977. "On the Proper Cost Tests for Natural Monopoly in a Multiproduct Industry." *American Economic Review* 67 (December):809-22.

Baumol, W.J., E.E. Bailey, and R.D. Willig. 1977. "Weak Invisible Hand Theorems on the Sustainability of Prices in a Multiproduct Monopoly." *American Economic Review* 67 (June):350-65.

Baumol, W.J., and D.F. Bradford. 1970. "Optimal Departures from Marginal Cost Pricing." *American Economic Review* 60 (June):265-83.

Baumol, W.J., and A.K. Klevorick. 1970. "Input Choices and Rate-of-Return Regulation: An Overview of the Discussion." *Bell Journal of Economics and Management Science* 1 (Autumn):162-90.

Beaulieu, P.L. 1897a. "Le gaz et l'électricité à Paris et le Conseil Municipal." *L'Economiste Français*, 18 December, pp. 793-95.

_____. 1897b. "Les compagnies d'électricité à Paris, à Berlin, et à Londres." *L'Economiste Français*, 25 December, pp. 829-31.

_____. 1901a. "Les divers systèmes de transportation commun dans les grandes villes." *L'Economiste Français*, 30 March, pp. 413-15.

_____. 1901b. "L'exploitation du gaz, les regies municipal et les concessions." *L'Economiste Français*, 14 December, pp. 809-11.

Behn, R.D. 1977. "The False Dawn of Sunset Laws." *Public Interest* (Fall): 103-18.

Beigie, C.E. 1974. "Telecommunications and the Regulation of Public Utilities." In L.H. Officer and L.B. Smith, eds. *Issues in Canadian Economics.* Toronto: McGraw-Hill.

Bernstein, M.H. 1955. *Regulating Business by Independent Commission.* Princeton: Princeton University Press.

_____. 1961. "The Regulatory Process: A Framework for Analysis." *Law and Contemporary Problems* 26:329-46.

_____. 1972. "Independent Regulatory Agencies: A Perspective on Their Reform." *Annals of the American Academy of Political and Social Science* (March):14-26.

"A Big Money Tap for Rural Electric Co-ops." 1976. *Business Week*, 29 November, pp. 77-78.

Blake, H.W. 1927. "Paris Revises Street Railway and Bus Franchise." *Electric Railway Journal* 70 (31 December):1185-89.

Bork, R.H. 1978. *The Antitrust Dilemma.* New York: Basic Books.

Brelay, E. 1897. "Le métropolitain à Paris." *L'Economiste Français*, 16 October, pp. 503-05.

Breyer, S.G. 1971. "The Ash Council's Report on the Independent Regulatory Agencies." *Bell Journal of Economics and Management Science* 2 (Autumn):628-37.

_____. 1977. "The Reform of Economic Regulation." Mimeographed. Cambridge: Harvard University.

Breyer, S.G., and P.W. MacAvoy. 1974. *Energy Regulation by the Federal Power Commission.* Washington, D.C.: Brookings Institution.

Buchanan, J.M. 1965. "An Economic Theory of Clubs." *Economica* 32 (February):1-14.

_____. 1968. "A Public Choice Approach to Public Utility Pricing." *Public Choice* 5 (Fall):1-17.

Buckler, W.H. 1906. "The French Method of Controlling Railway Rates." *Quarterly Journal of Economics* 20:279-86.

Burns, A.E. 1970. "The Tax Court and Profit Renegotiation." *Journal of Law and Economics* 13 (October):307-26.

Bussing, I. 1936. *Public Utility Regulation and the So-called Sliding Scale.* New York: Columbia University Press.

Callen, J.L. 1978. "Production, Efficiency, and Welfare in the Natural Gas Transmission Industry." *American Economic Review* 68 (June):311-23.

Capron, W.M., ed. 1971. *Technological Change in Regulated Industries*. Washington, D.C.: Brookings Institution.

Carman, H.J. 1919. *The Street Surface Railway Franchises of New York City*. New York: Columbia University Press.

Caves, R. 1977. *American Industry: Structure, Conduct, Performance*. 4th ed. Englewood Cliffs, N.J.: Prentice-Hall.

Centre Européen de l'Enterprise Publique. 1967. *Les Enterprises Publiques dans la Communauté Economique Européene*. Paris: Dunod.

Chadwick, E. 1859. "Results of Different Principles of Legislation and Administration in Europe; of Competition for the Field, as Compared with Competition within the Field, of Service." *Journal of the Royal Statistical Society, Series A* 22 (September):381-420.

Chandler, A.D. 1962. *Strategy and Structure: Chapters in the History of the Industrial Enterprise*. Cambridge: MIT Press.

Cicchetti, C.J., W.J. Gillen, and P. Smolensky. 1977. *The Marginal Cost and Pricing of Electricity: An Applied Approach*. Cambridge, Mass.: Ballinger.

Clark, J.M. 1939. *Social Control of Business*. 2d ed. New York: McGraw-Hill.

Clemens, E.W. 1950. *Economics and Public Utilities*. New York: Appleton-Century-Crofts.

Cleveland, H. 1956. "Survival in the Bureaucratic Jungle." *Reporter*, 5 April, pp. 29-32.

Clough, S.B. 1939. *France: A History of National Economics, 1789-1939*. New York: Charles Scribner's Sons.

Coase, R. 1960. "The Problem of Social Cost." *Journal of Law and Economics* 3 (October):1-44.

———. 1970. "The Theory of Public Utility Pricing and Its Application." *Bell Journal of Economics and Management Science* 1 (Spring):113-28.

Colberg, M.R. 1955. "Utility Profits: A Substitute for Property Taxes?" *National Tax Journal* 8 (October):382-87.

Comanor, W.S. 1970. "Should Natural Monopolies Be Regulated?" *Stanford Law Review* 22 (February):510-18.

Courville, L. 1974. "Regulation and Efficiency in the Electric Utility Industry." *Bell Journal of Economics and Management Science* 5 (Spring):53-74.

Crain, W.M., and R.B. Ekelund. 1976. "Chadwick and Demsetz on Competition and Regulation." *Journal of Law and Economics* 19 (April):149-62.

Crew, M.A., and P.R. Kleindorfer. 1978. "Reliability and Public Utility Pricing." *American Economic Review* 68 (March):31-40.

Cross, J.G. 1970. "Incentive Pricing and Public Utility Regulation." *Quarterly Journal of Economics* 84 (May):236-53.

———. 1972. "Incentive Pricing and Utility Regulation: Reply." *Quarterly Journal of Economics* 86 (February):145-47.

Currie, A.W. 1944. "Rate Control on Canadian Public Utilities." *Canadian Journal of Economics and Political Science* 10:381-90.

Cushman, R.E. 1941. *The Independent Regulatory Commissions.* New York: Oxford University Press.

Cutler, L.M., and D.R. Johnson. 1975. "Regulation and the Political Process." *Yale Law Journal* 84 (June):1395-418.

Davies, D.G. 1971. "The Efficiency of Public versus Private Firms: The Case of Australia's Two Airlines." *Journal of Law and Economics* 14 (April): 149-66.

_____. 1977. "Property Rights and Economic Efficiency—The Australian Airlines Revisited." *Journal of Law and Economics* 20 (April):223-26.

Davis, K.C. 1969. "A New Approach to Delegation." *University of Chicago Law Review* 36 (Summer):713-33.

Davis, M.G. 1944. "Regulation by Formula—New Jersey Adjustment Plan." *Public Utilities Fortnightly* 33 (25 May):681-85.

DeAlessi, L. 1974a. "Managerial Tenure under Private and Government Owner- ship in the Electric Power Industry." *Journal of Political Economy* 82 (May-June):645-53.

_____. 1974b. "An Economic Analysis of Government Ownership and Regulation: Theory and the Evidence from the Electric Power Industry." *Public Choice* 19 (Fall):1-42.

_____. 1975. "Some Effects of Ownership on the Wholesale Prices of Electric Power." *Economic Inquiry* 13 (December):526-38.

_____. 1977. "Ownership and Peak-load Pricing in the Electric Power Industry." *Quarterly Review of Economics and Business* 17 (Winter):7-26.

Demsetz, H. 1968. "Why Regulate Utilities?" *Journal of Law and Economics* 11 (April):55-65.

_____. 1971. "On the Regulation of Industry: Reply." *Journal of Political Economy* 79 (March-April):356-63.

H.J. DePodwin Associates, Inc. 1974. *Regulation of Utility Performance: A Proposed Alternative to Rate Base Regulation.* Report to the U.S. Federal Communications Commission, June.

Doades, R. 1978. "The Mentality of Management Audits." *Public Utilities Fortnightly* 101 (16 February):25-28.

Domar, E.D. 1974. "Optimal Compensation of a Socialist Manager." *Quarterly Journal of Economics* 88 (February):1-18.

_____. 1975. "The Effects of a Managerial Bonus (or a Subsidy) on the Quality and Quantity of Output." Manuscript. Cambridge: Massachusetts Institute of Technology.

Donahue, C. 1971. "Lawyers, Economists, and the Regulated Industries: Thoughts on Professional Roles Inspired by Some Recent Economic Literature." *Michigan Law Review* 70 (November):195-220.

Downs, A. 1967. *Inside Bureaucracy.* Boston: Little, Brown.

Drèze, J.H. 1976. "Some Theory of Labor Management and Participation." *Econometrica* 44 (November):1125-40.

Drèze, J.H., and K.P. Hagen. 1978. "Choice of Product Quality: Equilibrium and Efficiency." *Econometrica* 46 (May):493-514.

Dunham, A.O. 1955. *The Industrial Revolution in France.* New York: Exposition Press.

Dusansky, R., and J. Walsh. 1976. "Separability, Welfare Economics and the Theory of Second Best." *Review of Economic Studies* 43 (February):49-51.

Eckert, R.D. 1973. "On the Incentives of Regulators: The Case of Taxicabs." *Public Choice* 14 (Spring):83-99.

Edwards, F.R. 1977. "Managerial Objectives in Regulated Industries: Expense-preference Behavior in Banking." *Journal of Political Economy* 85 (February):147-62.

"The Effects of the English Tramways Act." 1895. *Street Railway Journal* 9 (February):99-100.

Elgen, R.E. 1940, "Profit Sharing, the Key to Regulatory Success." *Public Utilities Fortnightly* 25 (20 June):787-96.

English, H.E. 1965. "Other Policies Affecting Competition." In T.N. Brewis et al., eds. *Canadian Economic Policy*, rev. ed. Toronto: Macmillan of Canada.

Farris, M.T., and R.J. Sampson. 1973. *Public Utilities: Regulation, Management and Ownership.* Boston: Houghton Mifflin.

Faulhaber, G.R. 1975. "Cross-subsidization: Pricing in Public Enterprises." *American Economic Review* 65 (December):966-77.

"Features of the New Paris Franchise." 1921. *Electric Railway Journal* 57 (7 May):847-49.

Feldstein, M.S. 1972a. "Distributional Equity and the Optimal Structure of Public Prices." *American Economic Review* 62 (March):32-36.

_____. 1972b. "Equity and Efficiency in Public Pricing." *Quarterly Journal of Economics* 86 (May):175-87.

Feugère, E. 1918. "L'augmentation du prix du vente du gaz." *L'Economiste Français*, 30 March, pp. 390-92.

Firth, R.E. 1962. *Public Power in Nebraska: A Report on State Ownership.* Lincoln: University of Nebraska Press.

Foster, C.D. 1971. *Politics, Finance and the Role of Economics.* London: Allen & Unwin.

Foster, J.R. 1934. "The Public Utility Franchise in Missouri." *University of Missouri Studies* 9 (October):1-83.

_____. 1944. "Rationale of the New Jersey Adjustment Plan." *Public Utilities Fortnightly* 33 (25 May):673-80.

Foster, J.R., and M.G. Davis. 1944 "Structure and Mechanics of the New Jersey Adjustment Plan." *Public Utilities Fortnightly* 33 (25 May):666-72.

Friedman, M. 1962. *Capitalism and Freedom.* Chicago: University of Chicago Press.

Friedman, W.G., and J.F. Garner, eds. 1970. *Government Enterprise: A Comparative Study.* New York: Columbia University Press.

Friendly, H.J. 1962. *The Federal Administrative Agencies: The Need for Better Definition of Standards.* Cambridge: Harvard University Press.

Garfield, P.J., and W.F. Lovejoy. 1964. *Public Utility Economics*. Englewood Cliffs, N.J.: Prentice-Hall.

Glaeser, M.G. 1927. *Outlines of Public Utility Economics*. New York: Macmillan.

_____. 1957. *Public Utilities in American Capitalism*. New York: Macmillan.

Goldberg, V.P. 1976a. "Toward an Expanded Economic Theory of Contract." *Journal of Economic Issues* 10 (March):45-61.

_____. 1976b. "Regulation and Administered Contracts." *Bell Journal of Economics* 7 (Autumn):426-48.

_____. 1977. "Protecting the Right to be Served by Public Utilities." In R.O. Zerbe, ed. *Research in Law and Economics*. Greenwich, Conn.: JAI Press.

Goldschmidt, Y., and K. Admon. 1977. *Profit Measurement During Inflation*. New York: John Wiley.

Gordon, L. 1938. *The Public Corporation in Great Britain*. London: Oxford University Press.

Gouldner, A.W. 1954. *Patterns of Industrial Bureaucracy*. New York: Free Press.

Gray, H.M. 1940. "The Passing of the Public Utility Concept." *Journal of Land and Public Utility Economics* 16 (February):8-20.

_____. 1956. Testimony in U.S. Congress. House. Committee on the Judiciary. *Monopoly Problems in Regulated Industries*. Hearings before the Antitrust Subcommittee of the Committee on the Judiciary. 84th Cong., 2d sess., pp. 77-81.

_____. 1976. "The Sharing of Economic Power in Public Utility Industries." In W. Sichel, ed. *Salvaging Public Utility Regulation*. Lexington, Mass.: D.C. Heath.

Gray, J.H. 1900. "The Gas Commission of Massachusetts." *Quarterly Journal of Economics* 14:509-35.

Hagerman, R.L., and B.T. Ratchford. 1978. "Some Determinants of Allowed Rates of Return on Equity to Electric Utilities." *Bell Journal of Economics* 9 (Spring):46-55.

Hall, G.R. 1968. "Defense Procurement and Public Utility Regulation." *Land Economics* 44 (May):185-96.

Harberger, A.C. 1971. "Three Basic Postulates for Applied Welfare Economics: An Interpretive Essay." *Journal of Economic Literature* 9 (September): 785-97.

Harbeson, R.W. 1944. "The 'New Jersey Plan' of Rate Regulation." *Journal of Business* 17 (October):220-30.

Hardies, M.A. 1974. "The Inflation Dilemma and Legal Possibilities." *Public Utilities Fortnightly* 94 (29 August):23-27.

"Has Paris Solved the 'Incentive' Problem in Railway-City Contracts?" 1921. *Electric Railway Journal* 57 (7 May):840-41.

Hatta, T. 1977. "A Theory of Piecemeal Policy Recommendations." *Review of Economic Studies* 44 (February):1-22.

Hellman, R. 1972. *Competition in the Electric Power Industry.* New York: Praeger.

Henderson, A.M. 1947. "The Pricing of Public Utility Undertakings." *Manchester School* 15 (September):223-50.

Hendricks, W. 1977. "Regulation and Labor Earnings." *Bell Journal of Economics* 8 (Autumn):483-96.

Hendriksen, E.S. 1977. *Accounting Theory.* 3d ed. Homewood, Ill.: R.D. Irwin.

Higgins, E.E. 1900. "Some Differences Between American and British City Transportation Methods." *Street Railway Journal* 16 (7 April):357-60.

Hilton, G.W. 1972. "The Basic Behavior of Regulatory Commissions." *American Economic Review* 62 (May):47-54.

Hirschfeld, A. 1973. "The Role of Public Enterprise in the French Economy: Origin and Evolution." *Annals of Public and Cooperative Economy* 44 (July-September):255-69.

Hirshleifer, J. 1976. "Toward a More General Theory of Regulation: Comment." *Journal of Law and Economics* 19 (August):241-44.

Holcombe, A.N. 1911. "The Régie Intéressée du Gaz at Paris." *Quarterly Journal of Economics* 25 (August):742-46.

Hull, P. 1977. "Control Type and the Market for Corporate Control in Large U.S. Corporations." *Journal of Industrial Economics* 25 (June):259-73.

Hunter, M.H. 1917. "Early Regulation of Public Service Corporations." *American Economic Review* 7 (September):569-81.

Huntington, S.P. 1952. "The Marasmus of the ICC: The Commission, the Railroads, and the Public Interest." *Yale Law Journal* 61 (April):467-509.

Huntington, W.C., trans. 1922. "The French Transportation Act of 1921." Trade Information Bulletin No. 3, Transportation Division, Bureau of Foreign and Domestic Commerce, U.S. Department of Commerce. Washington, D.C.: U.S. Government Printing Office.

Hyman, L.S. 1975. "Rate Cases in 1970-1974: A Quantitative Examination." *Public Utilities Fortnightly* 96 (6 November):22-30.

Iulo, W. 1961. *Electric Utilities—Costs and Performance.* Pullman, Wash.: Washington State University Press.

Jackson, R. 1969. "Regulation and Electric Utility Rate Levels." *Land Economics* 45 (August):372-76.

Jaffe, L.B. 1954. "The Effective Limits of the Administrative Process: A Re-evaluation." *Harvard Law Review* 67 (May):1105-35.

Jaffee, B.L. 1972. "Incentive Pricing and Utility Regulation: Comment." *Quarterly Journal of Economics* 86 (February):143-44.

Jones, W.K. 1967. *Regulated Industries.* Brooklyn: Foundation Press.

———. 1976. "The General Revenue Proceeding and the Need for Regulatory Change." Paper presented at the Future Planning Conference of the Federal Communications Commission, Washington, D.C., July.

Jordan, W.A. 1972. "Producer Protection, Prior Market Structure, and the

Effects of Government Regulation." *Journal of Law and Economics* 15 (April):151-76.

Joskow, P.L. 1972. "The Determination of the Allowed Rate of Return in a Formal Regulatory Hearing." *Bell Journal of Economics and Management Science* 3 (Autumn):632-44.

_____. 1973. "Pricing Decisions of Regulated Firms: A Behavioral Approach." *Bell Journal of Economics and Management Science* 4 (Spring): 118-40.

_____. 1974. "Inflation and Environmental Concern: Structural Change in the Process of Public Utility Price Regulation." *Journal of Law and Economics* 17 (October):291-328.

_____. 1976. "Contributions to the Theory of Marginal Cost Pricing." *Bell Journal of Economics* 7 (Spring):197-206.

_____. 1977. "Electric Utility Rate Structures in the United States: Some Recent Developments." Paper presented at the Seventh Michigan Conference on Public Utility Economics, Detroit.

_____. Forthcoming. "Regulatory Activities by Government Agencies." In W. Starbuck, ed., *Handbook of Organizational Design*. New York: Elsevier.

Joskow, P.L., and P.W. MacAvoy. 1975. "Regulation and the Financial Condition of the Electric Power Companies in the 1970's." *American Economic Review* 65 (May):295-301.

Joskow, P.L., and R.G. Noll. 1978. "Regulation in Theory and Practice: An Overview." Working Paper No. 218, Department of Economics, Massachusetts Institute of Technology, April.

Kahn, A.E. 1970. *The Economics of Regulation, Vol. 1: Principles*. New York: John Wiley.

_____. 1971. *The Economics of Regulation, Vol. 2: Institutional Issues*. New York: John Wiley.

_____. 1975. "Between Theory and Practice: Reflections of a Neophyte Public Utility Regulator." *Public Utilities Fortnightly* 95 (2 January):29-33.

Kahn, A.E., and C.A. Zielinski. 1976a. "New Rate Structures in Telecommunications." *Public Utilities Fortnightly* 97 (25 March):19-24.

_____. 1976b. "Proper Objectives in Telephone Rate Structuring." *Public Utilities Fortnightly* 97 (8 April):20-27.

Kawamata, K. 1977. "Price Distortion and the Second Best Optimum." *Review of Economic Studies* 44 (February):23-30.

Kendrick, J.W. 1975. "Efficiency Incentives and Cost Factors in Public Utility Automatic Revenue Adjustment Clauses." *Bell Journal of Economics* 6 (Spring):299-313.

Kennedy, T.E. 1975. "Incentive Pricing and Utility Regulation: A Comment." *Quarterly Journal of Economics* 86 (February):311-13.

Keran, M.W. 1976. "Inflation, Regulation, and Utility Stock Prices." *Bell Journal of Economics* 7 (Spring):268-80.

King, C.L., ed. 1912a. *The Regulation of Municipal Utilities.* New York: D. Appleton.

_____. 1912b. "The Need for Public Utility Commissions." In C.L. King, ed. *The Regulation of Municipal Utilities.* New York: D. Appleton.

_____. 1912c. "State versus Municipal Utility Commissions." In C.L. King, ed. *The Regulation of Municipal Utilities.* New York: D. Appleton.

Klass, M.W., and W.G. Shepherd, eds. 1976. *Regulation and Entry.* East Lansing, Mich.: Institute of Public Utilities, Michigan State University.

Klevorick, A.K. 1973. "The Behavior of a Firm Subject to Stochastic Regulatory Review." *Bell Journal of Economics and Management Science* 4 (Spring): 57-88.

_____. 1974. "The Behavior of a Firm Subject to Stochastic Regulatory Review: Correction." *Bell Journal of Economics and Management Science* 5 (Autumn):713-14.

Kolko, G. 1965. *Railroads and Regulation.* Princeton: Princeton University Press.

Koller, R.H. 1973. "Why Regulate Utilities? To Control Price Discrimination." *Journal of Law and Economics* 16 (April):191-92.

Konopnicki, M. 1971. "Some Aspects of the Co-operative Movement in Latin America." *Annals of Public and Cooperative Economy* 42 (July-September):229-56.

Lalumière, P. 1975. "Note sur une expérience de financement privé des investissements publics: Les Sociétés Agréés pour le Financement des Télécommunications." *Revue de Science Financière* 67:617-47.

Landis, J.M. 1961. "Perspectives on the Administrative Process." *Administrative Law Review* 14:66-70.

Latimer, H.A. 1974. "The Cost and Efficiency Revenue Adjustment Clause." *Public Utilities Fortnightly* 91 (15 August):19-24.

Lee, D.R. 1977. "Discrimination and Efficiency in the Production of Public Goods." *Journal of Law and Economics* 20 (October):403-20.

Lefranc, G. 1930. "The French Railroads, 1823-1842." *Journal of Economic and Business History* 2 (February):299-331.

Leibenstein, H. 1966. "Allocative Efficiency vs. 'X Efficiency.'" *American Economic Review* 56 (June):392-415.

Leland, H.E. 1974. "Regulation of Natural Monopolies and the Fair Rate of Return." *Bell Journal of Economics and Management Science* 5 (Spring): 3-15.

Leland, H.E., and R. Meyer. 1976. "Monopoly Pricing Structures with Imperfect Discrimination." *Bell Journal of Economics* 7 (Autumn):449-62.

Lent, G.E. 1951. "Excess-Profits Taxation in the United States." *Journal of Political Economy* 59 (December):481-97.

Lewis, W.D. 1898. "The Lease of the Philadelphia Gas Works." *Quarterly Journal of Economics* 12:209-24.

Lindsay, C.M. 1976. "A Theory of Government Enterprise." *Journal of Political Economy* 84 (October):1061-78.

Lipsey, R.G., and K. Lancaster. 1956. "The General Theory of Second Best." *Review of Economic Studies* 24 (December):11-32.

Littlechild, S.C. 1970. "A Game-Theoretic Approach to Public Utility Pricing." *Western Economic Journal* 8 (June):162-66.

_____. 1975. "Common Costs, Fixed Charges, Clubs and Games." *Review of Economic Studies* 42 (January):117-24.

Littlechild, S.C., and J.J. Rousseau. 1975. "Pricing Policy of a U.S. Telephone Company." *Journal of Public Economics* 4:35-56.

Locklin, D.P. 1966. *Economics of Transportation,* 6th ed. Homewood, Ill.: R.D. Irwin.

Loehman, E., and A. Whinston. 1971. "A New Theory of Pricing and Decision-Making for Public Investment." *Bell Journal of Economics and Management Science* 2 (Autumn):606-25.

_____. 1974. "An Axiomatic Approach to Cost Allocation for Public Investment." *Public Finance Quarterly* 2 (April):236-51.

Lowi, T.J. 1969. *The End of Liberalism: Ideology, Policy, and the Crisis of Public Authority.* New York: W.W. Norton.

Lowry, E.D. 1973. "Justification for Regulation: The Case for Natural Monopoly." *Public Utilities Fortnightly* 92 (8 November):17-23.

Maass, A. 1951. *Muddy Waters.* Cambridge: Harvard University Press.

Macaulay, S. 1963. "Non-Contractual Relations in Business: A Preliminary Study." *American Sociological Review* 28:55-70.

MacAvoy, P.W. 1965. *The Economic Effects of Regulation.* Cambridge: MIT Press.

_____, ed. 1970a. *The Crisis of the Regulatory Commissions.* New York: W.W. Norton.

_____. 1970b. "The Effectiveness of the Federal Power Commission." *Bell Journal of Economics and Management Science* 1 (Autumn):271-303.

_____. 1971a. "The Regulation-Induced Shortage of Natural Gas." *Journal of Law and Economics* 14 (April):167-200.

_____. 1971b. "The Formal Work-Product of the Federal Power Commission." *Bell Journal of Economics and Management Science* 2 (Spring):379-95.

_____. 1978. "The Present Condition of Regulated Enterprise." Working Paper No. 5, Series C, School of Organization and Management, Yale University, April.

McCall, J.J. 1970. "The Simple Economics of Incentive Contracting." *American Economic Review* 60 (December):837-46.

McConnell, G. 1966. *Private Power and American Democracy.* New York: A.A. Knopf.

McCraw, T.K. 1975. "Regulation in America: A Review Article." *Business History Review,* 49 (Summer):159-83.

McKay, D. 1976. "Has the A-J Effect Been Empirically Verified?" Social Science Working Paper No. 132, California Institute of Technology.

McKie, J.W. 1970. "Regulation and the Free Market: The Problem of Boundaries." *Bell Journal of Economics and Management Science* 1 (Spring):6-26.

Macneil, I.R. 1974. "The Many Futures of Contract." *Southern California Law Review* 47 (May):691-816.

Mann, P.C. 1974. "User Power and Electricity Rates." *Journal of Law and Economics* 17 (October):433-44.

Mann, P.C., and E.J. Seifried. 1972. "Pricing in the Case of Publicly Owned Electric Utilities." *Quarterly Review of Economics and Business* 21 (Summer):77-89.

Manne, H.G. 1965. "Mergers and the Market for Corporate Control." *Journal of Political Economy* 73 (April):110-20.

Marshall, J.M. 1976. "Moral Hazard." *American Economic Review* 66 (December):880-90.

Massel, M.S. 1961. "The Regulatory Process." *Law and Contemporary Problems* 26:181-202.

"The Metropolitan Railway of Paris." 1900. *Street Railway Journal* 16 (1 September):797-806.

Meyer, H.R. 1905. *Government Regulation of Railway Rates.* New York: Macmillan.

Meyer, R.A. 1975. "Publicly Owned Versus Privately Owned Utilities: A Policy Choice." *Review of Economics and Statistics* 57 (November):391-99.

Mill, J.S. 1848. *Principles of Political Economy.* As reprinted by W.J. Ashley, ed. New York: Augustus M. Kelley, 1965.

Moore, F.T. 1967. "Incentive Contracts." In S. Enke, ed. *Defense Management.* Englewood Cliffs, N.J.: Prentice-Hall.

Moore, T.G. 1971. "The Effectiveness of Regulation of Electric Utility Prices." *Southern Economic Journal* 36 (April):365-75.

Morgan, C.S. 1923. *Regulation and the Management of Public Utilities.* Boston: Houghton Mifflin.

Munk, K.J. 1977. "Optimal Public Sector Pricing Taking the Distributional Aspect into Consideration." *Quarterly Journal of Economics* 91 (November):639-50.

Musolf, L.D. 1959. *Public Ownership and Accountability.* Cambridge: Harvard University Press.

Myers, G. 1900. *The History of Public Franchises in New York City.* New York: Reform Club Committee on Public Affairs.

Myers, S.C. 1972. "The Application of Finance Theory to Public Utility Rate Cases." *Bell Journal of Economics and Management Science* 3 (Spring): 58-97.

————. 1976. "Rate of Return Regulation—A Critical Appraisal." Paper presented at the Future Planning Conference of the Federal Communications Commission, Washington, D.C., July.

Nash, L.R. 1925. *The Economics of Public Utilities.* New York: McGraw-Hill.

Nebraska Legislative Council. 1974. *Nebraska Blue Book: 1974-75.* Lincoln.

Neuberg, L.G. 1977. "Two Issues in the Municipal Ownership of Electric Power Distribution Systems." *Bell Journal of Economics* 8 (Spring):303-23.

"A New Federal Hand on Electricity Rates." 1977. *Business Week,* 28 February, pp. 29-30.

"New Franchise Conditions in Paris." 1910. *Electric Railway Journal* 38 (1 October):505-07.

Nguyen, D.T., and G.J. Macgregor-Ried. 1977. "Interdependent Demands, Regulatory Constraint and Peak Load Pricing." *Journal of Industrial Economics* 25 (June):275-93.

Niskanen, W.A. 1971. *Bureaucracy and Representative Government.* Chicago: Aldine-Atherton.

Noll, R.G. 1971a. "The Behavior of Regulatory Agencies." *Review of Social Economy* 29 (May):15-19.

_____. 1971b. *Reforming Regulation: An Evaluation of the Ash Council Proposals.* Washington: Brookings Institution.

Normand, J. 1910. "L'exploitation du gaz et l'emprunt de 180 millions." *L'Economiste Français,* 26 March, pp. 152-54.

_____. 1916. "Les répercussions économiques de la guerre sur les deux grandes compagnies l'éclairage: Gaz et Electricité." *L'Economiste Français,* 29 July, pp. 152-54.

O'Brien, T.R. 1938. *British Experiments in Public Ownership and Control.* New York: W.W. Norton.

Okun, A.M. 1975. *Equality and Efficiency: The Big Tradeoff.* Washington, D.C.: Brookings Institution.

Owen, B., and R. Braeutigam. 1978. *The Regulation Game: Strategic Use of the Administrative Process.* Cambridge, Mass.: Ballinger.

Panzar, J.C., and R.D. Willig. 1977a. "Free Entry and the Sustainability of Natural Monopoly." *Bell Journal of Economics* 8 (Spring):1-22.

_____. 1977b. "Economies of Scale in Multi-Output Production." *Quarterly Journal of Economics* 91 (August):481-94.

Parris, H.W. 1965. *Government and the Railways in Nineteenth-century Britain.* London: Routledge & Kegan Paul.

Pashigian, B.P. 1976. "Consequences and Causes of Public Ownership of Urban Transit Facilities." *Journal of Political Economy* 84 (December):1239-60.

Pauly, M.V. 1967. "Clubs, Commonality, and the Core: An Integration of Game Theory and the Theory of Public Goods." *Economica* 44 (August):314-24.

_____. 1970. "Cores and Clubs." *Public Choice* 9 (Fall):53-65.

Payen, E. 1897. "Les moyens transports en commun a Paris." *L'Economiste Français,* 20 March, pp. 364-66.

Peacock, A.T., and C.K. Rowley. 1972. "Welfare Economics and the Public Regulation of Natural Monopoly." *Journal of Public Economics* 1 (August): 227-44.

Pegrum, D.F. 1940. "The Public Corporation as a Regulatory Device." *Land Economics* 16 (August):337-43.

_____. 1965. *Public Regulation of Business.* Rev. ed. Homewood, Ill.: R.D. Irwin.

Pellerzi, L.M. 1974. "A Conceptual View of the Regulatory Process." *California Management Review* 16 (Spring):83-86.

Peltzman, S. 1971. "Pricing in Public Enterprises: Electric Utilities in the United States." *Journal of Law and Economics* 14 (April):109-48.

_____. 1976. "Toward a More General Theory of Regulation." *Journal of Law and Economics* 19 (August):211-40.

Petersen, H.C. 1975. "An Empirical Test of Regulatory Effects." *Bell Journal of Economics* 6 (Spring):111-26.

Pettway, R.H. 1978. "On the Use of β in Regulatory Proceedings: An Empirical Examination." *Bell Journal of Economics* 9 (Spring):239-48.

Phillips, A. 1974. "Research on Rate Regulation in the Energy Industries." In H.H. Landsberg et al., eds. *Energy and the Social Sciences: An Examination of Research Needs.* Washington, D.C.: Resources for the Future.

Phillips, C.F. 1969. *The Economics of Regulation.* Rev. ed. Homewood, Ill.: R.D. Irwin.

Pigou, A.C. 1920. *The Economics of Welfare.* London: Macmillan.

Posner, R.A. 1969. "Natural Monopoly and Its Regulation." *Stanford Law Review* 21 (February):548-643.

_____. 1970. "Natural Monopoly and Its Regulation: A Reply." *Stanford Law Review* 22 (February):540-46.

_____. 1971. "Taxation by Regulation." *Bell Journal of Economics and Management Science* 2 (Spring):22-50.

_____. 1972. "The Appropriate Scope of Regulation in the Cable Television Industry." *Bell Journal of Economics and Management Science* 3 (Spring): 98-129.

_____. 1974. "Theories of Economic Regulation." *Bell Journal of Economics and Management Science* 4 (Autumn):335-58.

_____. 1976. *Antitrust Law: An Economic Perspective.* Chicago: University of Chicago Press.

Primeaux, W.J. 1975. "A Reexamination of the Monopoly Market Structure for Electric Utilities." In A. Phillips, ed. *Promoting Competition in Regulated Markets.* Washington, D.C.: Brookings Institution.

Pryke, R. 1971. *Public Enterprise in Practice.* London: MacGibbon & Kee.

Pryor, F.L. 1976. "Public Ownership: Some Quantitative Dimensions." In W.G. Shepherd et al. *Public Enterprise: Economic Analysis of Theory and Practice.* Lexington, Mass.: D.C. Heath.

Public Power in Nebraska. 1963. Depth Report No. 2, School of Journalism, University of Nebraska, September.

Radner, R. 1968. "Competitive Equilibrium under Uncertainty." *Econometrica* 36 (January):31-58.

Raffalovich, A. 1916. "L'avance de l'heure legale: Le prix du gaz." *L'Economiste Français*, 10 June, pp. 795-96.

Ram-Mohan, S., V. Salas, and A. Whinston. 1977. "An Automatic Price Adjustment for a Regulated Firm." *Applied Economics* 9 (September): 243-52.

Ramsey, F. 1927. "A Contribution to the Theory of Taxation." *Economic Journal* 37 (March):47-61.

"Recent Cases on Measures of Value." 1978. *Public Utilities Fortnightly* 101 (2 March):52-54.

Renshaw, E. 1958. "Utility Regulation: A Re-examination." *Journal of Business* 31 (October):335-43.

_____. 1978. "A Note on Cost and Efficiency Revenue Adjustment Clauses." *Public Utilities Fortnightly* 101 (5 January):37-38.

Robinson, G.O. 1970. "The Making of Administrative Policy: Another Look at Rulemaking and Adjudication and Administrative Procedure Reform." *University of Pennsylvania Law Review* 118 (February):485-539.

Robinson, J. 1933. *The Economics of Imperfect Competition.* London: Macmillan.

Robson, W.A., ed. 1937. *Public Enterprise: Developments in Social Ownership and Control in Great Britain.* London: Allen & Unwin.

_____. 1962. *Nationalized Industry and Public Ownership.* 2d ed. London: Allen & Unwin.

Ross, S.A. 1973. "The Economic Theory of Agency: The Principal's Problem." *American Economic Review* 63 (May):134-39.

Rowe, L.S. 1907. "The Relation of the City of Philadelphia to the Gas Supply." In *Municipal and Private Operation of Public Utilities*, part 2, vol. 1. New York: National Civic Federation.

Rural Electrification Administration. 1976a. *1975 Annual Statistical Report: Rural Telephone Borrowers.* Washington, D.C.: U.S. Department of Agriculture.

_____. 1976b. *1975 Annual Statistical Report: Rural Electric Borrowers.* Washington, D.C.: U.S. Department of Agriculture.

Russell, M., and R.B. Shelton. 1974. "A Model of Regulatory Agency Behavior." *Public Choice* 20 (Winter):47-62.

Sabatier, P. 1975. "Social Movements and Regulatory Agencies: Toward a More Adequate—and Less Pessimistic—Theory of 'Clientele Capture.' " *Policy Sciences* 6:301-42.

Samuelson, P.A. 1954. "The Pure Theory of Public Expenditure." *Review of Economics and Statistics* 36 (November):387-89.

San Pedro, J. 1971. "Electricity Co-operatives in the Argentine Republic." *Review of International Cooperation* 64:174-80.

Sargent, H. 1978. "Fishbowl Planning in Management Audits." *Public Utilities Fortnightly* 101 (16 March):22-25.

Scherer, C.R. 1977. *Estimating Electric Power System Marginal Costs.* Amsterdam: North-Holland.

Scherer, F.M. 1964. *The Weapons Acquisition Process: Economic Incentives.* Boston: Division of Research, Graduate School of Business Administration, Harvard University.

_____. 1970. *Industrial Market Structure and Economic Performance.* Chicago: Rand McNally.

Schiffel, D. 1975. "Electric Utility Regulation: An Overview of Fuel Adjustment Clauses." *Public Utilities Fortnightly* 95 (19 June):23-31.

Schmalensee, R. 1974. "Estimating the Costs and Benefits of Utility Regulation." *Quarterly Review of Economics and Business* 14 (Summer):51-64.

_____. 1977. "Income Distributional Concerns in Regulatory Policy-making: Discussion." Paper presented at the National Bureau of Economic Research Conference on Public Regulation, Washington, D.C., December.

_____. 1978. "A Note on Economies of Scale and Natural Monopoly in the Distribution of Public Utility Services." *Bell Journal of Economics* 9 (Spring):270-76.

Schwartz, D.S. 1976. "Regulatory Change in Non-Communications Industries." Paper presented at the Future Planning Conference of the Federal Communications Commission, Washington, D.C., July.

Schwert, G.W. 1977. "Public Regulation of National Securities Exchanges: A Test of the Capture Hypothesis." *Bell Journal of Economics* 8 (Spring): 128-50.

Seidman, H. 1970. *Politics, Position, and Power: The Dynamics of Federal Organization.* New York: Oxford University Press.

Selznick, P. 1957. *Leadership in Administration: A Sociological Interpretation.* New York: Harper & Row.

Sheahan, J.B. 1976. "Experience with Public Enterprise in France and Italy." In W.G. Shepherd et al. *Public Enterprise: Economic Analysis of Theory and Practice.* Lexington, Mass.: D.C. Heath.

_____. 1977. "Public Enterprise: Ideas from West European Experience." Paper presented at the American Economic Association Meeting, New York, December.

Shepherd, W.G. 1965. *Economic Performance under Public Ownership: British Fuel and Power.* New Haven: Yale University Press.

_____. 1966a. "Marginal Cost Pricing in American Utilities." *Southern Economic Journal* 33 (July):58-70.

_____. 1966b. "Utility Growth and Profits under Regulation." In W.G. Shepherd and T.G. Gies, eds. *Utility Regulation: New Directions in Theory and Policy.* New York: Random House.

_____. 1970. "Regulation and Its Alternatives." *Stanford Law Review* 22 (February):529-39.

_____. 1973. "Entry as a Substitute for Regulation." *American Economic Review* 63 (May):98-105.

_____. 1975. *The Treatment of Market Power*. New York: Columbia University Press.

_____. 1976a. "General Conditions of Entry." In M.W. Klass and W.G. Shepherd, eds. *Regulation and Entry*. East Lansing, Mich.: Institute of Public Utilities, Michigan State University.

_____. 1976b. "Objectives, Types, and Accountability." In W.G. Shepherd et al. *Public Enterprise: Economic Analysis of Theory and Practice*. Lexington, Mass.: D.C. Heath.

_____. 1976c. "British and United States Experience." In W.G. Shepherd et al. *Public Enterprise: Economic Analysis of Theory and Practice*. Lexington, Mass.: D.C. Heath.

Shepherd, W.G., et al. 1976. *Public Enterprise: Economic Analysis of Theory and Practice*. Lexington, Mass.: D.C. Heath.

Sherman, R. 1967a. "Club Subscriptions for Public Transport Passengers." *Journal of Transport Economics and Policy* 1 (September):237-42.

_____. 1967b. "A Private Ownership Bias in Transit Choice." *American Economic Review* 57 (December):1211-17.

_____. 1970. "The Design of Public Utility Institutions." *Land Economics* 46 (February):51-58.

_____. 1974. *The Economics of Industry*. Boston: Little, Brown.

_____. 1976. "Curing Regulatory Bias in U.S. Public Utilities." *Journal of Economics and Business* 29 (Fall):1-9.

Simon, H.A. 1957. *Models of Man*. New York: John Wiley.

Slesinger, R.E. 1971. "The Need to Modify Current Regulatory Processes." *Public Utilities Fortnightly* 88 (8 July):38-40.

Smiley, R. 1976. "Tender Offers, Transactions Costs, and the Theory of the Firm." *Review of Economics and Statistics* 58 (February):22-32.

Smiley, R., and W.H. Green. 1978. "Determinants of Effectiveness of Electric Utility Regulation." Mimeographed. Ithaca, N.Y.: Cornell University, August.

Smith, L. 1978. "State Utility Commissioners—1978." *Public Utilities Fortnightly* 101 (16 February):9-15.

Smithson, C.W. 1978. "The Degree of Regulation and the Monopoly Firm: Further Empirical Evidence." *Southern Economic Journal* 44 (January):568-80.

Solomon, E. 1970. "Alternative Rate of Return Concepts and Their Implications for Utility Regulation." *Bell Journal of Economics and Management Science* 1 (Spring):65-81.

Sorenson, J.R., J.T. Tschirhart, and A.B. Whinston. 1976. "A Game Theoretic Approach to Peak Load Pricing." *Bell Journal of Economics* 7 (Autumn):497-520.

Spann, R.M. 1974. "Rate of Return Regulation and Efficiency in Production: An Empirical Test of the Averch-Johnson Thesis." *Bell Journal of Economics and Management Science* 5 (Spring):38-52.

Spann, R.M., and E.W. Erickson. 1970. "The Economics of Railroading: The Beginning of Cartelization and Regulation." *Bell Journal of Economics and Management Science* 1 (Autumn):227-44.

Spence, A.M. 1975. "Monopoly, Quality, and Regulation." *Bell Journal of Economics* 6 (Autumn):417-29.

_____. 1976. "Product Differentiation and Welfare." *American Economic Review* 66 (May):407-14.

Spengler, J.J. 1969. "Evolution of Public-Utility Regulation: Economists and Other Determinants." *South African Journal of Economics* 37 (March): 3-31.

Spiro, P.S. 1978. "Alternative Methods of Inflation Adjustment in Utility Rate-Making." *Public Utilities Fortnightly* 101 (2 March):30-31.

Starrett, D. 1978. "Marginal Cost Pricing of Recursive Lumpy Investments." *Review of Economic Studies* 45 (June):215-27.

Stauffer, T.R. 1971. "The Measurement of Corporate Rates of Return: A Generalized Formulation." *Bell Journal of Economics and Management Science* 2 (Autumn):434-69.

Stelzer, I.M. 1969. "Rate Base Regulation and Some Alternatives." *Public Utilities Fortnightly* 84 (25 September):17-25.

Stewart, R. 1975. "The Reformation of American Administrative Law." *Harvard Law Review* 88 (June):1667-813.

Stigler, G.J. 1968. *The Organization of Industry.* Homewood, Ill.: R.D. Irwin.

_____. 1971. "The Theory of Economic Regulation." *Bell Journal of Economics and Management Science* 2 (Spring):3-21.

Stigler, G.J., and C. Friedland. 1962. "What Can Regulators Regulate? The Case of Electricity." *Journal of Law and Economics* 5 (October):1-16.

"Still Trying to Make the Post Office Work." 1977. *Business Week,* 21 March, pp. 133-41.

Strauss, R.P., and K.L. Wertz. 1976. "The Impact of Municipal Electric Profits on Local Public Finance." *National Tax Journal* 29 (March):22-30.

Stromberg, H. 1970. "The Public Corporation in Sweden." In W.G. Friedman and J.F. Garner, eds. *Government Enterprise: A Comparative Study.* New York: Columbia University Press.

Swidler, J.C. 1970. "Comments on the Case for Deregulation." *Stanford Law Review* 22 (February):519-28.

Telser, L.G. 1969. "On the Regulation of Industry: A Note." *Journal of Political Economy* 77 (November-December):937-52.

_____. 1971a. "On the Regulation of Industry: Rejoinder." *Journal of Political Economy* 79 (March-April):364-65.

_____. 1971b. "On the Regulation of Industry: A Correction." *Journal of Political Economy* 79 (July-August):932.

Telson, M.L. 1975. "The Economics of Alternative Levels of Reliability for Electric Power Generation Systems." *Bell Journal of Economics* 6 (Autumn):679-94.

Thomas, N.C. 1971. "Politics, Structure, and Personnel in Administrative Regulation." *Virginia Law Review* 57 (September):1033-68.

Thompson, C.W., and W.R. Smith. 1941. *Public Utility Economics.* New York: McGraw-Hill.

Tideman, T.N., and G. Tullock. 1976. "A New and Superior Process for Making Social Choices." *Journal of Political Economy* 84 (December):1145-60.

Tinbergen, J. 1956. *Economic Policy: Principles and Design.* Amsterdam: North-Holland.

Trebing, H.M. 1960a. "What's Wrong with Commission Regulation? Part I." *Public Utilities Fortnightly* 65 (12 May):660-70.

_____. 1960b. "What's Wrong with Commission Regulation? Part II." *Public Utilities Fortnightly* 65 (26 May):738-50.

_____. 1963. "Towards an Incentive System of Regulation." *Public Utilities Fortnightly* 72 (18 July):22-37.

_____. 1974. "Realism and Relevance in Public Utility Regulation." *Journal of Economic Issues* 8 (June):209-33.

_____. 1976a. "The Chicago School versus Public Utility Regulation." *Journal of Economic Issues* 10 (March):97-126.

_____. 1976b. "Market Structure and Regulatory Reform in the Electric and Gas Utility Industries." In W. Sichel, ed. *Salvaging Public Utility Regulation.* Lexington, Mass.: D.C. Heath.

Treves, G. 1970. "The Public Corporation in Italy." In W.G. Friedman and J.F. Garner, eds. *Government Enterprise: A Comparative Study.* New York: Columbia University Press.

Troxel, E. 1947. *Economics of Public Utilities.* New York: Rinehart.

Tulkens, H. 1976. "The Publicness of Public Enterprise." In W.G. Shepherd et al. *Public Enterprise: Economic Analysis of Theory and Practice.* Lexington, Mass.: D.C. Heath.

Tullock, G. 1975. "The Transitional Gains Trap." *Bell Journal of Economics* 6 (Autumn):671-78.

_____. 1976. "Regulating the Regulators." In S. Pejovick, ed. *Governmental Controls and the Free Market.* College Station: Texas A&M University Press.

Tzoannos, J. 1977. "An Empirical Study of Peak-Load Pricing and Investment Policies of the Domestic Market of Gas in Great Britain." *Applied Economics* 9 (June):133-54.

Ulen, T. 1977. "The ICC as a Cartel Manager: Was It Necessary?" Ph.D. dissertation, Stanford University.

U.S. Congress. 1975. House. Committee on Interstate and Foreign Commerce. *Electric Utility Automatic Fuel Adjustment Clauses.* Report of the Subcommittee on Oversight and Investigations. 94th Cong., 1st sess., October.

U.S. Department of Commerce. 1977. Bureau of the Census. *Statistical Abstract of the United States.* Washington, D.C.: Government Printing Office.

"A Utility's Experiment in Rate-Setting." 1977. *Business Week,* 26 September, p. 84.

Washington Public Utility Districts' Association. N.d. *Laws of the Public Utility Districts: State of Washington.* Seattle.

Washington Public Utility Districts' Association. 1976. *What Is a P.U.D.?* Seattle.

Waverman, L. 1975. "The Regulation of Intercity Telecommunications." In A. Phillips, ed. *Promoting Competition in Regulated Markets.* Washington, D.C.: Brookings Institution.

Weingast, B.R. 1978. "A Positive Model of Public Policy Formulation: The Case of Regulatory Agency Behavior." Working Paper No. 25, Center for the Study of American Business, Washington University, January.

Weintraub, S. 1968. "Rate Making and an Incentive Rate of Return." *Public Utilities Fortnightly* 81 (April):23-33.

Weiss, L.W. 1975. "Antitrust in the Electric Power Industry." In A. Phillips, ed. *Promoting Competition in Regulated Markets.* Washington, D.C.: Brookings Institution.

Welch, F.X. 1963. "Constant Surveillance: A Modern Regulatory Tool." *Villanova Law Review* 8 (Spring):340-61.

Wendel, J. 1976. "Firm-Regulator Interaction with Respect to Firm Cost Reduction Activities." *Bell Journal of Economics* 7 (Autumn):631-40.

Wenders, J.T. 1976. "Peak-Load Pricing in the Electric Utility Industry." *Bell Journal of Economics* 7 (Spring):232-41.

Wenders, J.T., and L.D. Taylor. 1976. "Experiments in Seasonal-Time-of-Day Pricing of Electricity to Residential Users." *Bell Journal of Economics* 7 (Autumn):531-52.

West, D.A., and A.A. Eubank. 1975. "Automatic Cost of Capital Model." *Public Utilities Fortnightly* 95 (22 May):27-32.

"Where Limited Franchises Lead." 1912. *Electric Railway Journal* 39:298.

White, L.D. 1921. "The Origin of Utility Commissions in Massachusetts." *Journal of Political Economy* 29 (March):177-97.

Wilcox, C., and W.G. Shepherd. 1975. *Public Policies Toward Business.* 5th ed. Homewood, Ill.: R.D. Irwin.

Wilcox, D.F. 1910. *Municipal Franchises.* Vol. 1. Chicago: University of Chicago Press.

———. 1911. *Municipal Franchises.* Vol. 2. Chicago: University of Chicago Press.

———. 1912. "Elements of a Constructive Franchise Policy." In C.L. King, ed. *The Regulation of Municipal Utilities.* New York: D. Appleton.

Williamson, O.E. 1967. "The Economics of Defense Contracting: Incentives and Performance." In R.N. McKean, ed. *Issues in Defense Economics.* New York: Columbia University Press.

———. 1970. "Administrative Decision Making and Pricing: Externality and Compensation Analysis Applied." In J. Margolis, ed. *The Analysis of Public Output.* New York: Columbia University Press.

———. 1971. "Administrative Controls and Regulatory Behavior." In H.M. Trebling, ed. *Essays on Public Utility Pricing and Regulation.* East Lansing: Institute of Public Utilities, Michigan State University.

_____. 1973. "Markets and Hierarchies: Some Elementary Considerations." *American Economic Review* 63 (May):316-25.

_____. 1975. *Markets and Hierarchies: Analysis and Antitrust Implications.* New York: Free Press.

_____. 1976. "Franchise Bidding for Natural Monopolies—In General and with Respect to CATV." *Bell Journal of Economics* 7 (Spring):73-104.

Williamson, O.E., M.L. Wachter, and J.E. Harris. 1975. "Understanding the Employment Relation: The Analysis of Idiosyncratic Exchange." *Bell Journal of Economics* 6 (Spring):250-78.

Willig, R.D. 1978. "Pareto-Superior Nonlinear Outlay Schedules." *Bell Journal of Economics* 9 (Spring):56-69.

Willig, R.D., and E.E. Bailey. 1977. "Incoe Distributional Concerns in Regulatory Policy-Making." Paper presented at the National Bureau of Economic Research Conference on Public Regulation, Washington, D.C., December.

Wilson, G.L., J.M. Herring, and R.B. Eutsler. 1938. *Public Utility Regulation.* New York: McGraw-Hill.

Wilson, J.Q. 1971. "The Dead Hand of Regulation." *Public Interest* (Fall):39-58.

_____. 1974. "The Politics of Regulation." In J.W. McKie, ed. *Social Responsibility and the Business Predicament.* Washington, D.C.: Brookings Institution.

Wrightington, E.N. 1912. "The Sliding Scale Method of Regulation as Applied to Gas Companies in Massachusetts." In C.L. King, ed. *The Regulation of Municipal Utilities.* New York: D. Appleton.

Yamey, B. 1974. "Monopolistic Price Discrimination and Economic Welfare." *Journal of Law and Economics* 17 (October):377-80.

Zank, E.E., and H.H. Bakken. 1959. *Light and Power: Rates and Costs of Service in Wisconsin R.E.A. Cooperatives.* Madison: University of Wisconsin Press.

Ziemba, W.T. 1974. "The Behavior of a Firm Subject to Stochastic Regulatory Review: Comment." *Bell Journal of Economics and Management Science* 5 (Autumn):710-12.

Index

About the Author

Richard Schmalensee is associate professor of applied economics in the Alfred P. Sloan School of Management at the Massachusetts Institute of Technology. He received the S.B. and Ph.D. degrees in economics from MIT and taught for a number of years in the Department of Economics at the University of California, San Diego. He is the author of *The Economics of Advertising* and *Applied Microeconomics* and co-author (with Edwin Kuh) of *An Introduction to Applied Macroeconomics*. Most of his numerous articles in professional journals are concerned with applications and implications of microeconomic theory.